T0365287

RUSH
LIMBAUGH,
"I hope he Fails,"
Bailed out America.

NDYFREKE NENTY

iUniverse, Inc.
Bloomington

Rush Limbaugh, "I hope he Fails," Bailed out America.

iUniverse books may be ordered through booksellers or by contacting:

iUniverse
1663 Liberty Drive
Bloomington, IN 47403
www.iuniverse.com
1-800-Authors (1-800-288-4677)

ISBN: 978-1-4502-7785-3 (sc)
ISBN: 978-1-4502-7786-0 (ebk)

Printed in the United States of America

iUniverse rev. date: 12/18/2010

Dedication

I dedicate this book to my parents, Professor Henty Nenty and Madam Felecia Nenty

Thanks

Much of my thanks goes to Rush Limbaugh, who is my chief mentor, Steven Howse, Apostle Excell, Anthony Henderson, Sean Hannity, Charles Scruggs, Stanley Howse, Pastor Bassey, Bryon McCane, all my mentors and of course, God in heaven.

Table of Contents

CHAPTER ONE

Obama the candidate: Revisiting the Historical 2008 Presidential Campaign

Illinois Demagogues: Obama's sketchy associations

<u>Who is Barack Obama?</u>

"I am the son of a black man from Kenya and a white woman from Kansas," Obama introduced himself to America.

<u>Various definitions of Barack Obama</u>

Former Bush aide Karl Rove said he thinks Obama is "arrogant." Karl Rove elaborated, "Even if you never met him (Obama), you know this guy. He's the guy at the country club with the beautiful date, holding a martini and a cigarette that stands against the wall and makes snide comments about everyone who passes by." Conservative legend Rush Limbaugh said that Obama is an "angry" fellow. Fox News' highly rated anchorman Sean Hannity summed it all up by saying: "Obama is a radical."

First character: Bill Ayers. Ayers the professor or Ayers the terrorist- makes no difference

Bill Ayers is a former domestic terrorist, a Chicago professor and a hardcore radical leftist. Obama had made it clear that he was only eight years old when William Ayers committed a number of domestic terrorist acts. When Ayers published a piece in the New York Times, Obama was an adult. He wasn't eight years old. Ayers said he wished he and his Weather Underground domestic terrorist group had done more destruction. On April 12, 2002, Ayers said "I considered myself partly an anarchist then and I consider myself partly an anarchist now. I mean, I am as much an anarchist as I am a Marxist, um, which is to say I find a lot of the ideas in anarchism, you know, appealing and I'm very open about what I think, nobody here surprised by what I think. The struggle over various religious fundamentalism it's jihad being, you know, the most visible. But the religious fundamentalism of the Christians and of the Jews is equally troubling. Is one of the regrets that I took extreme measures against the United States at a time of tremendous crisis? No, it's not. I don't regret that."

Rush said, in response to Ayers' remark: "He's lying through his teeth!" Ayers is unrepentant, and it wasn't a coincidence that Obama worked with him seven days after he made this remark. Rush discarded the notion that Obama thought Ayers was rehabilitated.

"Ultimately, I ended up learning about the fact that he had engaged in this reprehensible act 40 years ago, but I was eight years old at the time and I assumed that he had been rehabilitated," said Obama about Ayers.

Regardless of Ayers' despicable act, Obama had the moral courage to work with Ayers. Obama said he "assumed" that Bill Ayers was rehabilitated, meaning that Obama knew about Ayers' past deeds when Obama accepted the opportunity to work with him – but he never actually asked Ayers if he was rehabilitated.

Rush said Ayers was probably one of the most "formative influences" in Obama's life. This is an individual that tried to bomb the Pentagon. Ayers coached and fundraised Obama's first political undertaking. He introduced Obama to ACORN and gave Obama one hundred and fifty million dollars to head an education foundation (the Annenberg Challenge).

What we should be concerned about in regards to Ayers is not his past terrorist deeds; it is what he's doing in the present. He's part of the radical bunch that wants to socialize the US education system. Rush had always said that about Ayers.

Ayers released the following statement denouncing capitalism: "Capitalism promotes racism and materialism, turning people into consumers, not citizens. Participatory democracy by contrast requires free people coming together voluntarily, as equals, who are capable of both self-realization and, at the same time, full participation in a shared political and economic life."

Rush translated that Ayers' motive is to overthrow capitalist education and replace it with socialist education. They want everyone to be equal and the same. That is socialism rather than capitalism, which is the antithesis of socialism. Therefore, the unfair and unjust capitalism must be corrected.

Ayers is Obama, Obama is Ayers. They're inseparable

For Obama to have worked with Ayers for all of those years and then deny knowing about the domestic terrorist act Ayers committed until Obama was campaigning for office is the height of dishonor.

Rush said that just like OJ Simpson, Ayers is unrepentant for his acts. Maybe Simpson was remorseful for what he had done, but Ayers wasn't. Ayers wished he had done more damage, he wished he had blown up more federal buildings. Rush said Obama will certainly not mimic the destructive part of Ayers, but he will follow his radical ideas. There is no way Obama's associates didn't bring Ayers' terrorist act to Obama's attention. The op-ed Bill Ayers and Bernardine Dohrn published in the New York Times stated that Ayers was unrepentant. Yet Obama befriended these "slimeballs." Rush talked about Ayers having "the aura of respectability" because he grew from a terrorist, he is a professor and he is of course a surrogate to Obama.

Ayers was an unrepentant terrorist. He was involved in the bombing of the Pentagon and bombing a judge's house, among others "Guilty as hell, free has a bird what a great country," Ayers proudly proclaimed.

If William Ayers were African American, do you think Obama would have rubbed shoulders with the distinguish professor? Obama thought dealing with a white guy would go unnoticed and undetected, but Sean Hannity brought to light and unmasked Ayers's connection with Obama.

During one of the presidential debates, Obama stressed that "I was only eight years old" when Bill Ayers and his entourage blew up the pentagon. But how old was Obama when he got involved with Prof. Ayers? Hannity influenced ABC's George Stephanopoulos to ask Obama about his ties with Bill Ayers.

What was the consequence of George Stephanopoulos asking Obama a so-called "irrelevant question?" George Stephanopoulos and Charlie Gibson were excoriated because they asked Obama a question Hannity proposed. The repercussion was that ABC was not included as one of the four mainstream media companies to host a 2008 presidential debate.

How many Americans still want to be a liberal professor after professor Ayers has preceded them? Please stand up. Americans are still waiting for the real Obama to stand up. Chuck, the state senator from Missouri, already stood up for Joe Biden. Eventually, the real Obama stood up when he claimed that Bill Ayers was just "a guy who lives in my neighborhood." It has since been revealed that Obama shared an office with Ayers for three years. He chaired Ayers's Chicago Annenberg Challenge and launched his local political career at Ayers' home. However, the "State run media" swept Obama's "just a guy in my neighborhood" comment under the rug.

Bin laden, al-Zarqawi and the blind sheik, all terrorists, may also be so-called distinguished professors, living in caves somewhere in Afghanistan. One of them is serving a life sentence. You have professor al-Zarqawi calling Condoleezza Rice a house Negro, and you have Professor Ayers attacking Hannity left and right.

Second character: Rev. Wright

Reverend Wright's Controversial Remarks

Reverend Wright is one of Barack Obama's mentors. A sermon that Rev. Wright once preached was the title of Obama's latest autobiographical book, "The Audacity of Hope". This is what Rev. Wright had to say: "The government gives them the drugs, builds bigger prisons, passes a three-strike law, and then wants us to sing God bless America? No, no, no! Not God bless America! God damn America! -- it's in the Bible -- for killing innocent people! God damn America for treating her citizens as less than human! We bombed Hiroshima! We bombed Nagasaki, and we nuked far more than the thousands in New York and the Pentagon, and we never batted an eye. We have supported state terrorism against the Palestinians, and black South Africans, and now we are indignant (cheers) because the stuff we have done overseas is now brought right back into our own front yards! (cheers and applause) America's chickens are coming home...to roost."

Rush made it clear that the category of radicalism that Wright spewed is foreign to America. It is what the rest of the world practices. Rush said there should be no place near the podium for Wright. He used his position as a pastor to preach anti –Semitism, hate and racism. Rush claimed that Wright is using Christianity to advocate views that are "antithetical to Christian values and beliefs."

Rush went on to state that this is nothing but unadulterated "lunatic racism," and it's sad that Obama's church of preference is headed by a race-baiter.

Obama is Wright. Wright is Obama. They're inseparable

The fact that Wright's radical belief overwhelmed every other thing Obama believed in could explain why Obama wasn't repulsed by Wright's affinity towards a certain Louis Farrakhan.

Obama should not be given the benefit of the doubt in terms of his knowing about Wright's beliefs and that Wright was preaching these beliefs to the masses. He knew his spiritual leader was a hate monger, yet he had the audacity to be a member of the church for 20 years. The fact that Wright married Obama and Michele and baptized Obama's children should not be dismissed. Rush wasn't even upset with Wright cursing White people and the Jews. But he was concerned about this: "Do you think it's healthy for parents to let their young children listen to sermons like this where a pastor is using curse words against God?"

Obama said during the campaign, "Don't tell me words don't matter. I have a dream. Just words. We hold these truths to be self-evident, that all men are created equal. Just words. We have nothing to fear but fear itself. Just words, just speeches." Rush capitalized on Obama's statement and said in Obama's world words matter, but not when it comes to his spiritual leader; not when it comes to Rev. Wright.

Rush was still trying to wrap his mind around the fact that Obama sat on the pews of Wright 's church, listening to all manner of hate dispatched to Jews, White people and African Americans who disagree with his Pastor. However, when asked about it, Obama said he was unaware that Wright had said those despicable things.

The best the Black Church has to Offer

Obama said about his pastor, "Reverend Wright, uh, my pastor who I -- I speak about in a chapter in the book, I think represents the best of what the black church has to offer" After revisiting Rev Wright's speech: "No, no, no! Not God bless America! God damn America! -- it's in the Bible -- for killing innocent people! God damn America for treating her citizens as less than human!"

Just as Obama acknowledged, Wright is probably the most "formative person" in Obama's life. And Wright's ideology is the best the Black church has to offer. Rush stated that, according to Wright, "black liberation theology" is the motto for African Americans going forward. Rush claimed that it is a shame Obama didn't have the "moral courage" to leave Wright's church, instead choosing to expose his children to Wright's hatemongering speeches.

Conclusion

When Obama was pressured, he finally denounced his pastor for political benefits: "I can no more disown him {Rev. Wright} than I can disown the black community. I can no more disown {Rev. Wright} than I can disown my white grandmother." Obama then added that Wright is no longer "the man I met 20 years ago."

Traditionally, a preacher is supposed to preach the Word of God. Any preacher that spews hate shouldn't be given space at the pulpit. Thank God judgment begins at churches.

How many Americans still want to be a Reverend after Wright has preceded them? Please stand up. Americans are still waiting for the real Obama to stand up. Chuck, the state senator from Missouri, already stood up for Joe Biden.

The real Obama stood up when he claimed that for 20 years, he didn't know the radical views of his pastor, Rev. Wright.

A spokesperson for Wright wrote: "After 20 years of loving Barack like he was a member of his own family, for Jeremiah (Wright) to see Barack saying over and over that he didn't know about Jeremiah's views during those years, that he wasn't familiar with what Jeremiah had said, is seen by Jeremiah as nonsense and betrayal."

Unlike Bill Ayers, Wright was a US Marine, so Americans should cut him some slack.

Rev. Wright's sermon
Venue: Trinity United Church of Christ
Notable attendants: Barack Obama, Rev. Ottis Moss, Michelle Obama

Rev. Wright, while screaming, uttered: "Barack {Obama} knows what it means to be a black man living in a country and a culture that is controlled by rich white people! The Reverend proceeded "Hillary {Clinton} ain't never been called a nigger." He persisted, "Bill {Clinton} did us (African American Democrats) just like he did Monica Lewinsky!"

As the congregation cheered, Wright kept the sermon going on strong: "He {Bill Clinton} was riding dirty. Without any hesitation, the right reverend continues "In white America, US of KKKA: black men turning on black men. I am sick of Negroes who just do not get it. No no no not God bless America, God damn America! It's in the Bible. For killing innocent people, God damn America!"

The Reverend's screaming sermon continued: "And now we {Americans} are indignant because of stuff we have done overseas is now brought right back into our own front yards!" And finally, he concluded: "America's chickensssss are coming home to roost."

As the cheering from the audience sitting in the pews finally ended, Wright exited the pulpit and said, stand up (audience) and let us pray.

Other Prominent Characters: Louis Farrakhan and Father Pfleger

Pfleger received national attention when he made belittling and divisive statements about Hillary Clinton. Father Pfleger, like Jeremiah Wright, shares a twenty year relationship with Obama. After Hillary Clinton lost the Iowa primaries, she struck a chord. Father Pfleger discussed Hillary's meltdown and provocatively said: "Hillary was crying, and people said that was put on. I really don't believe it was put on. "I really believe that she just always thought, "This is mine! I'm Bill's wife, and this is mine! I just gotta get up and step into the plate… And then out of nowhere came, Hey, I'm Barack Obama and she said, 'Oh, damn! Where did you come from? I'm white! I'm entitled! There's a black man stealing my show!"

Pfleger shouted, as he continued to mock Hillary: "She wasn't the only one crying," There was a whole lot of white people crying….? I'm white! I'm entitled! There's a black man stealing my show!"

Minister Louis Farrakhan

He is the head of the Nation of Islam. Farrakhan, a New Yorker who resides in Chicago, has been labeled as an anti-Semite because of his racial remarks. In particular:"Now that nation called Israel never has had any peace in 40 years and she will never have any peace because there can be no peace structured on injustice, thievery, lying and deceit and using the name of God to shield your gutter religion under His holy and righteous name," Farrakhan said.

"Injustice, thieving, lying and deceit," doesn't only exist in Israel, it happens all over the world. In addition, using the term "gutter" religion is way beyond the pale. We should always remember that the Israeli are still God's chosen people. For many years, Farrakhan has launched a jihad against the Jews.

Rush recalled a Democratic presidential debate between Obama and Clinton. Rush said that when Hillary started uncovering Obama's damaging statement about Farrakhan, Obama just laughed it off. Obama said "You know, I have to say, I don't see a difference between 'denouncing' and 'rejecting.' There's no formal offer of help for Minister Farrakhan that would involve me rejecting it, but if the word 'reject' Senator Clinton feels is stronger than the word 'denounced,' I'm happy to concede the point. I'll reject and denounce."

There was only so much Hillary Clinton could take after she lost the Iowa caucus. On Super Tuesday, Obama got the lion's share of the delegates in play. Clinton couldn't take it anymore; the gloves came off. Obama was on the verge of feeling the wrath of a woman scorned. Hillary brought Obama's association with Louis Farrakhan to the forefront. At the end of it all, Hillary's case against Obama was irrelevant.

Million Man Match

Barack Obama attended Louis Farrakhan's Million Man Match: "What I saw was a powerful demonstration of an impulse and need for African-American men to come together to recognize each other and affirm our rightful place in the society. There was a profound sense that African –American men were ready to make a commitment to bring about change in our communities and lives," Obama said during the controversial Million Man Match.

"That is the change we need," Obama said.

Louis Farrakhan's affinity for Jeremiah Wright was evident when Wright uttered the Million Man Match's opening prayers. Why is Obama's mentor/moral compass all religious? Farrakhan, a chief Islamic leader, Wright, a prominent reverend and father Pfleger, a Parish pastor: "The white man is our mortal enemy, and we cannot accept him. I will fight to see that that vicious beast goes down into the lake of fire prepared for him from the beginning, that he never rise again to give any innocent black man, woman or child the hell that he has delighted in pouring upon us for 400 years. And I'm home to stay!" Farrakhan made the comment in 2002. That is who Obama looks up to.

Farrakhan praised Obama

Farrakhan praised Obama: "You are the instruments that God is going to use to bring about universal change. And that is why Barack has captured the youth. And he has involved young people in a political process that they didn't care anything about. That's a sign. When The Messiah speaks, the youth will hear. And The Messiah is absolutely speaking."

Farrakhan called Obama the messiah. Other pundits have gone as far as to refer to Obama as God. Democratic media pundit Evan Thomas said: "I mean in a way Obama's standing above the country, above – above the world, he's sort of God." God is everlastingly impeccable. What a shame to call a flawed human being God.

Conclusion

The decimation of the Israelites since the days of old isn't enough for an anti-Semite like Farrakhan, Wright and President Ahmadinejad. They want the total annihilation of Israel. They want Israel to be wiped off the map. Psalm 83 verse 4 said: "They have said, come, and let us cut them off from being a nation; that the name of Israel may be no more in remembrance." That's what Farrakhan, Rev. Wright and other comrades of Obama desire.

Tony Rezko

"This isn't the Tony Rezko I knew."

Rezko was said to be up to his ears in dubious dealings. There was a lot of evidence when he was convicted. Tony Rezko is a wealthy business man and a very close comrade of Obama's for over twenty years. As a major benefactor to the Democratic Party, Rezko donated significantly for the Obama during his run for the US senate. After Tony Rezko was found guilty on sixteen charges of corruption, Obama released a statement saying: "I'm saddened by today's verdict. This isn't the Tony Rezko I knew, but now he's been convicted by a jury on multiple charges that once again shine the spotlight on the need for reform."

Rush was indignant: "What Tony Rezko did Obama know?" Due to the fact that Obama had previously claimed not to know Ayers and Pfleger, Rush then asked how many other people had Obama thrown under the bus? There is definitely no room left under that bus.

Rush sums up Tony Rezko and Obama's dealings

Rush said the lesson we should learn from Obama's dealing with Rezko is that people no longer do things on their own. Hard work and ambition is not the way forward. They way forward is through connections and sweetheart deals, etc, even if the connection is a felon and thus Tony Rezko comes into the equation. Rezko was hugely involved in Obama's purchasing his home at below asking price.

Rush's Summary of Obama's Mentors and left-wing radical activists

Rush was satisfied and had heard enough of Obama and his radical associates: "All right, let's go through a little timeline here."

Jeremiah Wright said, "America's chickenssss-ach are coming home to roost." Jeremiah Wright also said, "God-bleep America!" Barack Obama responded, "Well, I was in the church for 20 years; I never heard that." Bill Ayers participated in trying to blow up the Pentagon. Barack Obama said of Ayers, "He's just a guy in my neighborhood. I was a young boy when he was doing those despicable acts."

When addressing the Blagojevich's corrupt deeds in the selling of a Senate seat, Obama said, "I had no idea this was going on."

Rush stated that the sixties radical gangs and the 1984 ideas of Saul Alinsky have finally infiltrated America. He feels that they will run the country to the abyss.

Final notes

It is difficult to dissect Obama's mentors and educators. The mainstream media barely scratched the surface in reporting Obama's radical associations. You had to look long and hard to find any damaging stories about Obama. And the stories were buried at the bottom of the back pages. Fox News and conservative radio dug deep and exposed the real Obama.

Wright and Ayers are trying to disseminate liberal and radical philosophy to the American people. Would young Americans rather have Obama and the likes of Farrakhan, Wright and Ayers be their role models, or are they queuing up to positive role models like Rush Limbaugh and Sean Hannity?

After spending 20 years in Rev. Wright's church and the nexus of Ayers, Rezko, Farrakhan and Pfleger, we can comfortably conclude that Obama is susceptible to making the wrong decisions.

Obama is a messiah to the illiterates, the uninformed and to the liberals, but a phony to the conservatives.[1]

Code Words

Is every word racially connoted?

Rush observed that throughout the 2008 campaign, the media assigned any phrase they distaste against Obama as code words. Community organizer, socialist, spreading the wealth: these were all considered by the left to be code phrases. Obama's middle name, Hussein, was a code word. Any conservative that talked about Obama's past radical associations, about Obama's Muslim ties, and about Michelle Obama, would be called a racist.

Michelle Obama

During the latter part of the 08 campaign, conservatives in the media were childishly threatened by Obama to leave Michelle's name out of their mouth. It got so heated that mentioning Michelle Obama's name became referred to as a code word.

"The conservative press-Fox News and the National Review and columnists of every ilk went fairly deliberately at her (Michelle) in a pretty systematic way," Obama fingered out. Candidate wives "didn't sign up for this, they're supporting their spouse. So it took a toll. If you start being subjected to rants by Sean Hannity and the like, day in and day out, that will drive up your negatives," Obama said. "I don't have a thick skin when it comes to criticism of my wife," Obama revealed.

Only a naïve presidential candidate would send his helpmate to the spotlight and not expect her to be attacked, especially after she has made absurd comments. Michelle Obama's patriotism was in question after she shockingly said: "Hope is making a comeback and, let me tell you, for the first time in my adult life I am really proud of my country. Not just because Barack is doing well, but I think people are hungry for change."

How many countries has America liberated during Michelle's adult life? Mrs. Obama was not proud of America when we liberated the world from Nazism, fascism, communism and Imperial Japan. Mrs. Obama isn't proud of America's exceptional achievements. Michelle Obama's unpatriotic attitude wasn't all that she wrote she specifically debased the United States, calling America a "just downright mean country."

When asked about the possible attacks on Michelle Obama by Republicans, Illinois's Senator Durbin replied: "The hottest ring in hell is reserved for those in politics who attack their opponents' families. And if there are some Republican strategists who think that's the way to win the election, I think they're wrong" Rush took offense with the Majority whip's comment. Rush said, how about the hottest ring in hell being reserved for the Hitlers and Bin Ladens of the world? Or murderers and child molesters? Or those who orchestrated in killing thousands of Americans on 9/11? No, a ranking Democratic senator wants the hottest ring in hell reserved for Republicans that verbally attack Obama's wife.

Mrs. Obama reproved the private sector and then pleaded to the supporters: "Don't go into corporate America. You know, become teachers. Work for the community. Be social workers. Be a nurse. Those are the careers that we need, and we're encouraging our young people to do that." Michelle's remarks did not sit well with Rush. In Michelle Obama's world, the sky for average Americans is no longer the limit. In Michelle Obama's world, community organizing and nursing is the pinnacle because it is all about helping people and communities. In Michelle Obama's world, as long as the average American remains in the underclass category, everything is fine and dandy.

Obama vs. the Muslim Religion

Is Obama a Christian or a Muslim? He claimed to be a Christian, but he was born into a Muslim family. His father was a Muslim. Obama revealed: "Although my father had been raised a Muslim, by the time he met my mother he was a confirmed atheist, thinking religion to be so much superstition." Barack seemed to conceal his true religion. He doesn't appreciate what God gave him. He threw the whole Muslim religion under the bus, as if being a Muslim is a curse. There was a reason why he was elected to be fathered by a Kenyan Muslim citizen. There is nothing wrong to be transformed from a Muslim to a Christian, but you have to admit that you were once a Muslim. Let's give Obama the benefit of the doubt that he is a Christian. Even so, the fact of the matter is that Barack Hussein Obama (all three names) are typically Muslim names, compared to Jeremiah Wright.

Middle Name

On the campaign trail, we also couldn't use Obama's middle name. Again, he doesn't like his forefathers' name. But why is Obama so incensed about people calling him Barack Hussein Obama? If he had a chance to erase Hussein from his birth certificate and his passport, he would have done so 20 years ago. What if Saddam Hussein, the former Iraqi dictator, never existed? Would Obama still forbid his own middle name?

Brother's Keeper

The story of Obama's brother living in a tent in Kenya was first thought to be a hoax. However, the story is as real as it can get.

Obama's family

It's not on Rush's radar to discuss an opponent's family, but the news served as an example of who liberals are, Rush stressed that Obama's message is based on helping each other. But how do we explain the fact that Obama's half brother lives on less than $20 a year? How can we accept the fact that Obama, who's a multimillionaire, has a brother living in a six-by-nine foot hut? Hypocrite is the most suitable term to describe who Obama is. Rush said all Obama needs to do is send his brother $40 and that his brother would consider that to be a fortune. That amount would certainly double his brother's annual income. If Obama can't take care of his own blood brother, how can he take care of the American people? Rush proceeded no further, "His brother lives in a dirt floor hut. Most of your bathrooms are larger than that."

Is Obama practicing what his preaching?

Obama talked about caring: "I think most people understand, uh, that if you're not, um, caring for your family, uh, then you're probably not, uh, the kind of person who's going to be caring for other people." Rush tried his best to eschew the issue. Rush said we need to look no further than George Onyango Bodongo Hussein Obama in order to answer that question. And that have begs the question: how many more family members of Obama live in squalor?

Family tree

It was also revealed that one of Obama relatives, Zeituni, lives in a Boston slum. Is there another Obama relative living in abject poverty? Obama is talking the talk but is not walking the walk. You have George Onyango Bodongo Hussein Obama living in a dirt floor hut and another, Aunt Zeituni, living in a slum in Boston.

Times Online wrote: "She {Auntie Zeituni} is a frail woman who walks with the aid of a metal sick. Neighbors said she lived alone in a ground floor flat, normally set aside for people facing physical hardship." Rush indicated that, according to Times Online, Auntie Zeituni walks not even with a cane, but with a metal stick.

Brother's Keeper

Obama said the following about "brother's keeper:" "It is that fundamental belief -- I am my brother's keeper, I am my sister's keeper -- that makes this country work." This story on Obama and his immediate family proves how heartless Liberals are. Don't judge a book by its cover. The so-called great, caring and compassionate person America deems Obama to be is vastly exaggerated. But Rush gave Obama the benefit of a doubt, saying that perhaps Obama has recently reached out to help his relatives. But his relatives haven't spoken out in defense of Obama. It's more than a crying shame that Obama isn't covering the nakedness of his brother, his aunt and his other relatives in the same abysmal conditions.

Obama on sex education

In Obama's world, a woman giving birth out of wedlock is a punishment she has been given: "I've got two daughters—9 years old and 6 years old. I'm going to teach them first of all about values and morals, but if they make a mistake, I don't want them punished with a baby," Obama spoke. Good for Obama, anticipating the teaching of values and morals to his offspring. Whether Obama was referring to abortion or sex education, his statement is clear. It can't be taken out of content.

No rights for babies at moment of conception

Rick Warren from the Saddleback Church asked Obama in an interview: "At what point does a baby get human rights in your view? Obama responded: "I think that whether you're looking at it from a theological perspective or, uh, a scientific perspective, answering that question with specificity, uhhhh, you know, is above my pay grade." Rush asserted that it is very telling that a person that voted three times for infanticide during his time in the Illinois House could not answer a simple, straightforward question. Just for the sake of winning the 2008 elections, Obama, when asked the question "At what point does a baby get human rights in your view?" answered "is above my pay grade."

Marxisant radical emerges
Rush said during the campaign: "Radicalism comes dressed in many ways." In 2008, radicalism was being "dressed up"
as President Obama. Rush said Obama, like all radical extreme leftists, will hide from the public who they really are.

Radicalism and Collectivism in tandem
Obama has cemented collectivism as a liberal identity. Collectivism is under the canopy of liberalism.

Talking about Lucifer for a moment, Saul Alinsky, another of Obama's mentors, dedicated his 1971 book 'Rules for Radicals: A Pragmatic Primer for Realistic Radicals' to Lucifer. A quote on Saul's book: "Lest we forget at least a over –the-shoulder acknowledgment to the very first radical: from all our legends, mythology, and history, the first radical known to man who rebelled against the establishment and did it so effectively that he at least won his own Kingdom (is) Lucifer."
"That's the change we need," Obama reiterated.[2]

The Obama/Biden ticket: Gaffe, Arrogant and Condescending

Obama's 57 States
Obama made an egregious error when he said: "It is wonderful to be back in Oregon. Over the last 15 months, we've traveled to every corner of the United States. I've now been in 57 states? I think one left to go. Alaska and Hawaii, I was not allowed to go to even though I really wanted to visit, but my staff would not justify it." Obama said, after fielding a comment from the media." There are 57 Islamic states. With the question of Obama being a Muslim constantly being debated amongst Americans, it was be hard to believe that Obama made a gaffe

about the 57 states in America. This was more than losing one's bearing. Rush said we haven't heard the end of Dan Quayle's 1993 misspelling of potato, but we have already heard the end of Obama's 57 states gaffe.

An imaginary reaction

When was the last set of states to make up the present 50 states established? There is no need to revisit history, because an Obama presidency might create 7 more states. All the Red states and the Swing States are saved. Only the Blue Democratic States will be cut. He will create seven more Blue states. Illinois will definitely be one of them, more precisely, the area covering the south side of Chicago. New Kenya might be a good name to call the new anticipated State.

The states of California and New York will also be in the reckoning. These changes will have an effect on the electoral map.

The double standard from the media was descried. Obama's comment didn't draw much scorn from the media. The media was much more scornful when Walker Bush's running mate misspelled potatoes.

"That is the change we need," Obama reiterated.
"Just words just speeches" Obama regurgitated. Just word, just speeches.

Obama's attacks on Rush Limbaugh

This was Obama's first direct attack on Rush Limbaugh: "A certain segment has basically been feeding a kind of xenophobia. There's a reason why hate crimes against Hispanic people doubled last year. If you have people like Lou Dobbs and Rush Limbaugh ginning things up, it's not surprising that would happen," Obama said at a fundraiser in Florida.

As if Obama wasn't satisfied, he vaporized Rush by releasing ads televising two of Limbaugh's more than a decade old quote, saying:

"Mexicans are stupid and unqualified" and "Shut your mouth or get out." The quotes were intentionally taken out of content.

Rush was cut to the heart. He didn't need a second invitation to launch at Obama. Rush claimed that Obama is the one that is "stoking racism" in America. And he's the one pitting people in groups against one another. Furthermore, Rush wasn't surprised that Obama aired race-baiting ads against him. "He is taking statements I've made entirely out of context. He knows they're out of context and is using them anyway to create division between people, in this case racial division.

Obama's Surrogates vs. Hannity

In the thick of his 08 campaign, Obama turned his attention to Sean Hannity. He attacked Sean on many fronts, one in particular during an interview with Bill O'Reilly.

Obama has frequently been asked to appear on either the Sean Hannity's radio program or Hannity's TV show. However, he continued throughout his campaign to turn down offers. If Hillary Clinton never made a cameo appearance on Sean's program, how on earth would Obama, then the most liberal US senator, darken the doorstep of one of the most conservative voices in the nation?

All of Obama's associates have attacked Sean on many different occasions. Bill Ayers and Rev. Wright took several swipes at Sean.

Wright scolded Hannity at a funeral in Chicago: "Sean Hannity's stupid fantasy will keep him forever stuck on stupid when it comes to comprehending how you can love a brother who does not believe what you believe."

Speaking at a conference for black journalists, Father Pfleger also reached out and belittled Sean Hannity: " I'm amazed that Sean Hannity who has- I don't know if he has any journalistic background is shaping media direction in this country. If he had the money out there and do what they're doing and so everybody else is responding, so ABC and NBC and CBS and CNN are {all} following Sean Hannity?"

Sean Hannity didn't take Pfleger's remark lightly. Sean instantly responded: "Father Pfleger come on the program. And you know something, Father Pfleger, you're the one that's friends with that racist and anti-Semite Louis Farrakhan. You're the one that's friends with Reverend Wright, and you're the one that takes a shot {at me}." The pastor of Trinity united church of Christ Rev. Otis Moss 111, also joined the fray in attacking Hannity: "For anybody who is tuning in the video screen, who normally doesn't tune in, you're looking for something, Reverend Jane. What's up Hannity."

Joe Biden's Blip

Joe Biden was chosen ahead of Hillary Clinton to be Obama's running mate. He served as a senator from Delaware for over thirty years.

Without even scratching the surface, here are some of Biden's absurd statements. While campaigning at Missouri, Joe Biden said, "I'm told Chuck Graham, state senator is here. Stand up Chuck, let'em see you. Oh, God love you. What am I talking about. I'll tell you what, you're making everybody else stand up though pal." After noticing that Chuck was confined to a wheelchair, Biden then changed his tune: "I tell you (the audience) what, stand up for Chuck."

This was Rush's reaction: "So he's (Biden) briefed that State Senator Chuck Graham is there, but nobody tells him that Chuck Graham is in a wheelchair. You can't make this stuff up. He needs a cocktail and a cigarette and a rim shot drummer." Rush then turned his attention to what vice presidential nominee Senator John Edwards said in 2004: "Let's go to John Edwards, folks, at the convention, at a debate, October 11, 2004. {Edwards said} 'When John Kerry is president, people like Christopher Reeve are going to walk-get up out of that wheelchair and walk again.'"

Before Biden's presidential election failed bid, he said this about Obama: "I think he can be ready, but right now I don't believe he is. The presidency is not something that lends itself to on-the-job training." They were asked during a presidential debate if candidates would be "Willing to meet separately, without precondition, during the first year of your administration, in Washington or anywhere else, with 'rogue' leaders of Iran, Syria, Venezuela, Cuba and North Korea, in order to bridge the gap that divides our countries?" Obama answered, "I would, and the reason is this, that the notion that somehow not talking to countries is punishment to them-which has been the guiding diplomatic principle of this administration-is ridiculous." Biden responded to Obama's precondition remarks, "Would I make a blanket commitment to meet unconditionally with the leaders of each of those countries within the first year I was president? Absolutely, positively no."

Biden, in 2006, summarized the state of Delaware in just one paragraph: "Better than everybody else. You don't know my state. My state was a slave state. My state is a border state. My state is the eighth largest black population in the country. My state is anything from a northeast liberal state."

Biden's next comment was more than a gaffe: "In Delaware, the largest growth of population is Indian Americans, moving from India. You cannot go to a 7/11 or a Dunkin' Donuts unless you have a slight Indian accent. I'm not joking."

Americans continued salivating for more racial slips of the tongue from Vice President Biden.

Joe Biden's diarrhea of the mouth continued. Knowingly or unknowingly, when introducing Obama, Biden uttered a racial slur: "The first mainstream African American {candidate} who is articulate and bright and clean and a nice-looking guy I mean that's a storybook, man."

Biden's comment basically threw Al Sharpton and Rev. Jackson, past presidential candidates, under the bus. His remarks ruffled African American people's feathers.

As the ranking Democrat in the Senate's Foreign Affairs Committee, Biden called for Iraq to be divided into three parts, namely Kurd, Shiite and Sunni, with the central government located in Baghdad. Biden, as vice president, might finally have his wish of splitting Iraq into three regions.

Days before the general election, Biden dropped clanger again when he said "John's (McCain) last-minute economic plan does nothing to tackle the number-one job facing the middle class, and it happens to be, as Barack says, a three-letter word: jobs, j-o-b-s, jobs."

Obama/Biden: arrogant and condescending

Finally, the real Obama surfaced. The genie was out of the bottle. He stood up in Nancy Pelosi's neck of the woods: "Bitter people in Pennsylvania clinging to their guns and religion with antipathy towards those who are not like them." Obama has nothing but utter contempt for the people in Philadelphia.

Condescension in the highest degree

Obama said confidently, "How many plumbers you know that are making a quarter-million dollars a year?" Joe Biden claimed, "I don't have any Joe the plumbers in my neighborhood that make $250,000 a year." All Obama and Biden have done is discredit plumbers. It's the height of condescension.

Rush blast elites in both parties

Rush blasted elites in both parties because they look down on average Americans. They are arrogant and condescending. They feel embarrassed to have average Americans around, save for Election Day.

Obama's Historical Victory

Regardless of all the manufactured self-made taint Obama faced during his presidential campaign, he was still able to cross the Commander-in-Chief threshold. Personally Obama might be a good father and a good husband, but his supporters should hope Obama's daughters will not be punished with a baby before they get married. After history was made, Rush uttered, "I would like to congratulate President-Elect Barack Obama, ladies and gentlemen." Rush said the good that came out of Obama's victory was bringing an end to Hillary's lurking for the White House.

Rush went on record

Rush responded to questions asked about America's historical moment. In precise words, Rush stated that he had been asked why he doesn't really sound deferential to the "historical consequences" of the election of the first black president. Rush said he doesn't care what skin color Obama is. It's Obama's radical ideology that bothers Rush. And he will oppose his ideas. Rush said he got past the seminal moment the day after Obama's victory. Rush said Obama is "my president of the United States." And whether he is black or white or Mexican or Asian American or Islamic is not his concern. Rush doesn't see Americans as groups of people. Rather, he sees Americans as human beings and individuals.

Rush explained why Obama won the presidency
Obama's landslide victory over McCain didn't tell the whole story. Before the election, subversive groups like Acorn circumvented the law with ease. Acorn was alleged to have registered dead and underage people as voters. Platitudes are pure ruses to get people's vote.

Rush stated point blank that Obama knew he won the 2008 election by fooling Americans to vote for him. Obama knows he was a far cry from being honest to the American people. Rush claimed a majority of Americans voted for an image; they voted for a "mythical thing called change."

Signs of the Times
Obama won because he ran a charade campaign. Rush said it's the sign of the times when a demagogue can hoodwink the majority of Americans to vote for him. It's the sign of times when a man that talks in platitudes was able to deceive the majority of Americans.

The main factors that led to the Obama victory
According to Rush, white guilt is the defining factor that caused Whites to vote for Obama. Rush went on to state that a contingent of pseudo-intellectual conservatives voted for Obama because they wanted someone that could communicate. George Bush wasn't satisfying their appetite. But the underlying factor for those who voted for Obama was race.

Obama's for infanticide
Rush stated that he is at a loss to explain how Obama, who is for infanticide, received way more Catholic votes than McCain in the 2008 election.

After studying Obama's associations, the majority of American voters still handed over the reins to Obama. We shouldn't discount the notion that Rev. Wright and Farrakhan, both Jews haters from Obama's neighborhood, will work with the president on religious issues. Similarly,

Ayers, also from Obama's neighborhood, will work on education issues. Show us who your friends are, Obama, (Wright, Ayers, Farrakhan, etc.) and we, the American people, will show you who you are.

Because of the genuine cloud of controversies surrounding his radical mentors, it is hard to believe Obama won the election.

As we can plainly see, the road to becoming an American president has been demeaned by the election of Obama. If Bush or even Clinton had the same radical nexus as Obama, they wouldn't have even gotten past the New Hampshire primary.[2]

In conclusion, Rush claimed that since the founding of America, no radical liberal has ever assumed the position of the commander-in-chief.

Acting President of America

Obama has been compared to Presidents Franklin Roosevelt, Abraham Lincoln and John Kennedy. Obama and Roosevelt both had excellent communicative skills, devastating economic tsunamis happened on their watch, and they all had to deal with record unemployment. President Obama, acting as President Franklin Delano Roosevelt, would serve 4 terms. Roosevelt said: "To announce that there must be no criticism of the President, or that we are to stand by the President, right or wrong, is not only unpatriotic and servile, but in morally treasonable to the American public." President Obama would reject the latter part of the quote.

Obama and JFK both talked about change. They were both charismatic, and they both delivered vibrant speeches.

"There is a wisdom there and a humility about his approach to government, even before he was president, that I just find very helpful," Obama said about Lincoln.

Of all three, Lincoln was the most identical to Obama. His resume is parallel to Obama's. They were both from Illinois. Both served in Congress, except one didn't finish his term. Lincoln abolished slavery, so maybe Obama will end racism. Most importantly, they both nominated political foes. Obama's choice of Hillary Clinton was a typical example of what Lincoln did in his time as president.

At the end of his presidency, Obama will be judged as a famous but unpopular president.[4]

Obama's entourage: Daley, Emanuel and Blagojevich

Who's the Black Sheep?
Gov. Rod Blagojevich, the governor of Illinois, tried to sell Obama's vacant US senate seat to the highest bidder. With the prospect of a cabinet position in Obama's administration slipping away, the governor opted for some kickback. The scandal was of monumental proportions. It involved the governor, the president-elect and a couple of Illinois US Congressmen, among others. Rush when discussing the Blagojevich deeds said Mayor Richard Daley runs Chicago politics. For over 2 decades, he has been at the helm. Daley runs the "cesspool that gave birth to Obama." Rush was surprised Daley wasn't being questioned by investigators.

For hours, Obama was interrogated by the FBI. Emanuel and Blagojevich were at sword's point over all of the proceedings. Democrats did everything to disassociate Obama from the Blagojevich scandal, Rush said the Democrats did everything under the sun to protect Obama from the scandal. "You know, Jesus walked on water." Obama walked on cesspool, but somehow he's untainted by the sewage.

Rush noted significantly that for two years, Fitzgerald tried the whole nine yards to convict one of Bush's surrogates, Scooter Libby. In the Blagojevich scandal, Fitzgerald, the prosecutor, "stops an ongoing crime spree, in the middle of the crime spree."

US prosecutor, Patrick Fitzgerald, could uncover the shenanigans in the Valerie Plame versus George Bush's White House case, but he couldn't uncover the shenanigans in Chicago. He tried the whole nine yards to mar former Bush's Deputy Chief of Staff Karl Rove, but he eluded the chase of an Obama and Emanuel interrogation. Maybe the corrupt politics in Chicago were too complicated for Fitzgerald.

After Libby, the former Chief of Staff to Cheney, was indicted, Charles Schumer said, "Mr. Fitzgerald is a prosecutor's prosecutor. He does not have a political bone in his body."

The Blagojevich Scandal has been put to rest. Liberal Democrats heaped opprobrium on Democratic governor Blagojevich. He was a scapegoat while Obama, Jackson and Emanuel were all immune.

Chicago politics

In light of the much maligned shenanigans going on in Chicago, Illinois, Hillary Clinton, a native of Illinois was able to discern the cesspool of Chicago politics. Chicago politics is the White House. Saul Alinsky's radical philosophy is the White House. The philosophy of Bill Ayers and Jeremiah Wright is the White House. The Chicago machine led by Mayor Richard Daley, Gov. Blagojevich, Rahm Emanuel, Alexi Giannoulias and Valerie Jarrett is the White House. What motivated Rahm Emanuel to resign from his powerful House position to become White House Chief of Staff for Obama? Whether it was a pay cut or pay increase, Rahm Emanuel was in line to be Speaker of the House. The former Illinois congressman was viewed by many at a replacement for Nancy Pelosi. A popular saying in Illinois is "You can take the politician out of Chicago but you can't take Chicago-corrupt politics out of the politician." Jeremiah Wright is Obama and vice versa. Bill Ayers is Obama and vice versa. Valerie Jarrett and Alexi Giannoulias are fresh products of Chicago politics. They're left-wing ideologues. Valerie Jarrett, whose name was withdrawn from Obama's vacated senate seat, was Obama's choice to replace him. Obama is Valerie Jarrett but Jarrett is not Obama. Jarrett still has a lot to learn before she could be held in the same corrupt Chicago cesspool politics status of Blagojevich.[5]

President Obama's First Twenty- one Months

Twenty- one months have passed, and America is going and getting nowhere fast with Obama in charge. Rush has brought Americans up to speed.

National security

Iraq: A War of Choice: Undermining American Troops' morale
Obama said in Egypt, "Unlike Afghanistan, Iraq was a war of choice that provoked strong differences in my country and around the world." By saying that the war in Iraq was a war of choice, Rush felt Obama has dampened the morale of our troops fighting in Iraq.

Rush's accurate prediction on the Iraqi war
Rush said time after time that the Democrats will not saddle themselves with a defeat in Iraq.

Obama said on June 2009: "Those who have tried to pull Iraq into the abyss of disunion and civil war are on the wrong side of history."

Rush reminded Americans that Obama, when he was a senator, predicated back in 2007 a civil war in Iraq if our troops stayed in Iraq.

And Rush was right, because on February 10, 2007 Obama said: "It's time to admit that no amount of American lives will resolve the political disagreement that lies at the heart of someone else's civil war."

So according to Obama's 2007 message, he would have immediately pulled out of Iraq after his inauguration. During the Iraq surge, Democrats accused the ranking commander in Iraq, General Petraeus, of being a rubberstamp to Bush. It was this same Democrat, Harry Reid, who said the war is lost and over. It was this same Democrat, John Murtha that accused our troops of rape in Haditha.

Rush maintained repeatedly that Obama won't saddle himself with defeat, and on June 2009 Obama declared victory: "Through tour after tour of duty our troops have overcome every obstacle,... to extend this precious opportunity to the Iraqi people. We've made important progress in supporting a sovereign, stable, and self-reliant Iraq; and everyone who served there, both in uniform as well as our civilians, uh, deserves our thanks." According to Rush, when Bush was president, Obama condemned every word he said in his above statement. How things have changed from Obama calling for a retreat to saying that as of 2009, the war is the piece de resistance.

America sacrifices values over the Fight against Terrorism

Rush claimed the constant preaching by Obama against our approach on terrorism really grates on him. Obama makes us believes the United States has lost it values. During the tenure of Bush and Cheney, "The moral beacon" that was the United States of America, had completely disappeared.

31

Sound Advice from Cheney: Teacher to Student Approach

A valuable piece of advice from Cheney: "The administration seems to pride itself on searching for some kind of middle ground in policies addressing terrorism. But in the fight against terrorism, there is no middle ground, and half measures keep you half exposed. You cannot keep just some nuclear-armed terrorists out of the United States. You must keep every nuclear-armed terrorist out of the United States. Triangulation is a political strategy, not a national security strategy. When just a single clue that goes unlearned or one lead that goes un-pursued can bring on catastrophe, it's no time for splitting differences. There is never a good time to compromise when the lives and safety of the American people hang in the balance."

Obama Apology Tours: Obama shunned Rush Limbaugh

What Obama is doing is apologizing for the Bush/ Cheney administration and America at large, but he is exempting himself for the apology. He is exempting himself from having done anything that made the rest of the world hate us. Rush said, "Obama's willing to go talk with all the anti-American tyrants he can find. He won't talk to me. He will not talk to any conservatives. He tells America not to listen to me. He tells members of Congress not to listen to me." "You're not supposed to listen to people like Rush Limbaugh," Obama said to Americans. Americans should listen to brutal dictators like President Chavez, who called Obama an ignoramus. And Daniel Ortega, President of Nicaragua who went on to bash America for almost an entire hour in a speech. And after Ortega's rant, Obama upheld everything Ortega said about America. Rush said the Democrats treat him and other conservatives as a greater enemy than brutal dictators worldwide. Obama found it pleasant to sit down for a 55 minutes diatribe against America by Socialist Nicaraguan President Daniel Ortega: "He goes and accuses me of exporting terrorism: the least I can say is that he's a poor ignoramus; he should read and study a little to understand reality," Hugo Chavez of Venezuela said about Obama. And Obama still went ahead and accepted a gift from a virulent dictator like President Chavez.

Rush denounced Obama's friendly meetings with Third World dictators Daniel Ortega and Hugo Chavez: "I would not want to be caught dead in a picture laughing, smiling, and yukking it up with Hugo Chavez," Rush said.

"For Obama is all about fame and adulation. Obama is fixated with himself," Sean Hannity said, "America is not about one person." Obama is totally focused on himself. He can't hide his narcissist attitude.

Rush delves into the mindset of terrorists

Rush said with Obama's tour of apologist, America's enemies see a sap and a weakling in Obama. Rush said these dictators "thrive on being hated." They don't care about being adored by their people. They are a Stalin and a Mao in the making. They are "loved by the people" they imprisoned. They bestow fear upon their people.

President Obama's approach to terrorism emboldened enemies

Rush feels that for years, Democrats have thought that America is unjust and immoral. And that belief was further compounded by the eight year presidency of George Bush. Rush said it's absurd to believe that by talking to a dictator like Mahmoud Ahmadinejad, he would have a change of heart on how he views America and Western civilization.

America cut down to size: End of World Order

President Obama said: "Given our interdependence, any world order that elevates one nation or group of people over another will inevitably fail. So whatever we think of the past, we must not be prisoners to it." Rush pushed back against Obama's remark. "Freedom will elevate people above tyranny." Rush believes that when you have the type of world order that Obama is proposing, the end results will be socialism and fascism. Rush said America happened to be the greatest country in the world, but we weren't appointed or elevated to that position.

Israel: A moral equivalence to the Holocaust

Obama, when comparing and contrasting Israelis and Palestinians, said: "Around the world, the Jewish people were persecuted for centuries, and anti-Semitism in Europe culminated in an unprecedented Holocaust. Six million Jews were killed -- more than the entire Jewish population of Israel today. ..."

A guilty conscience would not allow Obama to praise Israel. Obama declaimed on the subject: "On the other hand, it is also undeniable that the Palestinian people -- Muslims and Christians -- have suffered in pursuit of a homeland. For more than sixty years they have endured the pain of dislocation. Many wait in refugee camps in the West Bank, Gaza, and neighboring lands for a life of peace and security that they have never been able to lead. They endure the daily humiliations -- large and small ..." Rush claimed it is outrageous for Obama "to draw a moral equivalence between" the Palestinians pursuit of a homeland and the six million Jews that were slaughtered.

Obama is reluctant in his support for Israel's causes, unlike George Bush. It seems he doesn't want Israel to finally bury the hatchet with other Middle Eastern counties. There is no robust support from his administration. The Palestinians who were without a homeland were put in that position by their own leaders. Rush said the six million Jews that were killed were not terrorists. They never tried to wipe Germany off the face of the world like Iran wants to wipe Israel off the map. Rush said it is striking that Obama could draw a moral equivalence.

Rush visited history when he said without the United States, most of the countries in Asia and Europe wouldn't have existed. Around the world, the United States has "Maintained an umbrella of security." Rush said weakness would certainly "invite aggression" if America is judged by the world as a "paper tiger" like the former Soviet Union was.

Lone Wolf: Texas Massacre

Before November 5 2009, Major Nidal Malik Hasan was a Muslim US Army officer. After November 5 of 2009, Nidal Hasan will be known as an Islamist extremist who ran riot and committed the deadliest act of terror since 9/11. What a transformation from a U.S Army Major to an Islamist terrorist.

After the smoke cleared, the results of the carnage were in. Over a dozen innocent Americans died, and 30 Americans were hospitalized. This radicalized Muslim gunman was alleged to have connections to al-qaeda. Major Hasan was said to have been upset that President Obama didn't pull American troops from Iraq, Afghanistan and other Middle Eastern countries. One can conclude that Hasan, if he voted in the 2008 election, voted for candidate Obama. President Obama said he was going to pull out of Iraq if he became president. Obama still has not withdrawn American troops from the Middle East. So Obama is the primary cause of the Texas Ford hood massacre. Obama's unfulfilled rhetoric during his campaign for president compelled Hasan to plan and execute his rampage. Hasan, the man behind the trigger, was impatient and unsettled. He couldn't even wait for Obama's first term to expire. He acted at the tail end of Obama's first year in office. Maybe he would have witnessed Obama pulling our troops out of those regions before 2012 and would have not taken the life of our brave military personnel. But is it a fait accompli for Rtd Major Hasan? Because he wasn't planning on living after November 5, 2009, especially after he shouted his allegiance to Allah before opening fire. President Obama didn't call Major Hasan's deed an act of terror. Instead, Obama said it was a man-made disaster. What Hasan did was utter terrorism, absolute jihadism.

Obama's national security agenda

Rush's predictions remain to be seen

Obama announced that he would close Guantanamo Bay (A detention camp). He also granted the Miranda right to be read to foreign terrorists.

Rush stated: "He's (Obama) not going to close Guantanamo, and he's not going to get out of Iraq in 16 months." Rush had confidence in his prediction because he said Obama would not saddle himself with defeats.

Threat to America

May 18, 2008, Obama said, "Iran, Cuba, Venezuela, these countries are tiny compared to the Soviet Union. They don't pose a serious threat to us the way the Soviet Union posed a threat to us." A much tinier country, Afghanistan, caused the most devastating catastrophe Americans has ever experienced. So Obama's statement is baseless.

Russia and Iran are a threat to America. Putin is an Eastern Europe threat to America. George Bush was able to shackle and confine Putin to a paper tiger status. Bush's tenure as president is over, but Putin's bully pulpit is still prominent. The whole of the Middle East is a threat to America. President Mahmoud Ahmadinejad of Iran is not toeing the line. He's resolved in seeking a nuclear program for Iran, despite warnings from United Nations Security Council and the United States.

Full-fledged incompetence

You have rogue nations like Iran still harboring hopes of getting nukes, and yet Obama isn't taking any drastic steps in defusing Iran of global threats. And Obama hasn't given Hillary the green light to take concrete steps toward peace in the Middle East.

Sec. Rice warned Obama and Hillary Clinton: "The last time we left Afghanistan, and we abandoned Pakistan, that territory became the very territory on which Al Qaeda trained and attacked us on September 11th. So our national security interests are very much tied up in not letting Afghanistan fail again and become a safe haven for terrorists. It's that simple; if you want another terrorist attack in the U.S., abandon Afghanistan."

The Iraq debacle

Obama was asked, "What's the most gut-wrenching decision you've ever had to make?" Obama replied, "Opposing the war in Iraq was as tough a decision that I've had to make, not only because there were political consequences but also because Saddam Hussein was a bad person and there was no doubt he meant America ill."

Rush whistled Obama for a foul; he said Obama didn't vote against opposing the war in Iraq because Obama wasn't, at that time, a United State senator.

Demoralizing our troops

Former Democratic Congressman from Pennsylvania Rep. Murtha said, "There was no firefight. There was no IED (improvised explosive device) that killed those innocent people. Our troops overreacted because of the pressure on them. And they killed innocent civilians in cold blood."

In 2006, Obama specifically targeted the American troops: "We've got to get the job done there and that requires us to have enough troops so that we're not just air-raiding villages and killing civilians, which is causing enormous pressure over there." "Just air-raiding villages and killing civilians," speaks volumes about Obama. What Obama meant by "just" is beyond frightening. Is that all our brave men and women do, air-raid villages and kill civilians?

Harry Reid was next: "This war is lost, and that the surge is not accomplishing anything."

Durbin, the Senate Majority Whip, fell prey to believing that damaging photos that fell into his lap about our troops were genuine. And with the eagerness to impugn our brave men and women, he said: "If I read this to you and did not tell you that it was an FBI agent describing what Americans had done to prisoners in their control, you would most certainly believe this must have been done by Nazis, Soviets in their gulags, or some mad regime—Pol Pot or others—that had no concern for human beings. Sadly, that is not the case. This was the action of Americans in the treatment of their prisoners."

Colonel Khadafy praised Obama

After twenty- one months, we have witnessed a presidency that is filled with an avalanche of world tour apologies on behalf of the United States. We have witnessed Obama making numerous churlish comments about the greatness of America. We have witnessed an American president getting warm wishes from a fruitcake terrorist like Muammar al-Gaddafi, the leader of Libya.

"We are content and happy if Obama can stay forever as the president of America," Gadhafi said. Colonel Moammar Gadhafi was asked why he thinks Obama should be president forever. Moammar Gadhafi responded, "Because the vision he has would save America, would save the world. His vision." Gadhafi intends for Obama to be handed the role of a judge, jury and executioner with a view to remake America.

Mohammed vs. New York

How judicious is Obama that he wants the 9/11 planners to be on trial in New York? Khalid Shaikh Mohammed, the mastermind behind the worst act of terrorism on American soil, and his cohort are to be on trial in New York? This is beneath the office of the presidency. This is disrespectful to the office once held by George Washington, Abraham Lincoln and Roland Reagan. Vice president Biden was right when he said the presidency is not "on the job training." This proceeding further proved that Obama's judgment is too impaired to be the president.

Al-Qaeda more optimistic than ever

Is Obama a wolf in sheep's clothing, or is Obama a paper tiger? Obama's dithering and taking too long to decide when to send troops to Afghanistan made it evident that the war against terrorism is an inconvenience for Obama. Americans have been gagged. On Obama's watch, we are banned from saying that America is engaging in a war on terrorism. Mirandizing enemy combatants and treating them like criminal defendants instead of war criminals sums up Obama's national security achievement. The whole of Obama's twenty- one months as Commander in Chief has emboldened al-Qaeda. American citizens around the world have been endangered by Obama and his national security policies. Since 9/11, there haven't been any attacks on Bush's watch. After the tragedy of September the eleventh, Cheney and Bush rolled up their sleeves and got ready for a fight against terrorism. And they won that battle. But Obama is the opposite. Cheney and Bush took a hard-line approach against terrorism. Obama believes that because he is president, al-Qaeda will repent from attacking America. He's respectfully running around like a chicken with his head cut off and apologizing left and right to people that George Bush won't even welcome to enter America. Al-Qaeda was extremely happy when McCain lost the presidential election. They knew that McCain would have been a carbon copy of Bush. Bin Laden is strategizing. He has seen a loop hole. Bin Laden's fingers are already on the trigger, he is just looking for a good aim. But God is in control, and America is the land of the free. America is God's land. And God will save Americans.

Afghanistan

The war in Afghanistan is an inconvenience for Obama. His speech on the war in Afghanistan was a far cry from a morale-boosting speech. He didn't send the requested number of troops. And he set a time-table for withdrawal. Al-Qaeda is watching, observing and taking notes on Obama's weaknesses. It's really blood in the water for America and the Western world. Al-Qaeda's breeding grounds for terrorism are established throughout the Middle East. That wouldn't happen if Bush was still in the Oval Office.

Bush's national security policies were much maligned by the Obama administration. However, there are signs that Obama may have heeded some of Dick Cheney's advice.

Conclusion

Obama's imperatives and leadership abilities in the war against terrorism are weak. The reading of Miranda rights to terrorists and enemy combatants is more evidence of that fact. His desire to close Guantanamo bay is also more evidence of his lack of leadership abilities.

We can take it to the bank that America single-handedly over the 200 plus years has liberated many countries from coast to coast. "We have saved the world from totalitarianism again and again and again," Sean Hannity reminded Americans.

Obama's original national security agenda was a recipe for disaster. But just as Rush predicted, Obama is being force to heed to Bush and Cheney's advice, especially in regards to Iraq and Afghanistan.[6]

Economy

How do we grow our economy?

Before Obama took office he said: "The American people understand that the way we grow this economy is from the bottom up." Rush was stunned: "Is that really right? We grow the economy bottom up?" Rush claimed that if economies were built from the bottom up, Mexico and Cuba would have the best economy in the world. They would be the international superpowers. He added that if economies were built from bottom up, Africa and the Soviet Union would be booming economically. Rush asked, how do poor people cause the economy to boom? When was the last time people with no money hired workers? How in the world do the unemployed contribute to the growth of the economy? Rush said you don't need a degree in economics to understand that economies can't be built from the bottom up. According to Rush, all Obama wants is the transferring of wealth from the rich entrepreneurs and the risk takers to the poor. He stated that working, and not the transfer of wealth, is the way "the lower income quintiles" move up the economic ladder. It's a playbook for spreading the wealth around. It's about pitting the upper class against the middle and poor classes.

Stimulus package: Obama Ignores Rush's Stimulus Plan

Drastic times call for drastic measures. Rush, in his formerly nicotine-stained fingers, drafted his own Stimulus Plan of 2009 that was published by World Street Journal. His plan was a stepping stone to a vibrant economy, yet Obama seemed to ignore Rush's bipartisan stimulus bill. Rush said Obama's stimulus plan is a far cry from a bipartisan plan. But Rush's plan is a step to correct the labyrinth Obama has created for himself. Rush said his plan is about the United States not failing, and he's not interested in taking the platitude so long as America would not fall.

The Truth behind Obama's stimulus package

Rush went on to state that Obama's stimulus package is done to solidify power to the Democratic Party and to stimulate the state government. There was no serious intent to create jobs and no concrete measures to solve the unemployment problem.

In regard to Obama's stimulus bill, Rush couldn't wait to experience the rubber hitting the road. Rush said America is in debt even to those who have not yet been born. He feels that the Democratic Party's objective is to stimulate and nationalize the private sector. He said that is not the concept that founded the country. It will only serve as a detriment to entrepreneurs.

The Bail out of Corporations
Goodbye to Capitalism, welcome to the city of Socialism
Rush said that the United States, under the leadership of Obama, is on the highway ignoring the speed limit, heading to the "city of socialism," The Obama administration is hiding under the pretext of not wanting unstable companies to go south, so that means they have to bail the private sector out.

Obama Protects CEO
Rush noted that what Barack Obama meant by "I'm the only one standing between you and the pitchforks," is if these private sector entities aren't in line with Obama, the "angry mobs" will come for them.

Is Second Stimulus on the Horizon?
Obama treated the stimulus package as monopoly money. And talk of a second stimulus bill is in the air. A second stimulus bill will worsen and add to the economic malaise. Free market capitalism will prevent further sabotaging of the economy. Obama said briefly: "I did not run for office to be helping out a bunch of, you know, fat cat bankers on Wall Street."

Democratic Representative vilified the Economy
Congressman Barney Frank asked, "Here is my problem. I cannot find a villain. Now, many of my colleagues have found various villains. They tend to be private sector or public sector, depending on the ideology of the finder. But, as I look at what happened, what I see is a very difficult

situation that threatened further severe damage to an economy already damaged." Rush answered Frank's puzzle. Rush said all Barney Frank has to do in order to find a villain is to look in the mirror.

Obama Worsens the Economy

There is no objecting to the fact that Obama inherited a deficit. However, Obama has been acting like he was tossed a curveball by the economic plight. And that gives him the freedom and the excuses to keep blaming the previous administration for his difficult first year in office. "He inherited it." Rush agreed that Obama inherited a bad economy, but that he has also aided in worsening what he inherited. And the sad truth is that Obama hurt the economy on purpose, in order to implement his radical agendas.

Obama Abhors Private Sector

Obama's policies are punitive to the private sector. Many businesses have filed for bankruptcy and eventually closed up shop. Rush claimed that Obama regards profit as evil. He views the private sector as a golden goose that lives forever. As such, it put a monkey wrench in Obama's economic plans.

Economic 101

Rush Elaborates on State of Economy

The outlook for the American economy is pessimistic, Rush counseled. So long as Obama is in charge, the crumbling of the greatest economy in the world is at hand. Trillions of dollars can't be accounted for. Rush said the United States government by itself can't support our economy. He went on to say that Washington DC's solutions, ideologies, philosophies and theories aren't working. All they do is usurp the entities that make America a thriving nation.

Obama Role Model to Socialism

Obama said, "The thing that we can do most importantly is serve as a good role model and that's why for example closing Guantanamo from my perspective as difficult as it is." Rush vehemently reacted: "Screw Guantanamo!" According to Obama, serving as a good role model is kneecapping and taking over the private sector. And that would be kneecapping General Motors and Chrysler. According to Rush, Fascism and Socialism is looking to be the role model for Obama. Rush said everything that Obama is implementing, from transferring of wealth to raising taxes, has been tried by the rest of the world and has failed dramatically.

What a real leader would do in a recession

In a dire situation, where unemployment is spiraling out of control, Rush stated that a real leader would seize the opportunity of our bad economy to significantly explain how the free market works. And he or she would be sincere in their presentation about how America can get out of the doldrums that the economy is facing.

America in Throes of Recession

Obama said about the recession: "If nothing is done, this recession could linger for years." Rush claimed that, if left alone, history has proven that recessions will come "out of their cycles in a 24 month period."

Obama's Administration pleading for opportunities

Opportunity presented itself, and Rahm Emanuel said: "You never want a serious crisis (Recession) to go to waste. What I mean by that is it's an opportunity to do things that you think you could not do before. This is an opportunity. What used to be long-term problems -- be they in the health care area, energy area, education area, fiscal area, tax area, regulatory reform area -- things that we had postponed for too long that were long-term are now immediate and must be dealt with. And this crisis provides the opportunity for us, as I would say, the opportunity to do things that you could not do before." Rush weighed in and said what the Obama's administration wants to do is to destroy the private sector and grow the state government so that people's first, instead of last, resort would be the state government. Rush said the opportunities the Obama's administration are talking about involve implementing their socialist agenda, not the opportunity to salvage the American economy from the abyss.

Can you believe that Rahm Emanuel wants to experiment with our bad economy? Is this the time for tinkering and experimenting or the time to call on experience? So Obama's Stimulus Plan jump-started Emanuel's experiment. In Obama's administration's experiment, some Americans have to bite the bullet and work for lesser paying jobs.

And what is experience in this economic tsunami that American is facing? The answer is free market. But Obama and Emanuel don't want the free market to be free, they want to experiment when Americans are fighting to keep their heads above water. They're not fazed with the mounting underlying problems. They want nothing to get in their way of experimenting. They will continue serving paper over the cracks while maintaining that the economy is recovering. The economy is already in a tailspin, yet Rahm Emanuel is skating on thin ice.

The Stock market got stock

Obama said about the stock market: "What I'm looking at is not the day-to-day gyrations of the stock market, but the long-term ability for the United States and the entire world economy to regain its footing. And, you know, the stock market is sort of like a tracking poll in politics. It bobs up and down day to day, and if you spend all your time worrying about that, then you're probably going to get the long-term strategy wrong." A few months after his comment, the stock market got stock.

Jobs created by the White House

Obama's laser-like focus on jobs is on the horizon. Rush was stunned to hear that the White House plans to imprison Guantanamo Bay detainees at a facility in the United States. And Senate Minority Whip Senator Richard Durbin said, "Eighteen hundred good-paying jobs with full benefit packages is a dream come true for many families in that part of the state. And then think of what those jobs lead to in terms of businesses, new schools, new hospitals, new libraries, new opportunities."

Rush asked, "Do you believe this? Bringing Gitmo terrorists to Thompson, Illinois, will be "a dream come true" for the people there!" So transferring Guantanamo Bay terrorist detainees to jails in America is one of the ways Obama wants to create jobs.

In Closing

The Obama administration will continue to slough the economic downfall off on Bush's administration. Rush claimed they will continue to undersell how bad the American economy is because they can't afford to make Obama look incompetent. "He has to borrow," Dick Morris said "To pay for the stimulus that didn't stimulate." That sums up Obama's twenty- one months of economic disaster. Throughout Obama's tenure as president, Americans have been sleeping and repeatedly waking up to sobering news about our economy; unemployment skyrocketing like no man's business, corporations going south, etcetera. A second stimulus plan will smother our economy. American continues to navigate through precarious and difficult times. There is nationwide angst and unsettlement among Americans. Obama makes you believe that our economy is hunky-dory. The economy is on the edge. Job causalities are skyrocketing; businesses have folded, there has been a huge amount of outsourcing of American's jobs and mass layoffs and furloughs are occurring statewide. Capitalism has the recipe for prosperity. Obama's policies are the antithesis; a war on prosperity if you will.

Rush final words: "Obama is destroying the best economic system ever created. And the results are in."[7]

Media bias

The truth about the liberal media

Rush stated that the mainstream media are all "on the same page" because none of the mainstream media outlets are interested in the truth. Liberals run away from the truth.

Fair and Balance: Refuting Mainstream media

The main duty of conservative radio is to counter the drivels, lies and bilges of mainstream media. News is disseminated by the template the liberal media sets on a daily basic.

How long will the media be in bed with Obama?

The Democratic Party is totally aided by a compliant media. The mainstream media, CNN, MSNBC, CBS, NPR, etcetera grovel to Democrat politicians. According to Rush, the media "has become slavish and sycophantish" to President Obama.

Rush said that journalism has deteriorated. The media had to "check its integrity at the door," to humbly and faithfully "become propagandists for" Obama, his administration and the Democratic Party. They are not reporters. Rather, they are repeaters and they do their utmost to "give credence" to Obama's lies.

Obama: defended like a Demon

If you oppose and criticize Obama you are considered a racist and a bigot, but if you uphold his view, you are considered intelligent. Silencing the critics of Obama is working everywhere, save Rush Limbaugh's EIB Network and conservative talk radio.

Obama: given a free pass

Rush said conservatives' criticism of Obama is solely aimed at alerting Americans about Obama's radical beliefs. But Rush also said if Obama is able to shun and not respond to all the critics, "then you've got the old question, well, if a tree falls in the forest and nobody's there, does it make a sound?" Rush asked, if Obama keeps saying things that are strange and he has not been criticized by the hard left for the strange things, then did he say those things?

Media favored Obama, but 2012 will be a whole new ball game

They were able to segregate all those who participated in criticizing Obama as racists and hate mongers. And they wouldn't report any deleterious news about Obama because it would contradict them portraying him as a messiah.

The media is no longer what it used to be. They are one of the Democratic Party's "ideological adjuncts." Rush's final words for the extreme liberal media, he said: "Orwellian and Machiavellian" are understatements to describe how despicable the media has become.

The media have been steadfast and faithful in their support of Obama. Apart from conservative talk radio and Fox News, there has been a drought of genuine news. The majority of the American people are being daily propagandized by the "Drive by Media" and the "State run media." These propagandizers have praised Obama to the hilt and it would be difficult for them to criticize him. They only report what fits their template. That wasn't the case when Bush was at the helm. Americans that are searching for real news should tune into conservative talk radio or Fox News because, "Everybody else in the state-controlled media is an echo chamber," Rush said. The echo chambers have to report what fits the template. MSNBC, CNN and the rest of the "State run media" repeats the same talking points. They wait for Rush's take on an important issues before they substantively delve into them.[8]

Supreme Court

The GOP bickering over Obama's Supreme Court nominee was predominately because they had to constantly be looking over their shoulders, making sure they don't agitate a certain Rush. The nominee, Sotomayor is best known for her racial comment: "wise Latina woman with the richness of her experience would more often than not reach a better conclusion than a white male who hasn't lived that life." Rush reacted by calling her a "reverse racist." And Rush came in for a hail of criticism for his comment. The truth is hard to swallow.

Obama needs a radical in the Supreme Court

Obama is hell-bent on desecrating America's Constitution, so the cold, calculating president selected Sonia Sotomayor as a nominee for the Supreme Court to help his cause. Obama is a man with a chip on his shoulder, not the cool, calm, collected individual that the world portrays him to be.

Rush reminds Republicans

Rush said that during Sotomayor's confirmation, the Republican Party in Congress forced their lawmakers to go easy on Sonia Sotomayor. Rush said the Democrats tried to destroy Clarence Thomas, but they still did not lose the black votes. You can also parallel that with Miguel Estrada and the Hispanic votes.

Appease critics for Hispanic votes

Rush said just to appease and ward off critics, the GOP are putting "duct tape on their mouths." Rush stated that George Bush nominated a number of Hispanics in his administration, but that they were all attacked by the Democrats. Yet that didn't prevent the Hispanic Americans from voting for the Democratic Party. Therefore, the notion that attacking a Hispanic for the Supreme Court on substance would drive away Hispanic voters from the Republican Party doesn't hold water. Rush said the GOP is "becoming extinct by virtue of its actions"

The media blamed Rush for the GOP treading water on Sotomayor's confirmation. Rush said, "It's getting so routine that I'm responsible for everything Republicans do."

Rush responded to Democratic senatorial threat to block Sotomayor's nomination

The Republican lawmakers' actions provoked Rush. It's sad to see the GOP buying into the premise that attacking a Hispanic or black nominee would drive away votes from both groups. Menendez and Schumer, both Democratic senators, said to their Republican counterparts, "they vote against her {Sotomayor} at their peril."[9]

Constitution

America is a nation of individuals, not a collection of individuals

Obama said from his point of view, "We are not a nation of individuals. We're not a collection of individuals." Rush profoundly disagreed: "Well, yes, we are." Our identity, what differentiates America from the rest of the world, is our individual freedom and our personal liberty. In Obama's thinking, working together for a common good is collectivism.

Madison on encroachment of liberty

James Madison, in 1788, said: "Since the general civilization of mankind, I believe there are more instances of the abridgements of the freedom of the people by gradual and silent encroachment of those in power than by violent or sudden usurpations." Rush said the birthright of every American is liberty. Eradicating liberty is what the Obama administration are scheming to do. And through their healthcare bill, they will seize the opportunity to usurp liberty.

Not all agree that we are endowed by our God

Rushed claimed that the left hate the notion that we are endowed by our Creator because Liberals "don't believe in God with certain inalienable rights." Rush said the reason why they hate the notion is because being endowed with certain inalienable rights is final and nothing can be built on that. Life, liberty and the pursuit of happiness are final. It can only be taken away.

According to Rush, the making of the Declaration followed by the Constitution in Philadelphia was a miracle. "There's no more perfect form of government that's been devised. I know Churchill's line is surviving, regardless. you can't go beyond certain inalienable rights endowed by our Creator."

"The source of our liberty and freedom was acknowledged in our founding documents as having come from God." The Founding document is an impediment to Liberals. The US Constitution limits them from implementing their agendas. Furthermore, they are seeking ways to render the US Constitution useless.

Independence Day or Dependence Day?

Conservatives are constitutionalists, Rush said the Declaration of Independence was started by seven words. Rush said those words also begat the United States. For 233 years, we have been guided by those seven words. For 233 years America has celebrated independence year, but how much longer will that be true?

According to Rush, we have to reject the promises of dependence. We have to reject the premise that a government takeover of the healthcare system is the way forward for the independence of America. Rush said 233 years of America's greatest has proved that independence tramples over dependence. We need to look no further than dependent countries in Africa and Asia for proof of that statement.

The US Constitution is mirrored by Republican views

Freedom, liberty and pursuit of happiness are the core belief of Republicanism, not Liberalism. Rush said humans were created into freedom, that the natural state for human is freedom, but tyrants and dictators tried to "curtail, lasso and constrain" that freedom. Rush said we are individuals, not a collective, and therefore we are at our best working for our own self interest. Individual liberty and freedom are part of our creation, and therefore they will "never go out of style." Our liberty is what puts us on the pinnacle on society. It is what makes us different from the rest of the world. "We have acknowledged that our creation comes from God, not from government, that our freedom is a natural yearning of our creation."

Abandoned what we believe in

Rush said that Liberals do not want us to believe in risk, reward and learning real life lessons from failures.

Obama's opposition to the US Constitution

Obama lamented: "The Supreme Court never ventured into the issues of redistribution of wealth and sort of more basic issues of political and economic justice in this society." Rush stated that Obama looks with disdain upon the US Constitution. According to Obama, if the Constitution can't be changed through the judicial system to suit his policies, it has to be ignored.

Obama went on to say: "Generally the Constitution is a charter of negative liberties. Says what the states can't do to you. Says what the Federal government can't do to you, but doesn't say what the Federal government or State government must do on your behalf." In response, Rush said the reason why Obama says the Constitution is a charter of negative rights is because it doesn't include the redistribution of wealth. And the Constitution doesn't outline what the federal government can do on our behalf. So Obama is constrained because there is no Marxism and socialism defined in the Constitution.

In precise words, Rush stated that rights come from God and the Democrats wish they could take them away from the people. Anything the government can't stop you from doing in a free society is a right. Life as in abortion, Obama is trying to take away. Liberty and freedom as in healthcare, Obama is trying to take away. Rush said young people have given up on the pursuit of happiness because all they want to do is survive.

It doesn't document what the state and federal government can't do to us. Obama is upset because of the limitations placed by the Constitution on the role of government in people's lives.

Rush concluded that Obama wants the government to be involved in our everyday life. Rush said Jefferson, Madison, Lincoln and Reagan would classify what Obama is doing to America as the "abuses of monarchy," despotism and the "tyranny of socialism."

Rush read the preamble of the United States Constitution to illustrate his point

"We the people of the United States, in order to form a more perfect union, establish justice, insure domestic tranquility, provide for the common defense, promote the general welfare," not insure it, "promote the general welfare, and secure the blessings of liberty to ourselves and our posterity, do ordain and establish this Constitution for the United States of America." Rush said the US Constitution is being abrogated and ripped by Democrats from section to section.

How was America founded?

Rush pointed out that America's past leaders believed that the government or the state should have limits so that the American dream will not have limits. The Founders rejected authoritarianism because they believe each individual has the potential to do great things if they are not obstructed by the government.

53

Democrats are ripping the Founders and all the unsung heroes that fought for the solid foundation of this country to shreds. It seems Obama is on the brink of pulverizing this country's constitution, and what has been enshrined by Americans might lose its venerable status. The Legislative and the Judiciary branches of government might be stumbling blocks for Obama wanting to desecrate our constitution, but he might have authority to abrogate certain sections of the constitution. Just with his intention on bastardizing our constitution, he has thrown the Founders and their original work under the bus.

Conclusion

America was founded on the concept that each and every individual has certain inalienable rights from God. Liberals want to rip the Constitution to shreds and "use it for toilet paper."[10]

Healthcare Reform

Obama's healthcare proposal was at the forefront of everybody's mind. And it was definitely a can of worms to the majority of Americans. All the Washington D.C protestations proved that his plan antagonized the American people.

Despite the steady erosion of support, Obama continued feinting and lying to the American people about the real purpose of his healthcare policy. The way the Democratic Party lionized Obama's healthcare bill was typical of their eagerness to control the American people's lives. Obama continued sandbagging Americans into believing that his healthcare reform has nothing to do with freedom for Americans to have a choice of doctors. They want to be the ones who would determine our medical options.

Nancy Pelosi, Harry Reid and other congressional leaders, had clandestinely tried to railroad Obama's healthcare bill through Congress. The passage of this bill comes with heavy implications for the future of America.

Obama made numerous transparent promises

Obama failed to air congressional negotiations on C-Span as he had promised. But of course, all those promises were just platitudes. Rush said the Democrats are the ones having meeting in secret; they keep the content of the bill from the common people. Obama, without coercion, promised transparency on many occasions. Obama said "we'll have [healthcare reform] negotiations televised on C-SPAN, so the people can see who is making arguments on behalf of their constituents and who is making arguments on behalf of the drug companies or the insurance companies." Rush said Obama didn't delivered his promises. There were no negotiations aired on C-Span.

Right or Privilege: Crossing the line of Demarcation

Senator Harkin is adamant that healthcare is a right, not a privilege. And his fellow Democrats will do anything to finally cross a demarcation line. Harkin said boldly: "We're trying to cross a demarcation line, this is the way I put it. On one side is health care as a privilege, on the other side is health care as a right. We will cross that line finally and say that health care is a right of all Americans."

Everything but the kitchen sink to pass Healthcare Reform

Democratic senate leader Harry Reid compared GOP lawmakers who withstand the passage of the senate healthcare bill to White Americans who supported slavery. During Republican Dwight Eisenhower's presidency, Democratic Senator Strom Thurmond was the lone wolf who lengthily opposed the Civil Right Act of 1957. And it was the Republicans who, without a hitch, came to a consensus for the passage of the Civil Rights act of 1964.

Majority Leader Harry Reid said, "Instead of joining us on the right side of history, all Republicans have come up with is this: Slow down, stop everything, let's start over. If you think you've heard this excuse before, you're right. When this country belatedly recognized the wrongs of slavery, there were those who dug in their heels and said, "Slow down, it's too early, let's wait." Rush reacted to Reid's efforts of retooling the history of slavery. Rush claimed that somebody needs to remind Reid that is was Democrats that stonewalled both the 1957 and 1964 civil right acts and, as such, the Democrats stalled the progress of ending slavery. But Rush is sad that Americans think it is the Republican Party that wanted to preserved and prolong slavery. Rush said the GOP came into existence due to the fight against slavery. The Democratic Party fought to preserve slavery. Senator Harry Reid's remark was based on flagrant dishonesty. The Democrats' unflinching determination to ram through health care reform legislation never ceased.

Borderline Criminal

After Rush read the Senate healthcare bill, he said the bill had liberalism written all over it. Rush knows where all the bodies are buried because of his longevity in fighting constantly against liberals:

"And as I read through this," Rush said, "It's an unmitigated disaster. It is irresponsible. It's almost criminal. "Rush said the bill was simply insidious.

Behind closed doors meetings, back room deals: How Historic?

Democrats conducted closed door meetings on the passage of the health care legislation and in the process left their counterpart out of the loop. Democrats were saying that the passage of the healthcare bill was going to be an historical moment, just as the election of Barack Obama was. After the Democratic senate held night sessions to push through the healthcare bill, Rush asked why the Democratic senators were having meetings "under the cover of darkness, in the middle of night like rats?"

Rush said the passage of Social Security and the 1964's Civil Right act weren't done under the cover of darkness. Reid's leadership of the Democratic senate certainly did not make him a heroic statesman like LB Johnson and Speaker Thomas O'Neill.

The upshot

The New Deal wiped out the black family. Obama's healthcare bill is aimed at wiping out the rest of America "Welfare, the war on poverty, {was} supposed to wipe out poverty and all we did was wipe out the black family," said Rush.

The Democratic Senate was shy by 60 votes until a few of its members were whored out by Majority leader Harry Reid. Hounded by their Party leadership, the few Democratic senators were on the verge of breaking ranks with the Democratic leadership. But after they laughed all the way to the bank, they decided to walk the plank for the leadership. So the passage of the senate version of the healthcare bill is a false consensus. What is the political fallout for the bribed senators? The 2010 midterm congressional election will determine the answer.

Being that they are United States' senators, they have the utmost healthcare plan in the country. So why are they so eager to pass a bill that they would be grandfathered from? And why do they act like rats in the night? Because they know it's an atrocious piece of legislation that the American people would reject outright. These Democratic partisan hacks ignored the outrage that has been effervescing because of their contemptuous view of the American people.

A plurality of American voters agreed that our healthcare system doesn't need an overhaul, but Congress overrode their wishes and passed a debacle of a healthcare reform bill.[11]

Obama's Reign

Rush on an Obama presidency

According to Rush, Obama is the most unqualified and the most unaccomplished candidate a major party has nominated for president. Rush said the Democratic Party is a "camouflage mask" and their leader Obama is "100% Machiavellian."

Obama's biography

Obama introduced himself: "I worked as a community organizer in Chicago. I was very active in low income neighborhoods, uh, working on issues of crime and education and employment, uh, and seeing that in some ways certain portions of the African-American community, uh, are doing as bad, if not worse, and recognizing that my fate remained tied up with their fates, that, uh, that my individual salvation, uh, is not going to come about without a collective salvation for the country."

Politically, who is Obama?

Rush defined Obama as a partisan leftist and a radical politician. Rush claimed that in order to get the truth from the mouth of a Democrat, you have to always take the opposite of what they say. Rush said Obama, in every waking moment, practices illusion: he's "an illusionist."

Rush claimed that Obama is a "charismatic demagogue" and a rigid ideologue that hasn't achieved anything meaningful in life.

Clinton retreads

Excluding defense secretary Gates and Timothy Geithner, the treasury secretary, the rest of Obama's top cabinet positions were Bill Clinton's associates. The Clinton retreads have been recruited to work in Obama's administration.

After Obama assembled his cabinet, Rush pointed out that all throughout the 2008 campaign, Obama ranted against appointing the "same old Washington people" in the same position. So when the ball was in Obama's court, what did he do? Change evaporated quickly.

Obama then went on to say: "Understand where the vision for change comes from first and foremost. It comes from Me. That's my job, is to provide a vision in terms of where we are going and make sure then that my team is implementing it."

Rush took into account all of Obama's appointees and then stated that Obama's "cross section of opinion" ranges from liberal to very liberal. Rush asked where are the moderate and conservative cross sections of opinion? Rush said Obama assembled only those who would implement his ideas and that is the vision Obama was talking about.

Obama's domestic agenda

Rush asserted that Obama's agenda is based on "readdressing wrongs" and the redistribution of wealth. Rush said Obama "peddles class warfare" and disseminates "human envy."

Returning the nation's wealth to its "rightful owners" is the bottom line. For Obama those who are wealthy, those who have accomplished got their wealth in an "ill-gotten way," and as such their wealth must be redistributed.

Obama's anger

Rush believes that on Obama's watch, the majority, the Whites has to pay for its racism. And the wealthy have to pay for their wealth. In Obama's adult life, we can chronicle a consistency in Obama's willingness to dither from his unapologetic ways. Racial division has grounded Obama in rage and anger. His anger over racial discrimination constitutes his beliefs. Rush is not one of the political figures that believes that Obama is a cool, calm and collected person. Rush said Obama is angry at Great Britain over the "colonization of Africa," and he's also angry at the United States over slavery. Obama doesn't believe the right price has been paid for the whites that were involved in slavery.

Obama's resentments

It's obvious that Obama has resentment for the wealthy. And as such, higher taxes for the wealthy in order to punish the rich and the achieved, should be enacted. Rush said it's hard to swallow the fact that the US government is purposely assaulting the country's private sector.

Chip on Obama's shoulder

Obama, like Wright, believes that America was "constituted as unjust." And Obama wants to make sure the "unjustness permeates" no further. Because of the racial discrimination that the minorities were subjected to, Rush said in Obama's world, a minority is allowed to be a racist.

The media claimed Obama is cool, calm and collected. He is actually quite the contrary. He is cold, unhinged and only wants to rob Peter to pay Paul. Obama has been disingenuous to the American people.

Judge not a book by its cover

Can we undo Obama's staged questions and planted audience? He often sounds incoherent without the use of a teleprompter. Rush believed there is no doubt that Obama is highly educated, but his intelligence has been exaggerated. Rush said Obama is an empty suit. He takes a teleprompter wherever he goes because they have to keep him on message. But without a teleprompter, Obama is simplistic: he is all over the place in his speeches.

Obama's leadership style: Saul Alinsky

Obama uses words he knows uninformed Americans want to hear. Rush asserted that what Obama says in private contradicts what he says in the public. According to Rush, Obama practices the "low art of political seduction." And Rush said that is pure narcissism. Everything about Obama is an "appeal to popular sentiment." Rush tells Americans not to pay attention to what Obama says because it's the hope and change that got him the Oval office.

Rush proceeded to say Obama "speaks within the realm" of his "audience's experience." In other words, he uses the language that his audience is comfortable with, though in the back of his mind, the exact opposite is his objective.

Obama's power
Rush said that first and foremost, Obama believes that America is an unjust and an immoral country. "We're in a position here, we don't have the power to stop Obama, so he's going to have to stop himself. And with nothing to stop him, there's nothing to stop him. And as there's nothing to stop him he's going to continue to try to get away with as much as he can, and at some point people are gonna go, "Wait a minute, I didn't think I was going to have to go to DMV to withdraw money from my bank," or some such thing."

Rush, while having a dialogue with Sean Hannity, stated that he never thought there would come a day in America where a United States president would dictate the types of cars automobile companies should make. Rush said he never imagined a day in America where a United States would dictate how much money Wall Street's CEO should earn. Rush said he never envisioned a day in America where a United States president would control the country's subprime industry. Rush said America under Obama is not the America he grew up in. Rush said if Al-Qaeda are planning to destroy America, they better do it swiftly because Obama "is beating them to it."

Remaking America or preserving America?

Rush asserted that every day Obama is in office is an "unmitigated disaster." Maintaining America as a beacon of liberty and freedom will be a tall order so long as Obama is at the helm.

Americans' sacrifice

Rush feels the American dream is as good as dead for the middle class citizen. It has been brought to a screeching halt by Obama's policies. Barack Obama is a wrench to the future of all Americans.

Rush's perfect analogy

Rush's analogy: Obama loves attention, so he goes into your house and starts a fire. He thus becomes an arsonist. He then goes outside and waits for the smokes before he yells fire, fire, and he gets the hose and sprays your house. Rush claimed Obama does this so that he can get the credit and be proclaimed as a hero. So he quenches the fire that he started but leaves you with a mess and damaged property.

Nobel Peace Prize: an Intrigue against America

Due to Obama being awarded with the Nobel Peace Prize, Rush said Obama is not only the first post-racial president of America: he's also the first post-accomplished president. Rush said just having good intentions can land you the Nobel Peace Prize. Accomplishing something of substance to win the prize is obsolete. Rush believes the reason why Obama was awarded the prize was due to an effort by global liberal elites to "manipulate Obama to the detriment of the United States." Rush said the liberal global elites know they have a "kindred spirit" in Obama. And their aim is to destabilize America as a world superpower.

Rush's prediction

Rush is the most reliable Republican soothsayer, largely because of his 20 years of experience countering liberals. Substantially, Rush has never come short in his predictions of what liberals have planned in the offing. On November 12, 2008, Rush predicted that he wouldn't be surprised if Obama stepped down from running for reelection. If Obama successfully implements his socialist agenda, then there wouldn't be any reason to run. "And that's a big "if.""

Rush would take his hat off to Obama if?

Rush said he would be the first to applaud Obama if he does the right thing like cutting taxes and taking action in booming the economy.

Twenty- one months have gone by, so is Obama just naïve and fundamentally misleading Americans, or is he just devious and is it a purely purposeful manipulation? There is lots of evidence that the latter is what he's practicing. Obama's personality gives him a cunning ability to deceive the American people outright.

The Obama bloom is largely off the rose. There is genuine opposition to Obama's policies. Ignorant liberals have been hoaxed. Others have been betrayed, and they are now being awakened. Never in the history of America has a newly minted president been so radioactive and so unpopular. But as long as moderates keep flocking to Obama, he will always have the capacity to talk to America.

America's first autocratic president

Obama is on the brink of being American's first despot, especially coming from a background where power is being exercised tyrannically. And you have Libya's dictator president begging Americans to give Obama the right to an absolute monarchy rule. Yes, Muammar Gadhafi wishes Obama to be an autocratic leader just as he is in Libya. America is not ready to be an authoritarian country; the town hall melees are evident. "We are on a collision course," Pat Buchanan, former presidential candidate, voiced his concerns: "He {Obama} wants to de-Christianize the nation; want it to be a secular nation," Pat Buchanan concluded.

The failed Chicago Olympic bid

Obama is so vigorously opposed to lobbyists. However, if that is truly the case, then what was he doing flying to Copenhagen? Wasn't he trying to lobby Chicago's bid for the Olympics? And who were his lobbyists? The answer is, first lady Michelle Obama, generous billionaire Oprah Gail Winfrey and the Mayor of Chicago. Obama's actions were unconventional. Rush said, "Just like I predicted: The Olympics go south, the bid, it's Bush's fault! It's residual hated for Bush, Bush's fault."

Obama voters, the aftermath

Obama's historical victory was a memorial moment for his voters, but how long did the Obama supporters enjoy the celebration of it? How will Obama deal with the magnitude of his broken promises to his supporters and fellow Democrats? The confidence that Obama's voters placed on him is incrementally ebbing away before his very eyes and ears. When it comes to trying to appease his critics, Hannity said, "Obama does just enough to tick the box."

Obama's enemy list

During the campaign, the Democratic media said Obama is an above party partisan. But his administration is sending out enemy lists which include Rush Limbaugh and Fox News. For twenty- one months, he hasn't lived up to the billing. Don't be fooled. Obama's White House attacks on Fox News is not about Fox News. It is about Sean Hannity and Glen Back. Without the impact of Hannity and Glen Back, Fox News could easily be mistaken for CNN or MSNBC. A moderate Fox News would be fine and dandy for the White House and Obama. The US Chamber of Commerce also fell on Obama's enemy list.

Closing Remarks

Nothing could be further from the truth when it comes to Obama's real agenda in his healthcare and stimulus bills. And because Obama is not similar to the core of the American people, he has to govern by lying to the American people. If he were honest with the American people, he would be rejected by a landslide.

Even though we have to judge a horse at the end of the race, Obama's reign in America is a disaster that has already happened. About every problem on earth has a silver lining. In America's situation, the silver lining is that there are under three years before Obama is done in office. But how much damage has been done to the country? Will America be the next Soviet Union? So the silver lining is really in limbo under the first black president.

Will all our Founding Founders' struggles, blood, sweat and tears that they went through to establish this county finally be in vain before human eyes? Will it be vanquished and defeated by Obama? America is heading from a capitalist oriented country to a nanny states utopia and socialist country.

Obama's administration

Let's not count our chickens before they've hatched and completely condemn Obama as the worst president in the history of America in the making. Having said that, it will be a miracle for Obama, his cohorts and his inner circle to dig themselves out of this hole.

To Obama's die-hard supporters

Obama's supporters are crossing their fingers that all the promises that Obama proclaimed will come to fruition. But his healthcare proposal is a major scale disruption that is threatening the majority of the American people.

To Americans as a whole

George Bush left America with a Richter scale of 5.0. Obama, within 21 months, has already increased that to a 7.0. Obama failure in 21 months as president is a microcosm of what we will have to deal with for the next 2 years. The insolvency occurring in California may also be a microcosm of what will happen to the other 49 States or, according to Obama, 57 States. Rush had the final word, and he said of an extremely radical Obama presidency: "There may be something lurking beneath the surface that we are all unaware of."

Rush is millions of miles away from the lemmings that support the Democratic Party's policies. In Rush's closing remarks, he issued an ominous warning about the future of America: "We're heading to a disaster here, and depending on how deep this disaster penetrates our country, it could take a generation to turn this stuff around. Elections have consequences. Okay, yeah, we're in a hole. But I'm not going to be on the bus when it goes over the cliff."[12]

Barack Hussein Obama
Mmm, mmm, mm!

END.

CHAPTER TWO

Rush's Unscripted Biography

Rush Limbaugh leads the conservative movement and also reluctantly leads the Republican Party. Rush is on a mission impossible because he wants every American to agree with him before he retires. It will really be a cold day in hell before Rush converts hard -core liberals. Rush is undeniably, indisputably and unarguably the wisest American in the 21st century. He is well-versed and a virtuoso in all areas of study. One would run out of superlatives to describe Rush. Adjectives are not enough to describe Rush's intelligence. Towering Democratic and Republican intellectuals have all fallen prey to Rush's wisdom. For about 2 decades now, Rush's political obituaries have been written, erased, re-written and the cycle continues. Within that period, Rush has found himself on the receiving end of contempt and considerable criticism.

Rush vs. Barack

Rush has been around since the latter days of Ronald Reagan's presidency. In the early nineties, when Rush was chiefly well-known nationwide, Barack was a community organizer. He probably heard the name "Rush Limbaugh" but never dreamt that he would be the number one opposition to Rush. Since declaring to test the water for a White House run, Obama has publicly belied Rush twice. He released an ad completely lying about Rush's stance on Mexicans and then alienated Rush by saying Rush is against immigrants. Obama's subliminal attacks on Rush were a testament to Obama's true character.

Like every other American he may have the privilege of calling out Rush's name, but regardless of his capacity as the United States president, he would never achieve the worth Rush is worthy of. Obama will never be able to look into the eyes of Rush. Obama is like a local elementary school teacher compared to Rush, who is a senior lecturer at an elite university. Mentality wise, no elected Democrats can see Rush Limbaugh. They can't see what Rush sees. Rush is a leader, while Obama, like every other president, is the boss. People are obedient to the boss because they are coerced. But Americans are not obligated to follow Rush Limbaugh. They do so because of Rush's true leadership abilities.

Limbaugh's audiences have been reading tomorrow's headlines too soon by listening to Rush constantly predict in advance what Obama and his administration will do. And most of Rush's predictions, especially Obama's national security and economic agenda, have been implemented or trial ballooned by Obama and his administration. Americans have to sincerely thank Rush for the weekly heads- up, especially in a time where many are unsettled and all at sea about the state of the economy. Rush said, "I, as a highly trained talk specialist, somebody that can read the stitches on a fastball as well as read between the lines."

As Obama hornswoggled the majority of Americans, Rush counters that by telling Americans the truth. The chance of ridiculing Rush's prediction about the Obama administration is remote. Rush's years of broadcasting experience dealing with liberals made his crystal ball predictions easy.

Who's the greatest, Limbaugh or Reagan?

Since the days of Reagan came to an end, Rush has matched or even surpassed the influences Reagan etched among Americans. But because of the no end in sight truthful and controversial remarks he makes, many Republican elected officials, during their campaigns, shy away from mentioning his name for the sake of the punishment of not being elected to office. They would rather resort to mentioning a dead president's name. Rush said, "Serving humanity, simply by showing up." Rush is on the air 3 hours every weekday, teaching and lecturing the American People. He has more than 25 million audience members, more than tens of thousands whom religiously listen to every single word and every syllable uttered by Rush. Reagan was the most principal politician that ever ran for president. And he was arguably the best president in the 20th century.

Having said that, it might not be popular to say Rush influenced Americans way better than Reagan did. Reagan never took questions from the average American and he never got directly insulted, disrespected or berated by uninformed Americans. If given a chance, Reagan might have been a decent talk radio host, but not to the heights of a well trained broadcaster. Reagan did effectively articulate the conservative principles, as does Rush.

Rush Limbaugh's 20 year message to Americans is not about saving face. Rush is about telling the genuine truth. But in the process, he became the greatest conservative icon in the nation. Rush years of unflagging industry have really answered a lot of questions for modern day conservatism.

In a tentative conclusion, conservatives have been banking on Rush's leadership more than they did on Reagan's.

Unprecedented: Rush's self-made success

Rush left no stone unturned to achieve his goals, his desires and his ambitions. And in the process, Rush was given the walking papers seven times. He didn't give in. He didn't traipse over to the government with his hands out for help. Rush was effervescent with ambitions. He continued struggling and searching until God answered his prayers. Rush's 20 years of fame in America has been sullied by death wishes, kidney failure, a 9/11 terrorist, by and large everything under the sun that is horrendous has been wished upon by the liberals. What did television host, Bill Maher, hope for for Rush? You have gubernatorial and congressional Republicans flocking to Rush as if Rush is a Father waiting to hear a confession. Their groveling attitude toward Rush is plain as day. When they meet Rush, it is like Steven Howse said: "prostituting." "{Rush} how are you doing?" These are heartless GOP politicians that only wish the worst case scenario for Mr. Limbaugh. They detest Rush; caring about Rush is probably in reverse, the penultimate thing on their mind, save only when it's time for fundraising during their campaign for office.

Rush reached his height in harness with limited quests. Rush's most notable guest was Richard Cheney. Rush seldom hosts politicians of Cheney's caliber. Gingrich, DeLay and a hatful of other high-profile political figures have been able to grace the Rush Limbaugh program. With Rush, it requires assiduous commitment to keep his loyal audience year in and year out. The big shot rivets his audience with the truth on a weekly basic. That is the principal reason his audience has expanded by leaps and bounds. Rush's show comes with lots of esoteric information: "I ignore conventional wisdom. I resist the tug of popular sentiment." Rush said he always resists the tug of conventional wisdom.

Rush is always on the cutting edge of societal evolution. His conspicuous success as a talk radio host will never be matched in this generation. Rush Limbaugh is a household name in all four corners of the world.

Obama vs. Limbaugh

An Obama – Rush interview can never be on the horizon. Rush wouldn't be caught dead involving himself in any of Obama's activities. However, Rush did confess to his millions of listeners that he had collided one on one with the newly minted president at a secret location. This was right before Obama took over the helm. Rush was left under no illusion as to what his audience thought after he had initially told them he never met with Obama. After he revealed his encounter with Obama, Rush made amends with his audience.

Compared to Rush, Obama was born with a silver spoon in his mouth. Rush had to vehemently strive to make it in the radio industry. His bully pulpit status was due to all the industry he had put into becoming a national talk radio host at California. Obama was a community organizer before he became a state senator. What is a community organizer? Anybody could organize a community.

Rush in the crosshairs of the White House

The White House have sent out their aides, Gibbs and Axelrod, to attack Rush on numerous occasions.

When Rush uttered, "I hope Obama fails," Obama responded and said Americans should stop listening to Rush Limbaugh. "You can't just listen to Rush Limbaugh and get things done," Obama said briefly. It was very detrimental of Obama to attack Rush in only his first week in office. According to Rush, the reason Obama's "calculated effort" didn't work is because conservatism is not fringe. Rush said Obama's plan wasn't lighthearted. Rather, it was a failed attempt to create animosity between GOP lawmakers in Congress and him.

Rush referenced President Clinton: "Clinton mentioned me all over the place, too. So, they (Obama administration) know that I am the direct route to conservative voters, and if they can discredit me and marginalize me, they think they have Republicans out of the way." Presidential candidate Patrick Buchanan claimed: "Rush is emerging as the de facto leader of the loyal opposition."

Obama's biggest domestic threat

Rush said Obama is willing to extend an olive branch to dictators like Ahmadinejad but he would not invite Rush for talks at the White House. For Obama, conservatism is a bigger threat than tyrannical dictators who are trying to destroy America. Conservatism represents an attempt to preserve America.

Rush has been bringing us up to speed with Obama and his administration's lackluster two years in office. Occasionally, Obama has been found behind the eight ball, and Rush has called time on those absurd moments. Rush's radio program is unscripted. His thoughts are amended within seconds and yet he doesn't ramble. He is coherent, unlike Obama, who is always simplistic and incoherent with the use of plants and staged questions. And the icing on the cake is that Obama uses a teleprompter. Obama has continued to buffalo the American people, but as the opposition, Rush has been unmasking Obama's every course of action. It's just divine the way Rush revealed the true meaning of Obama's agenda.[1]

Rush's Scripted Biography

Rush is still in his fifties. Way back in the mid 90's, he was at the summit of his career. Opportunities went begging left and right for Rush Limbaugh to abandon leading the conservative movement and instead accept a top cabinet position working for President Bush. Rush also could have easily run for the US Senate in the States of Florida, New York or Missouri, and be a victor without losing any sleep. But he dedicated his time to enlightening the American people with the real truth of American exceptionalism and American greatness. Rush won't dwell on or rue all of those opportunities that have not garnished his resume.

There has never been a leadership vacuum for the GOP since Rush has been on the horizon. The vacuum needs to be filled by a principal conservative politician who will willingly take up the bedrock conservative principles that have been harangued by Rush and run with it.

Rush resigned as the Titular head of the Republican Party

Sean Hannity interviewed Rush Limbaugh

Rush tendered his resignation as titular head of the party, but his resignation as been repudiated. Hannity asked Rush, "You came on the air one day, and you said, "I resign as the head of the Republican Party." Rush responded, "Titular head of the Republican Party," because I was not the head of the Republican Party. I was named the head of the Republican Party by the White House, by the Obama White House. What they were trying to do was get Republicans -- elected Republicans -- to throw me overboard, disavow me." Rush asserted that what the Liberals want to do is marginalize conservative talk radio. And Obama's plan of rallying the GOP lawmaker in Congress against Rush didn't worked out for Obama.

Rush finally resting on his laurels

Conservative Republicans know that Rush is at the zenith of his career. There is certainly time for everything, and the time will come when Rush will no longer be on the air. We reconcile on the fact that has to happen. For 20 years, Rush has been on the cutting edge of his field. He has paid his dues. For a century to come, conservatives will be indebted to Rush once he retires. Rush's contributions has been etched in stone.

Rush's Power

Rush is second to none. He takes a backseat to no one. It's diminishing or not enough to simply say that Rush is a talk radio host. Once upon a time, he was. Then he grew in stature to be preeminent. He single-handedly brought AM radio back to life. Some Democrats, instead of calling Rush by name, would rather refer to him as a conservative talk radio host.

Rush is the Solomon of our time. To use the words smartest or cleverest is an insult and an understatement in describing Rush. Rush is simply the most knowledgeable and most intelligent American in the 20-21 century, bar none. Although Rush never admits it, his mentality and wisdom are streets ahead of all others. Rush's brilliance is not tempered by any stretch of the imagination.

Rush has accepted numerous apologies from past and present congressional Republican politicians. Contrite politicians at Capitol Hill have either apologized for or recanted the criticisms they said about Rush.

No one holds more considerable power than Rush in the entire GOP. One could even go out on a limb to say Rush's power outweighs the whole US Republican senate, especially at a twilights phase for the GOP senate, where their opponents is one vote short of a filibuster proof senate.

Rahm Emanuel, the White House Chief of Staff and the former congressman with the sharp elbows, said this about Rush: "He is the voice and the intellectual force and energy behind the Republican party." Emanuel continued, "He has been up front about what he views and hasn't stepped back from that, which is he hopes for failure."

Just about everything Rush touches turns to gold. Rush's two hugely successful books were a benchmark for others in the political world to attain. For years, his radio program has been the envy of other talk radio hosts. He leads and others follow. Most of them that follow get lost in his tracks.

The mainstream media parrots everything Rush says. They waits for Rush's take on any issue before they are able to override, bash or reluctantly accept Rush's enormous understanding of an issue. Rush, "a talent on loan from God" and the most listened to talk radio host in the world, never knew any competition. For Rush, the most influential conservative voice in the country and the Institute for Advanced Conservative Studies, there isn't any competition. He is the most prominent American political icon that never ran for office and is a household name in all four corners of the world. Till the cows come home, no politician, journalist or American will ever surpass Rush's achievements.

The GOP will find themselves in an endless cauldron should Rush abandon the Party. Prominent Democratic political consultant James Carville said about Rush: "Rush Limbaugh's running this party. He is the most influential and important Republican in the country. Rush Limbaugh is the de facto head of the Republican Party right now. I congratulate Rush on his position as the number one Republican in the country. He is the most exalted Republican, he is, he is the leader of their party, they quake at mighty Rush. He's the one that's setting the Republican agenda. He is the most powerful person in that party. He is the daddy -- the daddy of the Republican Party, he has ascended to political power that's unseen, unheard of in American politics. He is the intellectual center of the Republican Party. I'm pointing out a fact. I'm a weatherman. No sense in getting mad at me if it rains, I'm just telling you what the weather is. Rush is very -- he's very popular. Rush is the person that they follow. The modern Republican Party has as its most influential member Rush Limbaugh."

Polling Rush

Rush has been scoring higher approval ratings than members of Congress. The groundbreaking talk radio host admitted that he doesn't have any executive nor any legislative powers "And yet they're polling me! I take this as a major career achievement."

Rush for office

Rush has earned an enviable reputation as the greatest conservative figure in the country. He confessed that he is tired of hearing, "When are we gonna hear Rush Limbaugh run for office?" It would be a walk in the park for him if Rush did run for the US senate, regardless of which state he chose to run in. Rush won't be shortchanged, and he won't take any shorts or losses. He won't tolerate a pay cut just to be called a senator. If Rush takes a pay cut, how will he maintain his EIB one Airplane?

Rush rejects running for Federal office: It's all about the Limbaugh Institute for Advanced Conservative Studies

Rush stated that the main reason why he can't run for office is because of the pay cut that he will be subjected to. Asked what he would say? Rush said what he would say "wouldn't last one day as a political candidate." In addition, Rush said he would tell the masses not to rely on him to solve their problems: rather they should look to themselves. Rush said to lie is not in his nature. He won't tell people something he doesn't believe just for the sake of getting their votes. Rush doesn't pander.

Rush preferred being behind the Golden EIB Microphone to being on the floor of the US Senate or at the Oval Office, awaiting a 3AM phone call

According to Rush, he won't accept freebies because he doesn't want to be obligated. Rush said accepting freebies comes with strings. And Rush wants none of it. Rush said there is an expectation attached when someone asks for fundraising. Because Rush doesn't want history to repeat itself, he said: "I have tried to set my life up, my whole life, so that I didn't need to depend on anybody, so that I didn't have to ask anybody for anything."

In all actuality, Rush ran for office on many occasions

Rush said although he's never on the ballot, he has run for president every four years since 1992, since Bush senior. Because if the Republican wins, Rush will be credited and if the Republican lose, Rush will be blamed.

Rush Limbaugh rushed out of New York City

Governor Paterson applauded as Rush bemoaned the tax situation in New York

Tax hikes and other reasons have propelled Rush to put his New York prize assets on the market. Rush has had it with New York and its massive taxes increases. Rush disclosed that he moved to Florida from New York in 1997, but he has been audited every year since 1997. Rush says he only works in New York State for 15 to 20 days. Yet he has to prove in 14 different ways his whereabouts every day including weekends for the entire year.

Rush said the audits constitute harassment and the only way out was to leave New York for good.

Governor Paterson, after Rush Limbaugh condemned New York's tax hikes and hinted at leaving the state, said: "If I knew that would be the result, I would've thought about the taxes earlier."

Attacks on Rush

Just after the historical inauguration of the 44th US president, Democratic pundits targeted Rush Limbaugh for Obama's difficult run to be the president elect. When Bush was president, the opposition party was able to censure Bush, Cheney and Limbaugh with what was wrong with America. When the Obama administration was eleven months old and not able to hit the ground running, not able to get off to the races, Democrats dispatched and laid the administration sluggishness on the feet of Rush Limbaugh.

Congressional Democratic heavy hitters en route to Obama's successful presidential run launched verbal broadsides at Rush on many fronts.

Since Bush/Cheney have no longer been in power, Rush has been targeted by Democrat and Republican moderates from all spectrum of the country. There is no end in sight to the baseless stigma on Rush. However, Sarah Palin and Sean Hannity have somehow been able to relieve Rush Limbaugh, as they are also being severely lambasted by the opposition. Rush also faced stinging criticism by members of the Republican establishment and by many prominent conservatives.

It's impossible for Rush to take time out of his busy schedule, a schedule that includes super secret location meetings, golf trips, delivering speeches and other important tasks to address all the daily withering attacks. It is unconscionable to start tabulating all the attacks Rush has received since he achieved superstardom status. Senator Harry Reid, whose approval ratings in Nevada stink, and who should be worrying about his reelection in 2010, again came out and pointed to Rush Limbaugh as the reason for Obama's stalled healthcare plan. Back in 2007, the Senate Majority Leader tried to slander Rush by claiming that Rush was calling our troops "phony soldiers," Harry Reid called Rush's EIB carrier to censure Rush.

Rush is the most amicable "lovable little fuzzball," and at the same time he is America's most dangerous figure. Yet for 20 years, the liberal media have blackened Rush. They soil his name as if he's a wanted terrorist. Ask an ordinary citizen what they think about Rush? "Oh he's very offensive; he's anti –American; he's extremely controversial," and other despicable takes. For 20 years, the Democrats have vilified Rush. They tried the whole nine yards to annihilate Rush's reputation. Liberals have gone berserk. His name has been all over the liberal media, whether it is an election year or not. Leftists like Gov. Howard Dean take pleasure in lampooning and ridiculing Rush.

It seems Rush might self-destruct with all the daily attacks he witnesses, but in all reality, they only make him stronger.

Harry Reid's second direct attack on Rush was just another day at the office for Rush.

Senator Reid hasn't yet recovered from the shame he felt in 2007 for attacking Rush on the Senate floor.

In August of 2007, Harry Reid and the rest of the liberal media accused Rush Limbaugh of impugning our brave military personnel by calling them "phony soldiers." Reid followed his accusation up by drafting a letter of disapproval to Limbaugh's primary syndication agent, Clear Channel. The letter, intended to condemn and punish Limbaugh for his remarks, was signed by more than 40 United States senators. The allegation from Harry Reid left Rush fuming. Right away, Rush gainsaid the allegation. Limbaugh never did call our military personnel as "phony." Reid calculatingly, swift boated Rush for the 08 Republican candidates. Rush's rebuttal to Reid's allegations wasn't enough for Rush. Being who Rush Limbaugh is, Reid wasn't going to get off scot free for libeling Rush.

Without waiting "to be wooed and wined and dined and begged and cajoled," Rush obtained Reid's letter and opted to put the smear letter up for sale on eBay.

What transpired after the auction? Limbaugh was able to net more than 2 million dollars off the Senator's letter. And without deliberation,

Rush matched the total sum of money with his own two million dollar donation and then donated all the funds to a foundation that provides scholarships to children of dead Marines. Rush demonstrated an extremely nice gesture.

After putting his foot in his mouth, Senator Reid ran back to the senate floor in what seemed to be a sudden rush of blood to the head and praised Rush for donating the proceeds of his smear letter to our military.

To those Americans that read what Rush did, it was unprecedented, unheard of and massive. But to Rush, it was nothing to write home about. Rush was just advertising how powerful he is. He was able to use a letter from the most powerful United States Senator, intended to besmirch his reputation, to raise money for the US Marines.

To sum it all up, since 1988, Rush gets criticized almost on a daily basis by the opposition. The attacks on Rush will never peter out.

Rush's Arrest

Rush was arrested and charged with Doctor shopping. It wasn't really an arrest; he turned himself in upon learning that he was wanted. Rush never spent a night in jail and the charges was substituted for a fine that came with a few months of probation. Rush was completely railroaded by the Florida state prosecutors. It was a golden opportunity for prosecutors to invade Rush's privacy. Rush was more sinned against than sinning. Eventually, he shrugged off the draconian, unjust and fierce criticism he receive during the whole process.

Regardless of what transpired, Rush's record is clean as a whistle. Rush's launch of Operation Chaos to aid Hillary Clinton's 2008 presidential campaign almost blemished his record. Rush was on the brink of being arrested for aiding and abetting voters to vote for Hillary Clinton.

Rush Limbaugh/Barack Obama's Biblical Gospel Character

Obama's biblical gospel character is better defined as one who, when he sees Christ carrying the cross, he would look at Jesus and just keep walking, passing Christ by. Unlike Simon, a man of Cyrene, who was compelled to bear Christ's cross, Obama would vehemently refuse to help. He first thinks about the race of Christ and then looks condescendingly towards Christ. Rush, on the other hand, is likened to Joseph of Arimathaea, a counselor and just man, who was also one of Christ's disciples, albeit he wasn't one of the original twelve disciples. After Jesus' Crucifixion, Joseph privately begged Pilate for the body of Jesus. After his request was approved he "laid Christ's body in his own new tomb, which he had hewn out in the rock: and he rolled a great stone to the door of the sepulcher, and departed,"-Matthew 27 v 60 Republicans are today's Publicans and Sinners, while Democrats are today's Pharisees and Scribes.

Rush's Depth

Rush participates in the unthinkable

African Americans in California voted overwhelmingly against the state's gay marriage amendment. And for some reason, there was no major outcry. Rush said: Rush stated: "I, of course, [am] a highly observant human being. It's my job. I sometimes participate in life by observing others doing what they do as they live. I have been observing something that's not happening. Now, you may say, 'Rush, how can you observe something that isn't happening?' Rush then went on to name the sources where he does his observation.

Rush's Charities

Most of Rush's good work and charities have been besmirched by the left. They can't bring themselves to accept Rush generosity.

For 19 years, Rush has been raising money for the Leukemia & Lymphoma Society. Rush spearheaded the proceedings and donated $300,000 to lead the 2009 Leukemia and Lymphoma Society Charity. Rush praised his audience for their constant donations: "I could not be more honored" to have the audience donate for the charity.[2]

Types of Republicans in America: Moderate Independent Republicans

This is where the RINO's and the moderate Republicans are nestled. Senator Joe Lieberman and Senator Lindsey Graham could easily unite with mavericks like McCain to form a branch of the Republican Party. The GOP establishment is sparged and spattered in this group.

Rush's harangue about the trio of moderate buddies in the US Senate: McCain, Graham and Lieberman

Democratic Media Picked GOP Presidential Nominee
Right from the get-go, Rush claimed the media nominated our 08 presidential nominee. Rush claimed that the so-called "brilliant pseudo-intellectual conservative intelligentsia" in the conservative media got the candidate and the campaign they advocated for. A politician that reached out to the Hispanics, to independents and to Democrats was just what the doctor ordered. Yet their candidate, McCain, lost badly in all those categories.

Rush scathingly launched at McCain

In precise words, Rush said that McCain's candidacy wasn't an attempt to capture and convert Liberals to the Republican Party. But he was going to bring them in just for their votes. Rush said if there is a genuine liberal Democrat on the ballot and a moderate Republican on the ballot, why would the Liberals vote for the generic? Why would they vote for the moderate Republican? Rush asked, what is the benefit of having Liberals vote for the Republican ticket when they are still Liberals? Rush said the McCain's campaign tried to avoid being called racist, but that didn't work out for them.

After McCain lost the 2008 election, Rush asserted that McCain was always looking forward to "mend fences" and make nice with the Democrats after the general election. Rush said Republicans are always eager to praise those lawmakers that cross the aisle and then at the end of the day are back with the Democrats. Rush said the bottom line is that if you're going to cross the aisle and dine with the Republicans, then stay a Republican. Rush said the same goes for a Republican that goes over the Democratic side. Rush claimed that our standard-bearer "didn't have a campaign." He didn't articulate the core conservative principles. He was campaigning as a war hero.

Rush admitted that the GOP got what they deserved. We got the candidate that the elitists in the Republican Party campaigned for. He did everything that was prescribed to him by the party elites, yet they lost by a landslide. He added that if it were not for Sarah Palin, McCain's landslide loss would have been in the double digits. Rush said prescribing to the "moderate path of appeasement" would end up in a landslide and wholesale defeats.

Rush issued a warning for a McCain-like party and said McCain's moderates are not welcomed in the GOP because they don't support conservatism. Rush stated that he doesn't want Democratic Senator Charles Schumer defining who the real McCain is.

Senator Joe Lieberman

Joe Lieberman, the Independent senator from Connecticut, was asked if there was a possibility for John McCain to abandon the GOP: "No, I don't think so at all. And, look, this is the problem. It's good for the Democratic Party, bad for the Republican Party that Arlen Specter left them and joined the Democratic caucus but overall it's not great for American politics 'cause both parties should have moderate or centrist wings in them that modifies the parties and creates more opportunity for common ground and less partisanship. So respectfully, I disagree with Rush."

On Lieberman's impact on the 08 election fallout, Rush asked of the moderate Republicans at the end of the day, what good came out of it? What good came out of reaching out to independents? Rush said with Lieberman we had the "model of moderation and independent spiritedness." Throughout the campaign, Lieberman had extolled the virtues of McCain and at the same time, though he had been critical of Obama, he did "preface his criticism" with warm words to Obama. After campaigning and praising McCain to a hilt, Rush asked where is Lieberman now? After McCain lost the election, Lieberman went back to the Democratic Party. Rush said Joe Lieberman would grovel to the Democratic Party in order to get back in good stead.

Rush said enough of Joe Lieberman casting his lot with the Republicans. Rush plagiarized himself. Rush stated that actions speak louder than words. All the praise from Lieberman to McCain went down the toilet because Lieberman is back caucusing with the Democrats. Rush asked the "brilliant wizards of smart" from the GOP, wasn't what Lieberman did meaningless? Rush said Lieberman owes Obama, due to the fact that he opted to caucus with the Democrats.

Senator Lindsey Graham

Crossing party lines to work with Democrats has landed Graham in a whole heap of trouble. The State Republican Party in South

Carolina has censured the senior senator on a host of issues. State party activists have basically called for Graham to be recalled. Rush claimed that Graham had devoted his time in the senate to be friends and in league with the Liberals and the media by attacking his own Party and by crossing the aisle to vote with the Democrats, but at the end of the day he has been called a "puppet of Rush Limbaugh" by the Democratic media.

Bipartisanship is tough, McCain said.

Graham was condemned by his voters for his bipartisan efforts. McCain is well known for his bipartisan maneuvering. Rush responded to McCain's statement that "Bipartisanship is tough." Rush echoed, "Bipartisanship is the easiest thing in the world." Compromising on your principles and agreeing with the Democrats equals bipartisanship. In contrast, partisanship is what is tough. Everybody will attack you because you are standing up for your principles. Just like liberalism, bipartisanship is gutless. "Bipartisanship is the most gutless choice" one can make. Just as being a liberal doesn't require any effort, the same rule applies when it comes to bipartisanship. When you stand up for what you believe in, you will be under assault. And that is the challenge. If you overcome that challenge, you overcome bipartisanship. People who hate partisanship are people who hate to hear the truth.

In Conclusion

Rush was vexed after the Democrats felicitated McCain, "Chuck Schumer and a lot of Democrats are saying it's great that the old John McCain's back."

Types of Republicans in America: Washingtonian Republicans

The GOP establishment is headquartered by this group. Rockefeller Republicans are the vast majority of this group. Colin Powell, Governor

Tom Ridge and Governor William Weld could conspire to form their own version of the Republican Party.

Rush asserted that Powell is not a Republican, rather he's a Washingtonian. Rush said Washingtonians' "culture and desire" are different from the rest of Americans. They want adulation from the media, and whether there is a Republican or a Democrat in the White House it doesn't matter to them. They simply want to be known as a cut above the rest. They want to amass as much power as they can and silence any opposition. Rush said if it comes to matters that should concern the American people, the Washingtonians are tone deaf. "General Powell claims to stand above politics as a big claim to fame."And when Powell goes out in public, he condemned the conservative wing of the GOP. Washingtonians "ingratiate themselves" with the Democrats by attacking the GOP. Rush said principle brought Powell out to the limelight, but moderation is his longevity. It is what gave him the great image without core belief and substance. "He lives in a bubble," therefore he is far from being in "touch with the public." He peddles his reputation and avoids criticism. Washingtonians derive their happiness from being adored and respected by their own colleagues. Rush ended by saying he remembered when Powell wouldn't let the public know if he was a Republican or a Democrat because he was scared his high poll numbers would drop.

Types of Republicans in America: Fringe/ Unsettled Conservatives

The GOP establishment exerts mediocre influence on members of this group. The most formidable contenders for president from the GOP like the Giulianis and the Romneys happened to fall into this branch.

They are not true conservatives. They are teetering at the edge because they ricochet from partially supporting gay rights constituents to partially supporting abortion rights constituents. While governing, they didn't have any problem placating gay and abortion rights advocates. But while campaigning for president, they both claimed to be true conservatives.

They are sojourners to the conservative movement. They only sing the conservative praises during the time they are campaigning for office. Fringes conservatives like Romney and Giuliani remain problematic for the progress of the conservative causes.

After giving them enough rope to politically hang themselves, we can fully concentrate on moving on with the conservative movement.

Types of Republicans in America: Traditional Conservatives

Mike Huckabee, Senator Sam Brownback and Senator Jeff Session are among the traditionalists. Newt Gingrich, the most prominent, is not an unadulterated conservative. He did a cameo appearance in an ad with Nancy Pelosi. And Newt finds it difficult to throw the betraying Colin Powell under the bus. The fact that he might be running for the Oval Office in the upcoming 2012 election may prevent him from undoing politicians and policies which conservatives loathe. Newt Gingrich, although he personally respects Rush Limbaugh, hasn't publicly spoken in glowing terms about Rush since the Republicans lost the 08 elections. For political reasons, Newt denounced Rush's "reverse racist" comments. Pat Buchanan also stamps his authority with the traditionalist.

Traditionalists dwindle until it reaches the ultra conservatives. It's difficult for one to be a conservative and a tall order to remain a true conservative. The rest of the Republicans strive to join the Rush Limbaugh lead conservative bandwagon. However, the leaders are keeping in mind that only a few will make it to the promise land.

Types of Republicans in America: Arch/ Ultra conservatives

Rick Santorum, Jim DeMint and other archconservatives make up this undiluted branch. Sean Hannity is probably a 99.5 % conservative. He has so much love for his fellow conservative friends that is difficult for Sean to denounce Newt and others like him when they are obviously wrong. In addition to that, Sean always comfortably hosts moderates GOP like 2008 presidential GOP nominee John McCain. However, he also made it clear that he voted against McCain during the bitter and animus 2008 Republican primary.

Rush Limbaugh, Tom DeLay and Sarah Palin are 100% conservatives. They take no prisoners in any way, shape, manner or form. Their loyalties are unabated. Hannity takes lot of prisoners. On his show, he hosts the likes of Bob Beckel and Juan Williams. He has also hosts radical liberals like Michael Moore and Al Sharpton.

To be a full fledged conservative might seems to be a fraught position, but that's why it's difficult to be a seasoned conservative. Rush has already set a benchmark.

American piñata

Rush said it's plain as day that he's America's piñata because everybody is attacking him. For Rino Republicans, Rush said he's the "new passkey," a passkey for them to get glowing praise for attacking him. By attacking Rush, they have been invited for sit down interviews on TV. Because of the volumes of attacks on Rush, Rush said that Democrats would no longer pursue the Fairness Doctrine to shut talk radio down. Powell, Cornyn and Ridge have all used Rush to "win a one night stand" with mainstream media outlets.

America's most prominent activist for freedom, Rush Limbaugh, has been vividly attacked by used up Democratic leaders. Hannity asked Rush: "The new game in the Beltway is the 'Bash Rush.'" You're in the news almost every day. What's going on?" Rush responded, and said those on conservative talk radio and TV are the focus and the target of the Obama administration. Those who opposed Obama in Washington aren't effective. Rush said Democrats need a villain and a demon to demonize, and since they can't find any from Congress, Rush is that villain.

The Weekly Standard's Bill Kristol, a prominent conservative pundit and a fervent McCain for president backer, killed two birds with one stone when he attacked two powerful conservatives in the country in an editorial piece. Tom DeLay, a consummate staunch conservative leader, and Senator Rick Santorum, a devout conservative, were the targets.

During the early primary 08 GOP presidential nominee search, William Kristol said: "It was an unattractive few weeks. In the rush to damn McCain, the movement paid obeisance to some dubious advisers. It listened to the pronouncements of Tom DeLay, who had previously done so much to convince his countrymen that conservatives could not be trusted to govern. It hearkened to the political counsel of Rick Santorum, who lost his Senate seat in the swing state of Pennsylvania two years ago by 17 percentage points."

Sarah Palin

Rush discussed why Republicans hate Palin

Rush feels that the media and those Rockefeller, blue- blood, country club Republicans despise Palin. They claim she's uninformed and inexperienced. Rush said they attack her because they are afraid she could beat Obama. He said no other GOP politician "energized the crowd" the way Palin did.

Rush called out the "Old guard, country club blue-bloods." He said: They are the ones that claim the "era of Reagan is over." And because Palin didn't attend Harvard or any other elite universities, they are embarrassed by Palin. She didn't follow the right prescription.

Palin's high approval ratings

Palin's approval ratings have been impressive amidst all the attacks. Talking about her high poll numbers, Rush said: They are livid at Palin's high approval rate. Rush said they hate Palin as much as the Democrats hate her too. The media picked our 2008 nominee, and after he was picked, they dumped him like a bad habit for Obama. Rush vented his anger by saying, "Political gurus and pundits -- these yapping yammerers all over TV; Palin trashers in the Republican Party; the sordid, looking-down-the-nose, low-wattage elitists."

Palin relates to Millions of Americans

Rush heaped praise on Palin. Palin knows the repercussion of having an unlimited government. She knows the repercussions of encroaching upon freedom and liberty. Rush says Palin "says the things he agrees with." She has the utmost ability to relate to the average American. She excited the crowd. Finally, Rush said that Palin epitomizes the American life. And thousands of Americans will vouch for Palin's life.

Palin's Attacks

The smear campaign against Palin is endless; there seem to be no end in sight. Rush was irritated to see trivial claims against Palin by the Republican Party. It was a situation that Rush finds unpalatable. He responded to the unnecessary and unconscionable attacks on Palin: "It has been a drumbeat" of never-ending "personal attacks."

Palin's effectiveness is the reason she is being treated badly. Rush pointed out that the hatred for Palin from Liberals and Democrats is visceral. They hate her as much as they hate Clarence Thomas because neither of them followed the liberal recipe for success. From the conception, Rush said Palin was just "minding her own business" in Alaska and all of a sudden, she was picked by McCain to be his running mate because the Republican Party needed a Hail Mary. And Rush said Palin and her family immediately got in gear and campaigned throughout the country for McCain. Palin was "unfailingly cheerful." Rush said 2008 was an abysmal year for GOP candidates running for federal offices and Palin was the only "spot of sunshine" for the Party.

It wasn't anywhere near sweetness and light for Palin and the John McCain campaign teams. With Gov. Palin in no man's land, being attacked by both parties, Rush claimed Palin was "Smeared worse than anybody in the McCain campaign went after Obama or any of his questionable allies."

And after the Republican 08 defeat Rush stated that when they lay the blame on conservatives, they lay the blame on Palin. Rush said everybody knows Palin was the one that excited the GOP campaign, and that is why they chose to lay the blame on her.

The attacks kept ratcheting up and Rush asked, what is the benefit of Palin being attacked by her own party? Is it because they want her image to be completely damaged?

Did Palin Betray the GOP Establishment?

Rush revealed his delight at Palin's bestselling book. For the ascendancy of conservatism, Rush said Palin's bestselling book was just what the doctor ordered: "One of the most substantive policy books I've ready by a politician in a long time." Steve McMahon, Democrat strategist, countered Rush's words of praise on Palin's bestselling book: "She traded her friendships, she traded her loyalty, she took the shekels like Judas, and she's selling everyone out along the way." The opposition is so obsessed with Palin and the fact that Rush thinks she is even more hated than he is. Rush refuted his claim, realizing that Palin has only been on the national scene for under two years: "They've hated me for 20 years and it's still going strong, still ratcheting it up," Rush concluded.

Jesus Christ sent away a number of disciples, but the original 12 were steadfast in standing by Christ. And Christ later said: "The harvest truly is plenteous, but the labourers are few." True conservatives have passed the litmus test on earth. However; no true conservatives are saved. But thank God for Peter, who asked Jesus a question. After Christ talked about the extreme difficulties of making His kingdom, Peter and other disciples asked who then can make it to the kingdom of God? Jesus replied, "With men it is impossible, but not with God; for with God all things are possible,"- Mark 10 verse 27. [3]

Before the Effectiveness of "I Hope He Fails"- CHAPTER 11: Republican Foreclosed Agents

Rush said of the GOP: "The whole Republican Party has gone south trying to become Mr. and Miss Moderate, Mr. and Miss Independent." On numerous occasions, Rush on his golden EIB microphone has predicted the demise of the GOP party. He has appealed to the party's hierarchy to grip and stay tuned to the conservative agendas, but his appeals have fallen on deaf ears. Taking a page from Steven Howse lyrics, Rush is, "Waking up every morning and feeling the pressure of living today," knowing that the America that he so loved is heading to be a socialist country under the vigilant watch of the Democratic Party. Rush is already involved in a never ending civil war against liberal Democrats and moderate Republicans. He is also having a skirmish against some conservative intellects who added enormously to foreclosing the Party.

John McCain

Right after McCain took Obama to the wire and eventually lost the 08 election, his campaign team attacked McCain's running mate, Governor Palin. The foreclosing Republican Party was officially jump-started with Senator McCain. The Arizonian didn't turned deaf ears on picking one of Rush's choices for Veep in the 08 presidential election. During the final third of the McCain campaign, damage was done when Palin was forced to mirror McCain's policies instead of the conservative policies. McCain never forced the issues that were accepted by conservatives.

John Kerry said about his senatorial colleague: "John McCain is a prisoner of the right wing, not a maverick." Rush Limbaugh holds the key to his nemesis' prison cell. The bipartisan McCain found it difficult to attack Obama during the last elections.

According to Rush, Lieberman will grovel before the Democratic Party until he's accepted. As long as McCain and Graham are still in Congress, Lieberman will continue to liaise between the Democrats and the Republicans. And that means compromising with the liberals.

David Brooks

McCain passed the baton to Reformers like David Brooks. Brooks, the New York Times house conservative columnist, argues that "Traditionalists" like Limbaugh and Hannity are: "people who believe that conservatives have lost elections because they have strayed from the true creed." And he said the Party could rectify the lost by "returning to its core ideas." That statement is right on the money. Having said that, Brooks highlighted that Reformers argues that for the Republican Party, "Priorities were fine for the 1970s but need to be modernized for new conditions." He continued, "The reformers tend to believe that American voters will not support a party whose main idea is slashing government." In analyzing Brooks' comments, the former is right; the latter is accepting liberal premises.

93

Brooks is a typical Reformer. He even went out on a limb to say: "The Republican party will probably veer right in the years ahead, and suffer more defeats. Then, finally, some new Reformist donors and organizers will emerge. They will build new institutions, new structures and new ideas, and the cycle of conservative ascendance will begin again." What are the new ideas? Conservatism is conservatism. The ideas of the past will always be the ideas of the present and the future.

David Brooks, who made us believe that McCain was the last beacon of hope for the GOP, said this about Obama: "What struck me is how incredibly even he is and how, frankly, reassuring he is. It's like you're camping and you wake up one morning and there's a mountain and then the next morning there's a mountain and then the next morning there's a mountain. Obama is just the mountain. He's there. He's always the same. He doesn't hurt himself. McCain can sometimes lob a cannon ball into the mountain but the mountain doesn't move and the mountain doesn't care. And the good part of the mountain is that he's reassuring and reliable."

So after two years of an incredible Obama presidency, how reliable and reassuring is Brooks' mountain?

The Republican Party was on life support because of conservative lap dogs like Brooks, Frum, Noonan and Bill Kristol. They were the stepping stone agents for foreclosing the GOP. Republicans are supposed to be united. David Brooks issued a withering rebuke to Rush, Sean Hannity and Glenback. All these give and take attacks on a fellow Republican are nothing but ways to lead the Party down the wrong path.

Michael Steele

Steel made the same blathering points like McCain by calling Rush an "entertainer." His comments speak volumes about the type of Republican he is. However, he immediately apologized and retracted his intended smear comment. Originally, Steele viewed Rush as an entertainer. He perhaps doesn't view Rush as a leader of the conservative branch of the GOP. Steele might be the RNC chairman, but Newt Gingrich wasn't really interested in the job. The permission of the party to name him as the GOP's dean is largely because he's an African American. Who will be used to slightly counter the African American president of America? Steele is anonymous nationwide. He is popular in the state of Maryland, where he narrowly lost a 2006 senate seat. The senate race was leaning toward his challenger and then became a dead heat. But the loss doesn't count because only the winner, Democrat Ben Cardin, got the glory. Can Steele afford to pay Rush to entertain his guests? Not in his wildest dreams. After dismissing Rush as an entertainer, the RNC chairman then added that Rush's "I hope he {Obama} fails" statement was "incendiary" and "ugly." Steele then released a statement saying, "My intent was not to go after Rush-I have enormous respect for Rush Limbaugh. I was maybe a little bit inarticulate. There was no attempt on my part to diminish his voice or his leadership." Steele continued, "What I was trying to say was a lot of people want to make Rush the scapegoat, the bogeyman, and he's not." A few months later, Steele attacked Rush again when Rush made the "reverse racist" comment. However, Rush had stopped accepting apologies. Steele and the GOP establishment have left the party in a dead end. And conservative leaders have to cut the deadwood out in order for the Party to turn things around.

Arlen Specter

Rush said he's surprised at the way Specter's defection was greeted by both parties. Rush said it is like a religious leader who abandon his religion. All we did, Rush said was getting rid of deadweight. Rush said Arlen Specter joined some radical Liberals to vote for the stimulus package, which Rush deems as an "irresponsible piece of legislation."

Obama's influence had an effect on a so-called member of Reagan's tent, Arlen Specter, who switched from being a Republican to being a

Democrat. The Pennsylvania senior senator is greedy for power. He, like most of the past and present senators, loves to be called "senator!" Arlen would rather be a sellout than to be a patriot. For many conservatives, Arlen's defection isn't like a deer caught in headlights. He was never a true Republican. He might have been one of Reagan's acolytes, but as time elapsed, his true identity was telling. There is a growing fear that Maine's Senatorial duo, Olympia Snowe and Susan Collins, might follow Specter's path. But if they can't beat them (the Democrats,) then they (Snowe and Collins) might join them. "Anybody who deviates toward the center, who departs from established doctrine, is a coward, and a sellout," David Brooks wrote, alluding to what Rush Limbaugh and Sean Hannity believe. Specter deflected because he wants to belong to the majority party in Congress. If McCain had won the presidential election of 2008, do you fancy Specter leaving the GOP? No, he would have continued masquerading as a Republican. Specter buckled under Obama's pressure.

We don't need checkmate Republicans who would only add impetus in foreclosing the party.

Obama checkmated Senator Specter, and Specter joined the Democratic Party. Obama has two or more years to checkmate the likes of Republican Senators Collins and Snowe. He already has them in his back pocket. Specter was the first GOP to walk the plank for Obama, so who is next?

Rush said, after Senator Specter deflected to the Democratic Party: "Hey, Senator Specter, if you're leaving, take McCain with you and his daughter."

Colin Powell

Powell is a Republican only because of his appointment by Republican presidents. Ronald Reagan elevated Powell to a four star general. Reagan's actions helped Colin feel at home with the Republican Party.

Further love was shown to Powell when George Bush became our nation's finest 41st president. Cheney and Bush were responsible for appointing Colin as the first African American Secretary of State. Powell paid Cheney back by attacking the ex-Vice President. Powell also attacked Rush Limbaugh. Rush said swiftly to Powell: "become a Democrat, instead of claiming to be a Republican." Powell still claiming to be a Republican was news to Cheney "My take on it was Colin had already left the party. I didn't know he was still a Republican," Cheney said. Feeling the pressure of being tag-teamed, Powell reacted: "Another version of the Republican Party waiting to emerge once again." Rush responded: "The only thing emerging here is Colin Powell's ego. Colin Powell represents the stale, the old, the worn-out GOP that never won anything."

How is the Republican Party going to keep hold of Powell? He served this country vehemently, and he received a deserved five star General recognition. But the GOP should get rid of him as an example for other encumbered GOP politicians on the horizon. The party is already self-destructing, why not go for broke? While the brickbats from the opposition party were flying for Rush and Cheney, Powell was always staying on the margin of everything that was happening in the Party. Powell has always been on the outside looking in. This is quite the opposite of what he used to do as a military man. During the I Lewis Scooter Libby criminal trial, back when Powell was State Secretary, Powell knew that the smoking gun was in his State Department's office, not in the office of Vice President Cheney. But because of the disconcerting aftermath of his UN presentation on proof of weapons of mass destruction against Iraq, Powell resigned his royalty to Cheney and instead opted for Cheney's top aide to be prosecuted. It makes no sense that Powell, who endorsed a Democrat over a Republican, is still sitting in the catbird seat of the Republican Party. We will be heading to an abyss that houses people like Powell, and there won't be time for an advisory warning.

Christ said: " In that day, he which shall be upon the housetop, and his stuff in the house, let him not come down to take it away; and he that is in the field, let him likewise not return back,"-Luke 17 verse 31.

Senator Cornyn

Many within the conservative hierarchy were astonished to hear Senator Cornyn, a marginal figure in the GOP senate, reprimand Rush Limbaugh and Newt Gingrich. When shall wonders ends? If Jeff Sessions, David Villa and other true elected senatorial conservatives attacked Rush, then Armageddon should be looming. Peter ended up denying Christ three times after he had said, in his free will, "Lord, I am ready to go with thee, both into prison, and to death,"-Luke 22 verse 33.

Cornyn won his reelection bid in 2008, so he has a four year cushion until he has to re-launch a reelection bid. Cornyn has all the time in the world to schedule an apology to Rush before 2014 comes knocking. Rush vehemently campaigned and fundraised for Cornyn when Cornyn was running for the senate. Politically, it's is not healthy for a genuine conservative to attack another, especially when the road to rebuilding the party is arduous.

The rest of the foreclosing agents are under the radar, so we'll turn a deaf ear on them.

Final Notes

The doldrums that we are experiencing in our party will only end when we first take over Congress in 2010. A Republican presidential loss in 2012 and in 2016 would be the final nail in the coffin for any support coming from Limbaugh. For all intents and purposes, conservatives might start thinking of a third party. We lost the 2006/2008 congressional election and the presidential election of 2008 because the Republican establishment was heedless to Rush's advice. Defeats will be staring GOP lawmaker's in the face in the impending

2010 elections if they don't give serious consideration to what Rush has to say. It's a crying shame that there is infighting happening within the GOP ranks. Thanks to Colin Powell and other liberal Republicans, the animosity is a momentous distraction away from searching for a standard bearer for 2012.[4]

Dead Weights

Dead weight Republicans

The GOP politicians that supported Obama thought the ship was sinking. They thought the GOP was going to hell in a handbasket. And as rats, they deserted a supposedly sinking ship. Accordingly, after the 08 election loss, Rush clarified the way forward. The objective is to reestablish the conservative movement and take it back from a bunch of deadweight Republicans who want to tailor their policies to suit their desires. Rush asked, why do Liberals never say the era of FDR is over? Why doesn't liberalism get redefined? Rush said balkanizing voters isn't the way forward. Rush said watered-down of conservatism led to the election loss. Watered-down conservatism means we are moderate and have no identity.

Limbaugh Sounds Alarm on Prototype Republicans who voted for Obama

Rush asserted that the GOP calling for a big tent is a code word for pro-choicers getting rid of pro-lifers. Rush said Governor Weld and former Bush aide McClellan shouldn't continue calling themselves Republicans. Rush said, Weid and the intellectual conservative media types should "stay a Democrat." For the sake of being invited to state dinners in the White House, they sided with the opposing party. Rush stated they steered the GOP to destruction and, like "little cowards," abandoned the Party. Rush knew this fate was going to be the outcome and that during the primaries, he warned the GOP. Rush said one of the good things that came out of the election loss was that those phony Republicans were flushed out.

Policy Wonk vs. Core Belief

Why should we drop everything we believe in because Obama got 52 % of the 2008 general presidential election votes? Rush said conservatives are not policy wonk, rather they are believers. Our core beliefs and policies lift everybody up. America was built on the concept of freedom and personal liberty. The 1980 and 1984 Reagan elections were a testament to that.

Misleaders

Rush was at a loss to explain the 2006 midterm congressional defeats. He did not have that same trouble in 2008. Rush said if the GOP wants to continue with the string of election losses, they should continue to listen to the advice of the likes of Chuck Hagel and EJ Dionne. Rush said the conservative media's wizards of smart think we weren't moderate enough. Rush said there weren't "any more moderate" Republican candidates like McCain.

Conservatism First, Wining Second

Rush noted it is a sign of how times have changed when some fraction of the conservative movement wants big government. Rush said politicians who try the whole nine yards to win elections by abandoning conservatives is a no no. "My point is, if you are a conservative but you throw it away in order to win, what have you won if you have to govern as a liberal in order to stay in power?" Rush said he's not sugarcoating the matter.

Conservatives are not Defeatists

Rush believes there are some defeatists in the GOP who would yield to liberal premises. Rush said bipartisanship entails accepting rather than fighting liberal premises. We should let the people know the repercussions of having socialized healthcare rather than accepting the premise from the left.

Senator Jim De Mint's Message for Dead Weight Republicans

Senator Jim DeMint said "I would rather have 30 Republicans in the Senate who really believe in principles of limited government, free markets, free people, than to have 60 that don't have a set of beliefs."

And when pressed by his fellow Republican colleagues, DeMint reiterated his comment. "I'd rather have 30 Republicans in the Senate who believe in freedom than 60 who don't believe in anything." De Mint continued "Let me make myself even clearer: I'd rather have 30 Marco Rubios in the Senate than 60 Arlen Specters." Rush said conservative Republican ideologues is the way forward for the GOP, not "wishy-washy" Republican moderates. Rush agreed totally with DeMint's comment because the GOP is in a "rebuilding phase." And we need to start from scratch to build a solid foundation. Rush said the 30 conservative ideologues will be foursquare on opposing Obama.

Conservatism is Timeless
The elephant in the Room: Abortion

Rush said pro-life and abortion is the elephant in the room. Rush said pro-life is what defines the Party. And any GOP politicians that are against abortion don't believe in conservatism. And as such, they want to reform and re-brand conservatism.

The elephant in the Room: Tax Cuts, Immigration

Rush made it clear that new ideas stem from liberalism. Rush has said listening tours and fresh ideas being catapulted by some conservatives is nothing but liberalism. So-called "fresh ideas" are ideas borrowed from Liberals. Rush said conservatism is timeless. They want to put an end to tax cuts and immigration debates.

The elephant in the Room: Social Issues Scare Liberal Republicans to Death

A true conservative wouldn't be worried about being on dangerous ground when talking about social issues. Social issues alienate fiscal conservatives. According to Rush, the mantra for the country club blue- blood liberal Republicans is getting rid of social issues. Because that is what they perceive is destroying the party at large. Rush said once a GOP politician says he or she is a fiscal conservative rather than a social conservative, it means they are a pro-choicer who doesn't want to be lumped with pro-lifers.

The elephant in the Room: Reaganism, old hat for Dead weight Republicans

Rush pointed out that the Republican Party's strategists don't want any Republican leader with a "tinge of Reaganism" being the spokesperson for the party. Therefore, Rush Limbaugh, Richard Cheney and conservative talk radio are banned from the pulpit. The strategists say Reaganism is obstinate, it's old hat.

Conservatism is Christianity

Rush said there is a "religious void" in the lives of many Americans. That void has been replaced by a belief in government, Democrats and liberalism. So it doesn't sit well with Rush when the GOP wants to believe in big government the way the Democrats do.

Class Politics are not in the Conservatism Agenda

Rush stated that it is a no no to follow the advice of pseudo-conservatives who want to segregate American voters into female Americans, African Americans, NASCAR dads and soccer moms. Rush said all that does is cause animosities and stall progress.

Leave the 2012 Presidential Election on the Backburner: Republicans free from Dead Weight's encumbrance

Rush noted that defining who conservatives are should take precedence over thinking of winning elections. According to Rush, there are many gutless fractions of the GOP. Rush said most rocky Republicans, after being elected to Washington, would abandon their conservative beliefs just to be accepted by their liberal colleagues. Rush feels to get rid of the conservative ideology is to ignore the "blueprint for landslide victory." That is what Republicans like Arnold Schwarzenegger believe the party has to do. "We've got our conservative intelligentsia wise men, these people in the media who also think that the worst thing that could happen to the Republican Party is to listen to me."

The GOP dead weights claimed to have Republicans' best interest at heart. It's quite the opposite. They supported McCain throughout the Republican primaries. Yet after McCain was certain to be the presumptive GOP nominee, they dumped him. And then they literally switched their support to Obama. They allied with liberal Democrats in fighting for Obama over Hillary Clinton. After Obama locked up enough delegates to win the presumptive Democratic nominee, they then inserted the final nail in the coffin by formally endorsing Obama over McCain. They excoriated McCain's running mate for no justified reason. In order to save face, they claimed Sarah Palin was the reason they opted to endorse Obama.

They are desperately trying to pulverize the conservative movement. As long as we have all these dead weight moderates and Republicans in our party, come election time, we will always be taken to the cleaners by the Democrats. The more we have different factions, the more the internecine within the party gets intensified. The GOP needs to purge from the party the politicians that voted against the Republican nominee for president during the general election. Obliterating the dead weights in our Party is the right course of action. Arlen Specter was the biggest dead weight of 2009. He was never a true Republican; he was teetering on the brink. Snowe and Collins's futures as Republican senator is thought to be hanging in the balance.[5]

Forerunners for 2012 GOP for President

The Republican Party has been jeremiad for too long since the post Reagan era. A number of pseudo conservatives said we can't keep reverting back to Reagan for our progress. Conservatives have to move forward. Doing everything to complete his mission on earth, God has already blessed conservatives with an oracle to listen to. That oracle is Rush Limbaugh. After twenty years, Rush is still the unwavering number one voice of dissent to the Democratic Party. And we have a 21st century true conservative politician in Sarah Palin. With those two in tandem, the Party will be successful for many years to come, and the conservative movement will be fueled to move on strongly. First things first: we have to get rid of the McCains, Powells and the rest of the dead weights and Rinos that are bringing down the party.

Rush has decried Obama's policies, and he will continue to criticize the president whenever he is wrong. Unfortunately, only Rush and a handful of Republicans are speaking out against Obama's misleading agendas. Republicans have to return to their conservative roots. Rush has already saddled the horse, but will the horse allow the rider to ride? With their massive audience, Rush and Hannity have elevated and brought to light Republican politicians.

GOP Standard Bearer
Potential presidential candidates

Let the race begin

"The jock jostling has already begun." Rush said about GOP potential candidates for president. Rush asserted that the "long knives" are out for Palin, Romney and Huckabee. They are all staying in the public eyes.

Those supposedly on the 2012 bandwagon

Sarah Palin

Picked by Rush to lead the Republican Party, Sarah Palin is an epitome of a down to earth true GOP politician. Her nationwide recognition speaks volumes. Conservatives owe McCain a debt of gratitude for bringing Palin to light. Before McCain picked her as a running mate, Rush Limbaugh had already brought up both Palin and Louisiana governor's Jindal's names as potential vice president candidates in the 08 elections.

Governors, who have an eye for a presidential run, can only seemingly speak for their state, unlike the Rush Limbaughs and the Richard Cheneys, who speak largely for the nation. But Palin stunned the political world when she resigned as governor of Alaska in July of 2009. She has joined the ranks of unattached conservative leaders. Palin draws both praise and disdain from Americans. Sean Hannity said "she has extraordinary commonsense, she draws big crowds and her statements are quintessential America." Senator Kerry called Palin a "Cheneyesque social conservative who's going to satisfy the base."

All the character assassinations that Bush and Cheney experienced have now been transferred to poor Sarah Palin. Bush and Cheney have been called all the names in the book, but Palin hasn't yet achieved that feat. Only time will tell, as we suspect the name calling from the liberals to eclipse what even Bush faced. "It's historical, the large crowd, record number of people tuning in to watch Palin." Sean Hannity noted. "She should remain in the federal stage. Palin has a bold distinct difference with what the GOP is offering."

Depending on the outcome of the 2012 elections, Palin might consider running for Alaska's US Senate seat: "My life is in God's hands. If he's got doors open for me, that I believe are in our state's best interest, the nation's best interest, I'm going to go through those doors," Palin said, while hinting a run for the US Senate to replace Senator Ted Stevens. Rush talked about the "defensive posture" that Palin put the Obama/Biden campaign on. Rush said the people attending Obama's rallies were cult people. And they were there just to be "part of the story," not to pay attention to what Obama was saying. Palin revved up people on substance because she lectured about American exceptionalism and American greatness.

Will Rush support Palin in the 2012 primaries? He didn't support any of the 2008 GOP candidates for president. There was growing speculation that Rush secretly supported Senator Thompson in the early primaries and then Gov. Romney in the latter part of the 2008 GOP primaries. Should Rush breaks his promise to not get involved in the primaries and thus endorse Palin, he will irritate the likes of Huckabee, Romney and even Giuliani if they run. We need to bring back the eleventh commandment and rally around a principal conservative like Palin. Palin was coached and constrained by McCain's campaign. Rush said: "She went out there and was mirroring what McCain was saying about reform this and reform that."

Because of Palin, Obama was forced to the wire. Only at the death of the 2008 general election was Obama able to be successful. Without Palin, Obama would have trounced McCain. The GOP tailored Palin's speeches to suit McCain's needs. Palin was forced to mirror McCain. So McCain's loss to Obama was surely expected. "Many just accept that lame duck status, and they hit that road. They draw a paycheck. They kind of milk it. And I'm not going to put Alaskan through that," Palin said, after she abruptly dropped the bombshell of her resignation from office of governor. Pundits like Dana Perino and Donna Brazile both indirectly told Sarah Palin to shut up because she expounded the reason why she resigned. They said she should save the rest of her message for her book.

The media scrutiny of Palin was unacceptable. After the 2008 presidential elections, there were more than a dozen ethics complaints against Palin. They tried the whole nine yards to destroy her credibility. The nature of the outlandish claims against Palin was just beyond outrageous. Palin devotes every waking day of her life defining what conservatism is all about. Palin's groundswell of support is equivalent to her groundswell of opposition. Palin is fast becoming a Rush Limbaugh.

Mike Huckabee

Huckabee is a Baptist minister and a social conservative. Huckabee can't wait to run again in 2012. He is the most prospective of all the bandied candidates penciled in to make a run. Mike is currently hosting a TV program on FOX News. He is trying to stay occupied and be in the public eye. Is he considering a run for the US senate? If he unsuccessfully runs for the presidency, then he will immediately switch his attention towards a seat in the upper chamber of Congress. "She brought electricity to the Party last campaign," Huckabee said briefly about Palin, keeping in mind that he might have to contend with Palin for the 2012 GOP presidential election nomination. Rush's refusal to galvanize his supporters to pick a presidential nominee caused melee in the 2008 GOP primary. It got very unsettling, and most conservatives were forced to support Romney over Huckabee. Illegal immigration was the issue that drove Rush Limbaugh's support away from Huckebee. Mike Huckabee's standpoint on illegal immigrants was that they were God's children.

Huckabee is way more conservative than Mitt Romney. Their records speak for themselves. Huckabee, as governor of Arkansas, was the benchmark for the rest of the GOP governors. Conservatives only rejected Huckabee because he was unpopular and too religious. In the 2008 presidential elections, his main supporters were the evangelicals. The fact that Huckabee refused to concede to John McCain even after the 08 GOP primaries was a dead rubber angered the GOP establishment.

Huckabee will always be an ideal fit to be president, and he would be brimming with confidence come 2012 that he would have a chance to be victorious.

Mitt Romney
Romney will definitely get support from the conservative base if he runs in 2012. He has all the money in the world to again campaign for the Oval Office. After Romney lost the 2008 primaries to McCain, speculation mounted that Romney was readying himself for the Veep position under John McCain. However, the bandying of his name was actually a decoy to deceive the Obama/Biden ticket. The former governor of Massachusetts' fundraising ability is outstanding. Mitt is well versed in the US economy. Pressure is being brought to bear for Romney to announce his candidacy for the White House. He might surpass the astronomic amount of money he spent in his 2008 campaign or stand a chance of ending up like his father; Governor George Romney, who also didn't get the GOP nomination.

As a governor, Romney governed as a liberal Republican. He hasn't had the chance to prove he is conservative enough to earn the conservative votes. Romney splurging tens of millions of dollars of his own money couldn't still buy him the GOP nomination. There is no doubt that Romney's religion might plague him again. As far as liberals are concerned, Romney's religion would be the elephant in the room for the former governor. Romney is as free as a bird. He doesn't hold a political office, so running for president suit him down to the ground.

Newt Gingrich

Speculation has also centered on Newt Gingrich, but will he put his hat in the ring for a presidential run in 2012? Even though Newt Gingrich has long left Congress, he has been running the GOP House of Representative from his home state of Georgia since DeLay left Congress in 2006. John Boehner, the Minority Leader in the House, can't press any important buttons until he gets orders from Newt. Newt is well read and his tremendous fundraising skills back in his short spell as Speaker of the House would be a plus if put to use. If he runs, he will certainly get most Republican lawmakers' endorsements. For the past decade, Newt has spent most of his time rebuilding and reorganizing the Republican Party. He has also been working on and influencing GOP grassroots organizations. Newt Gingrich belongs to the conservative folklore. He deserves to be put on the same pedestal as conservative politicians like Reagan and Goldwater. The grassroots contingency urged for Newt to go further than testing the water. This continued until the last minutes of the 2008 presidential election. And in 2009, he has been inundated with requests to make a bid for the presidency. The proceeds from his bestselling books would be a huge advantage for building a war chest for a possible 2012 campaign.

He is a powerful and popular figure nationwide. He is not as polarizing a figure as he was in his Speaker days, but his political baggage might be too heavy for him to make a run. If he does accept the request to run, he will certainly be one of the front-runners for the GOP nomination.

Mayor Rudy Giuliani

In the 2008 primaries, it seemed more like Giuliani was campaigning for senator or governor of Florida rather than campaigning for Commander in Chief. Giuliani put all his eggs in one basket, the basket being the state of Florida. Florida has 57 winner- take-all delegates, and Giuliani calculated and envisioned a victory in Florida would give him the edge he needed to win the GOP nomination. Giuliani's campaign strategy turned out to be a house of cards. Regardless of his dismal 2008 election campaign, to preclude Rudy from the 2012 election would be absurd. Giuliani is probably not enthused to make another run after his 08 campaign strategies was a complete rout. Rudy has been quizzed about his prospect of running again for the White House. Giuliani did just enough to tamp down rumors of a 2012 presidential run by hinting on settling to run for either the New York State governorship or the US Senate, where he stands a better chance to resurrect his political career. Although he tried running for the US Senate in 2000, Giuliani is suited most effectively for executive leadership, not legislative leadership. He was compelled to take on Hillary Clinton in 2000, but one problem led to another and he was forced out of the running. At the last moment, Giuliani finally weaseled out of running for both offices in 2010, thereby hitting millions of New Yorkers where it hurts. His reason for declining a statewide run might not hold water for New Yorkers, but his decision would enable him to concentrate on a presidential run. On the national front, should Giuliani decline to run in 2012, the anticipation of another awful election loss would take precedence. Giuliani will definitely play a significant role in shaping who will be our nominee. Giuliani's heroic 9/11 performance will never be forgotten. His name is already etched in stone as American's Mayor.

Tim Pawlenty

Pawlenty is another ambitious Republican who is speculated to make a run. The governor of Minnesota remains coy about whether he would prepare his way for the Oval office. For the sake of wasting citizen's taxpaying dollars, incumbent Governors and Senators shouldn't be allowed to juggle their gubernatorial or senatorial duties while campaigning for the presidency. They must step down from office before they can make a run. An example of this occurred in 1996. Bob Dole was forced out of Congress in order to concentrate on his run for the presidency, but in 2008, John McCain wasn't asked to step down. What happened to Dole in 1996 should have gotten the ball rolling so that we can conveniently avoid having a politician like Obama running for president after only two years in office as a senator. And then Obama spends 18 months as an incumbent senator campaigning to be president.

It should be incumbent upon them to relinquish their office if they want to run for the Oval office. A huge disadvantage for governors like Pawlenty is that they have limited foreign policy backgrounds. Governor Pawlenty's announcement that he won't seek reelection will enable him to get a head start on the scheduled 2012 presidential election. There have been flurries of speculation that he's on his way to make a bid. The loss of one of his important senatorial supporters, Senator Noel Coleman, who was bitterly bested by Al Franken, will be a dent to his supposed presidential campaign statewide. It will be difficult for Pawlenty to vault the likes of Romney and Palin to win the nomination.

Mike Huckabee was written off and out of the argument before the 2008 GOP primaries commenced, but Huckabee turned out to be a formidable candidate. In 2012, Pawlenty might be the Huckabee of 2008.

Haley Barbour

Barbour is the second ever Republican governor in the state of Mississippi since the Reconstruction. When asked if he will forsake the office of governor to run for president, Barbour answered point blank: "I am not. I don't have any plan to run for president. I don't have any intention of running for president." He gave the sort of broad answer that any politician with the intention of running will say at a very early stage. So will the GOP's most beloved governor run? After Sanford's salacious scandal, Barbour was appointed to replace Sanford as the Republican Governor Association chairman. The GOP presidential nominee, let alone the presidency, should be deemed beyond his reach. As early as 2009, Barbour has been touted as a possible Republican vice presidential candidate.

Bobby Jindal

He might run just to put his name on the national scene. The governor of the hurricane calamity stricken Louisiana is hugely popular in the state. The media labeled his response to Obama's 2009 congressional address as poor. Jindal has a serious career dilemma to make. Will he forgo running for reelection a year before the 2012 presidential election, or will he jump into the fray? Conservatives have begun agitating for Jindal to affirm his intentions.

Charlie Crist

He may be laying the foundation for a senatorial bid, but his interest in a presidential bid is not shrouded in secrecy. The Florida governor might be a plausible bet for the Oval office. In terms of Electoral College votes, Florida is one of the decisive states when it comes to general elections. The media has been inquisitive about Crist possibly running for president. It's certainly a bridge too far for the Floridian who remains coy for a run. And as days elapse, it is improbable the Floridian will make a run.

No Repeat of 2008, No Repeat of the Media Picking McCain as the GOP Nominee

Rush has always claimed that the liberal Democratic media "will go a long way in telling" the Republicans which of the major GOP candidates they are most afraid of. Rush said they aren't afraid of Huckebee or Ronmey because they spent less time talking about them. But Rush said everybody talks about Palin; everybody lambastes Palin. Rush claims hoping that one day the media will love a Republican candidate is a day that will never happen. Palin is our strongest candidate, that is why they constantly attack her.

No single individual, including Rush, has the sole power to have the final say on who our Party nominates. But the election has consequences, just as in 2008, voting in the primaries for a moderate McCain-like candidate had consequences.

NEVER SAY NEVER

Conservatives can never say never to prominent Republicans like Condoleezza Rice and Jeb Bush. Sean Hannity, Richard Cheney and Rush Limbaugh stand an outside chance of running.

Jeb Bush

Another Bush in the White House would definitely establish a Bush dynasty. It would be a long shot for that to occur, but the possibility of Jeb one day becoming vice president is not remote. In 2008 rumors were speculated that Mitt Romney, heeding to Walker Bush advice, would have picked Jeb as his running mate if he got the nod over McCain.

George Bush, the 43rd president, vowed to be taciturn and not reprobate Obama's presidency. George Bush's silence will be a positive boost for Jeb should he make an inquiry for the Oval Office. Jeb announcement that he won't run to replace Mel Martinez in the US Senate come 2010 may be viewed as him concentrating on a possible run for the presidency in 2012.

Like Newt Gingrich, Jeb Bush has been devoting and dedicating his time for the continual growth of the party: "I can play a role in helping to reshape the Republican Party's message and focus on 21st century solutions to 21st century problems," Jeb said. Jeb Bush is oriented towards executive leadership positions. He remains a popular figure in Florida, the state where he has governed for two terms. Continuous talk of him running for the Oval Office will definitely be in the pipeline within the GOP establishment. To forgo a race for the US senate in 2010 and to forgo a race for the presidency in 2012, having after governed as a governor for eight years, would really be unbecoming for a Bush. Lots of questions would be asked.

Rush Limbaugh

Rush is only focused on navigating the conservative movement to its core value roots. Rush would be negligent if he abandoned leading the conservative movement and instead made a run for the presidency. Despite being a well trained broadcaster, Rush can do both jobs with ease. Look at Silvio Berlusconi; he is a three time prime minister of Italy and also the president of the most successful soccer team in the world. Rush could juggle two jobs at the same time, regardless of perhaps having too many irons in his fire. Rush is a far cry from reaching the retirement age of 65. Rush will most certainly fundraise for GOP candidates.

Richard Cheney

If Cheney was greedy for power, he should have been the 2008 Republican nominee like Al Gore was in 2000. There is time for everything. What hasn't this true statesman from Wyoming achieved? Supreme Court judge might have eluded his resume, but Cheney has reached the pinnacle in both the legislative branch as House Minority Whip and the executive branch as Vice President. A hawkish diplomat when he was secretary of defense, Cheney is also the most accomplished Republican executive in the United States. Pundits claimed that Cheney broke with tradition by blasting Obama's presidency so soon after he left office. But Al Gore didn't break with tradition after the 2000 presidential election fallout? There was speculation that Vice President Richard Cheney and conservative icon Rush Limbaugh were secretly scheming on a possible run for president in 2012 as a formidable ticket. CNN's Wolf Blitzer asked: "Dick Cheney and Rush Limbaugh running together in 2012? What's going on here?" Mary Matalin, a former Cheney aide, responded, "Well, it is a conservative's dream. I would giving up this perch, Wolf, in a New York minute to go work for that ticket." Limbaugh has since moved to quell the rumors. The genuine hatred the Democrats have for Cheney could disseminate to GOP voters nationwide.

Sean Hannity

For Hannity to suspend lecturing his 15 million plus audience and focused on a potential run for the presidency is just what the doctor ordered. So far, Hannity isn't heeding what has been prescribed. He has turned a deaf ear on the blizzard of calls for him to make a run. Hannity is 3 months younger than President Obama. So he has between 2009 and the next 25 years to deny contemplating running for the Oval Office. All of the GOP 2008 candidates for president were interviewed by Hannity. Depending on how conservative the GOP candidates are, Hannity would be driven to do his level best in campaigning for them.

Eric Cantor

Cantor is far from being a plausible candidate for 2012. He's been getting enormous praises from Hannity. Cantor replaced Representative Roy Blunt as the Minority Whip of the US House of Congress. He might not run for the presidency until after he achieves the minority leader position. Cantor would be short listed as a vice president choice for the GOP nomination. The Virginian has been very outspoken against the Obama administration. Cantor's White House hopeful is definitely in the offing, but Cantor knows he needs to enhance his national profile.

Mark Sanford

Until June 2008 he was widely viewed as a potential presidential candidate, but all those hopes and ambitions suddenly went down the drain. Sanford confessed of an extramarital affair with a mistress in "don't cry for me" Argentina. Republicans were surprised to see Sanford commit political suicide days after appearing on Sean Hannity's show explaining why he was against Obama's stimulus package. Calls for the embattled governor to resign were escalating by the day after news of his affair surfaced.

The governor of South Carolina won reelection in 2008. Sanford's philandering might have been the twilight of his career. Sanford's deviance and perversion could surely end his hopes of running for any political office.

Although Sanford's self-inflicted damage might be his undoing, he has 2 years to get back on track. He should be advised to go moderate for some time before reverting back to being a social conservative. South Carolina legislature has already begun impeachment proceedings against Sanford. An impeachment would be the final nail in the coffin for Sanford, so it would be academic for Sanford to try to revamp his political career.

Condoleezza Rice

Calls for her to run could increase if Palin is reluctant to make a bid. Of all the potential candidates, she has the inside track to a successful presidential victory, having vehemently campaigned for George Bush in two occasions. Exhorted and pressed in an explosive interview with Sean Hannity, Rice, the former secretary of state, refused to be drawn into speculation about a move for the White House was brewing, but there's no smoke without fire. Rice's deafening silence might be suppressed as time elapses; Rice might defer her decision in running for president until the last minute.

Chuck Norris

He's a Hollywood Republican conservative and a Baptist minister. Like Mike Huckabee, Norris is an evangelical Christian who has been a cameo host on Fox News. Norris won't be flirting for a presidential bid, but he will be in the running as a possible GOP vice presidential candidate.

Rick Santorum

Senator Santorum needed a lot of time off from the national scene. When he was in the US senate, he was the most attacked Republican senator. There is talk that he could be a possible Veep for the expected presidential candidate for Sarah Palin. The Pennsylvanian would unequivocally get endorsements from Rush Limbaugh, Sean Hannity and the majority of Republican senators should he make a bid. For years, Santorum was the third highest ranking Republican senator.

John McCain

McCain is certainly not trying to go through the rigors of another presidential bid. But a war hero like McCain might throw down the gauntlet for his third crack at the Oval Office. Bob Dole, former GOP presidential nominee was forced to write a letter to Rush indirectly upbraiding Rush for reproaching John McCain in the 2008 presidential election. Age is nothing but a number. In McCain's case, however, that belief is an exception to the rule. McCain was supported to the hilt by the GOP establishment. Should McCain ponder on another run, he would be adjudged as a candidate who's well stricken in age.

Others

Alan Keyes and other nobodies might be in contention but, like Brownback in 2008, they will be the GOP's laughingstocks and will eventually get kicked off the bandwagon. Primarily, they are running to enhance their chances for other lesser offices. But as far as the GOP nominee is concern, they will be predisposed as also-rans and minnows just there to complete the numbers. Insufficient media coverage will cause them to drop out of the race as early as the Iowa primary.

Tabulating
GOP main candidates/running mates

Palin--------------Giuliani /Santorum

Jindal-------------Daniels

Gingrich--------------Armey-Hannity, DeLay

Romney----------------Jeb Bush

Huckabee------------Norris

Pawlenty ------------Barbour

?-------------------- Cheney, Limbaugh

Final Notes

Giuliani, Huckabee and Romney are all reputed to make another bid. They wouldn't be able to undo the record high capacity crowd that Palin drew in 2008.

Political cannibalism and Reagan's eleventh commandment that occurs during the primaries has to cease in order for us to rally around a principle conservative candidate.

As the GOP waits for presidential hopefuls to make a clear-cut decision on a run, Rush has already pinpointed Romney, Huckebee and Palin as the possible nominee for 2012. Rush's endorsement of Palin will rankle GOP presidential hopefuls, but Rush will do his damnedest to make sure Palin or any other genuine conservative secures the nomination.

Rush said it is a shame that "some stuffed shirts, blue blood country club types" in the GOP are upset that Palin is the most popular Republican candidate for president.

Rush doesn't want to get caught between the devil and the deep blue sea, so he decided not to get involved in any GOP presidential election primaries. But will Rush have a change of heart because of Palin? If Palin runs and wins the GOP nomination, all hands would definitely be on deck. Rush would fire on all cylinders to make sure Palin wins the 2012 presidency. All things being equal or not, fairness doctrine or not, golden EIB microphone or not, nothing will hinder a paramount Rush support for Palin. The GOP needs a genuine conservative candidate like Reagan. Sarah Palin, as the closest politician to the Reagan model, fit the bill.

Ignoring Rush's advice has lead the Republicans to sweeping congressional election losses and a dismal presidential election loss. And what is coming in the offing if we continue to neglect Rush's recipe for success? In 2008, we had a Republican candidate who was more populist than conservative. McCain was looking for some type of middle ground with the Democrats on every issue he was campaigning for. And that was one of Rush's disagreements.

"If they stay principal, focus and engage they will win," Sean Hannity talking about 2012 elections. We don't want a nominee who will find some type of common ground between liberalism and conservatism. We don't want a nominee who would, on the liberal premises, yield to the tug of popular sentiment. We don't need a candidate who would try to compromise with the Democratic Party. We don't need candidate who would be embroiled in horse-trading with the liberals.

And we certainly won't support a candidate who wouldn't dig in their heels, but rather compromise on their opinionated conservative beliefs. We won't support a candidate that would be looking for a second invitation before they opposed the liberal premises.

But thank God the GOP candidates for president know that they have to preface Rush before they could get that nomination. Rush is the last strenuous test they have to face.

"If you don't see what you like, like what you see," Celestine Mohammed said. In the 2008 elections, there weren't any true popular conservatives on the ballot. Virginia's Senator George Allen and Pennsylvania's Senator Rick Santorum were two popular conservative candidates that prior to 2008 were favorites to win the conservative votes.

Giuliani, Romney and McCain, who represented the GOP candidates for president, weren't conservative enough. They didn't warrant the conservative votes. The conservative voters didn't see what they liked, so they were forced to like what they saw. They were forced to like a candidate like Romney and a candidate like McCain. The conservative votes were split, and the damage had been done. When Palin was introduced, there was no time to reunite the conservative voters.

The GOP establishment dug their own grave and as such lost by a landslide to the most liberal senator. In 2012, Rush Limbaugh and Sean Hannity will try to prevent history from repeating itself.

Rush chided the GOP 2008 candidates for not being principle enough. Will that be the same fate come 2012? It will be a principle donnybrook for all the potential 2012 candidates for president.[6]

Conservatism is of the Essence

The Conservative Family

The modern conservative family started with Goldwater and Buckley through Reagan. From Reagan to baby boomers' Limbaugh, Gingrich and DeLay, conservatism was no longer fringe. From Gingrich and co. to Hannity, Santorum and Palin, the modern conservative family lives forever.

What is Conservatism?

1-Using a hint from Anthony Henderson: conservatism at it very best is when Hannity runs back to Limbaugh for an interview. That is conservatism.
2-Informed Americans cramming in droves to hear Sarah Palin speak. That is conservatism.
3-DeLay's book being credited by Limbaugh and Hannity. That is conservatism.
4-Reagan's letter of praise to Rush Limbaugh. That is conservatism.

5-Rick Santorum winning a US senate seat in a very blue State. That is conservatism.

6-Efforts from Gingrich, DeLay and Limbaugh for the GOP's 1994 historic congressional midterm election smashing victory. That is conservatism on display.

7-Reagan's 1980 and 1984 landslide presidential victories, including defeating a seating president. That is conservatism.

8-Goldwater spearheading the attacked on a fellow Republican corrupt president, Nixon. That is conservatism.

9-Buckley, Goldwater and Regan's momentous contributions to the modern conservative movement. That is conservatism.

10-Conservative Americans who steadily, in session and out of session, support our core ideas that were etched out by our Founders. That is conservatism.

11-Finally, and most importantly, believing in the resurrection of Jesus Christ and the worship of the one true God in heaven. That is conservatism.

Before "I Hope He Fails"- Conservatism 101
Conservatism is Original, Ageless and Biblical

Life and the Pursuit of Happiness is of the Essence

Conservatism is solely based on individual freedom and a small government. The sole purpose of the state is to protect the population. Conservatism doesn't need to be redefined, moderated or upgraded. Conservatism is about life, liberty and the pursuit of happiness. Therefore, pro-choice doesn't belong in conservatism. "The essence of innocence is a child in the womb who has no choice over what happens to it." The state doesn't recognize a baby's right to live, so it's left for conservatism to stand for that right.

Individual liberty and freedom is of the essence
Personal freedom and individual liberty is at the root of conservatism. And they will "never go out of style." Problems will always emerge, but freedom will solve any set of problems. Conservatism is nothing but "natural law, and at the root of it is freedom."

Truth about conservatism
According to Rush, conservatism is not focused on race, gender or religion. We are focused on personal liberty. Individual liberty is of the essence. Blood, sweat and tears brought individual liberty to Americans. What is foreign to us, Rush said, is tribalism. Conservatism doesn't objectify Americans. Rush said you won't win playing defense. You won't win if you don't stand up for your principles. You won't win if you worry about what everybody thinks about you. Rush confessed that whenever he gives political speeches all over America, all across the fruited plain, he doesn't get booed.

The fundamental conservative
The conservative ideology sees Americans as Americans. Not Americans as black, Hispanic or white. Conservatism has the best interests of Americans at heart. Conservatism wants everybody to be successful. Conservatism includes the belief that average people can achieve the extraordinary, so long as the state is not an obstacle to them. With whatever desires and ambitions Americans have, they have to ability to be the "best they can be."

Rush's Wining Formula
In order for conservatives to win office, Rush calculated: be "unapologetic pedal-to-the-metal conservatives" and get 40% of the votes. And for a 52% majority, seek after moderates to complete the vote count. Rush rebuked the notion that conservatism is in the wilderness. Conservatism is timeless, and the foundation of conservatism is freedom. And is those inside the Beltway media that is trying to derailed conservatism.

Conservatism Descended

Rush asserted that the "watering down" of conservatism and creating big tent is what led to conservatism descending. Rush said the blueprint for conservative landslide victories doesn't include creating a big tent; it doesn't include seeking moderate Democrats. Talking about Reagan Democrats, Rush said Reagan got many Democrats to vote for him but Reagan didn't pretend to be like them. Rush said an overwhelming majority of Americans "lives their life as conservatives" and if a genuine conservative is on the ballot, a landslide victory will emerge.

Conservatism near Death: Critical Condition
The diminishment of conservatism in America

Rush asked why is the hard left, the Democrats media, writing columns and editorials in an attempt to diminish the conservative influence in the GOP? "If we're dead, as they say we are," then why are the Liberals still trying to kill us politically? Rush said it is because we are a constant threat to them. They are a collection of liars and deceivers. And they can't stand the substance that conservatism is made up of. And as such, Rush, Sarah Palin, Newt Gingrich and those that perfectly articulate the principles and core beliefs of conservatism are being destroyed by the Democrats.

Conservatism Dead: Wake Keeping

Rush stated:"if we're dead," if Republicans are a "small pocket of renegades," then let the Americans left leave us alone and stop getting in the way of our follies. If the GOP is heading for destruction, let us continue on that path, don't obstruct us. Rush asked, why are they so vicious and demeaning in attacking us? For the left, trying to diminish the conservative movement is an everyday thing because they are afraid of opposition. Rush said conservatism should be looked as the "foundation for philosophy and ideas," not a "debating society." Rush said he left the "debating society" back in his high school days. Liberals want the McCains of the world to "muddle the waters" on what conservatism is all about. Rush said the left got their wish because the "Republicans have fallen to it hook, line, and sinker."

Conservatism Dead and Buried: RIP

"If conservatives are as dead as the left says we are," then why do they devote all of their time to "dancing on our graves?" Rush said as such, we have a golden opportunity to contrast conservatism with the most "quasi-socialist" American presidency in history. Rush said he has never experienced a period of time when Americans are afraid of their own government. Categorizing people is the language of Liberals. Rush said conservatism "lifts all boats" and conservatism policies don't result in pandering because they have roots.

The Reestablishment of Principled Conservatism: Rush

Rebuilding the Movement after McCain's General Election Defeat

A number of conservative intellects supported Obama in the general election. They believed the grass was much greener on the other side. Rush Limbaugh is determined to let them stay on the other side, to let them stay on the Democrat's side. According to Rush, rebuilding the conservative movement will be much easier because of the departures of those who abandoned the movement for Obama. Rush feels that in McCain, they got what they campaigned for. However, after things went south, these pseudo-conservatives flocked to Obama and the Democrats. Rush said those that abandoned the movement should be tarried on the other side. Using a football analogy, Rush said conservatism in the 2008 elections had the playbook but we "didn't run the plays." So it's high time for us to the start running the play without having sideliners or "draft choices" in our movement. Rush said those sideliners may make the bench, but they will have to "prove themselves in training camp." Rush said this is a golden "opportunity for cleansing." After the 2006 midterm elections and the 2008 presidential election loss, Rush was amazed that the conservative movement had fractured despite the fact that there is a blueprint for winning elections. Seeking moderates and yokels is not the blueprint for winning elections. Reagan's victories in the 80's and the Gingrich led congressional victory in 94 is the blueprint on how to win elections. McCain was not the blueprint.

The pickle that we found ourselves in is all because of Rockefeller Republican types, for the express purpose of destroying conservatism. The harmony that Rush and other conservatives forged within the Party is being severely threatened.

Conservatism relied excessively on Reagan in the 1980's, and it paid dividends. Regressing back to the Reagan era should be the first step taken. Why? Because Reagan's philosophy was the philosophy of our Founders.

In the 1990's and in the new millennium there hasn't been a drought of vital information, thanks to the voices of Rush Limbaugh and Sean Hannity. The paring of Rush and Sean to anchor the conservative movement can never be bettered. But they are both pamphleteers, not politicians. We need a pamphleteer like Rush Limbaugh to articulate the conservative message to a first tier political candidate like Sarah Palin to run with it. Reagan had his ear to many influential pamphleteers that were essential to his landslide victories. Paul Weyrich was a typical example. The combination of a Palin and a Rush is really a marriage made in heaven for the conservatives. Conservative ideology is fraught with sacrifice. Conservatism is original, and it can't be glossed over. There is nothing to be sanitized from conservative beliefs. Finally, conservatism is God's gift to America. That means it is etched in stone.[7]

End.

CHAPTER THREE

Democratic and Republican Parties

The Democratic Party

The Democratic Party is a no-holds-barred type of party. Anybody can just wake up and says "Oh I'm a Democrat." It's without limitation. You are always going to be welcome to the Party of JFK and FDR. Former Bush's White House press secretary, Scott McLellan, is a typical example.

The Democratic Party preys on the less fortunate Americans. We are talking about the disadvantaged, the have-nots, the underclass, by and large those without a pot to piss in. Those are the types of people who the Democrats crave for, just to get their votes.

The Democratic Party of the 21st century has become a cabal that is comprised of authoritarian imperialists. Freedom, liberty and all the core principles of conservatism is an obstacle to Democratic Party. Capitalism is an obstacle to liberalism.

Different types of Democrats
Rush said the Democratic Party is an "amalgamation of various coalitions:" the Big Labor, the teachers unions, the animal rights group, the global warming group, the Feminizes, the militant gay rights activists and the environmentalist advocacy groups, to name a few. Rush said they all have their demands from the Party's leadership.

Black Coalition in tandem with the Media Coalition

Rush claimed that at times, they rival each other. But what they all have in common is that they hate Republicans. And for financial benefits, they thrive on being close to the government. The Democratic Party has to give these coalitions their desires because when it comes to voting time, it will be a quid pro quo. Rush said the duty of the black coalition of the Democratic Party is to maintain 90% of the black votes. The media is the glue that holds all the coalitions together. They lionize the likes of Sharpton and Jesse Jackson. And although they are corrupt race-baiters, the media would never portray them as such. "Their corruption is legion," but the mainstream liberal media wouldn't dissipate their corruption.

The Democratic Party is one "giant den of thieves." Anti-freedom and liberty is the Democratic Party and its associates' agenda. Their main agenda is to deprive Americans of freedom and liberty.

Democrats' main goal

Democrats want feminism, which entails men and women in conflict. They want racism, which entails blacks and whites in conflict. They crave class envy, which entails the poor hating the rich. Rush said Liberals have done "their every living best to divide" as many Americans as possible. Rush admitted that to a great extent, they have succeeded.

Rush Summed up the Democratic Party Leadership

In closing, Rush said nothing could be further from the truth. The Democratic lawmakers must lie about their real agenda, for example the healthcare bill, because "at its core" Americans would reject the Party's agendas by a landslide. Democrats and Liberals avoid speaking outside their audience's comfort level so as to maintain that core group. They spend "every waking moment" scheming and conspiring against the American public. As a "narrow ideological party," lying to the American public is the main objective.

Democratic Party under Eleven Months of an Obama abject leadership

In 1992, President Bill Clinton, Speaker Tom Foley, Senate majority leader George Mitchell and House majority leader Dick Gephardt controlled both ends of Washington DC's Pennsylvania Avenue. History has repeated itself as radicals like President Obama, Speaker Pelosi, Senate leader Reid and House leader Hoyer are kneecapping everywhere in America, except occupants of Pennsylvania Avenue, with their taxes hikes, healthcare policies, etcetera.

Speaker of the House Nancy Pelosi, at a town hall meeting, claimed that local citizens were "carrying swastikas and symbols like that." Her comment drew much scorn from GOP. What type of country are we living in when the critic to Pelosi comment were lopsided? Reid also foisted insults on tourists. Harry Reid said: "In the summertime, because of the high humidity and how hot it gets here, you could literally smell the tourists coming into the Capitol." Reid egregious remarks were ignored by his Democratic colleagues.

The Democratic Party is in danger of spiraling out of control: "The train is already off tracks and its heading to a cliff, Pelosi, Franken, Reid all driving the train," Sean said.

Democrats hoped that after 11 months of diabolical and abject leadership that President Obama was over the hump. But that wasn't the case; it only got worse.

Schadenfreude moments for Democrats

Al Franken was finally accepted to represent Minnesota at the US senate. That was a sad day for the Republicans and a schadenfreude moment for the Democrats. The Democratic Party has 60 senators, but they can't explain the political gridlock in Congress. Sanford, the GOP governor from South Carolina, represents a reproach to conservatives and the Republican Party as a whole. Sanford was laughed to scorn by liberals. Sanford's extramarital affairs sum up the schadenfreude from the Democrats.

Enraged moments for Democrats

What made the Democrats all bent out of shape and filled with anguish within the eleven months of Obama regime? As expected, they reproved Rush for saying that he wants Obama to fail. The Democratic Party had a cow when Joe Wilson, a congressman from South Carolina, said Obama lied. Wilson's utterance drew widespread condemnation. There were calls for Wilson to be recalled and he was said to be on the verge of being reprimanded by his peers in Congress.

Obama's administration fit to be tied with Rush Limbaugh and Fox News. They were said to be on Obama's enemy list. The 2009 gubernatorial GOP election victories was a referendum on President Barack Obama's policies and the coup de grace for the Democratic Party.

Democratic Party: standard bearer for 2012

As the Republicans search extensively for a standard bearer, Democrats are also searching for a future standard bearer. After Obama's thoughtless eleven months as president, Hillary Clinton might be lurking dangerously. Obama has been constantly, for the past eleven months, campaigning for president, even though he is already the 44th United State president.

After Hillary lost the Democratic nomination, she was asked her chances of running for president again, Hillary said: "Probably close to zero. There's an old saying: Bloom where you're planted."

Before Hillary was appointed as State Secretary, Rush highlighted "Mrs. Clinton as secretary of state is not about Mrs. Clinton as secretary of state." Rush said it was Obama's political maneuvering that made it absolutely impossible for Hillary to challenge him in the 2012 presidential election.

Rush said that if Hillary wants to run for the oval office in 2012, she would have to start campaigning in 2010. It would be unprecedented should Hillary resign from her secretary of state post to run against Obama. Rush said Obama took in consideration the fact that he didn't want Hillary as senate majority leader. Hillary, on the other hand, didn't want to continue being the junior senator to Charles Schumer so she took the offer from Obama.

"I'm stunned that she took it," Rush said about Hillary's appointment as Secretary of State: "Hillary has always worked for herself. I think this is stroke for Obama. You know, the old phrase, you keep your friends close and your enemies closer?"

Obama outwitted Hillary Clinton in the 2008 Democratic primaries. Towards the end of the Democratic primaries, Hillary's attacks on Obama were at a premium. Hillary sensed that even waiting for the other shoe to drop would not salvage her path to the Democratic nomination. Hillary was reluctant to cave in to Obama. At the end of it all, she yielded by "suspending" her campaign. Of course Hillary Clinton, being the most powerful woman in America, would not openly surrender to a mere junior senator from Illinois.

Hillary Clinton's supporters did cut Obama some slack because he elected Hillary as Secretary of State. The fact that Obama's choice for veep, Joe Biden, was a foregone conclusion, while Obama's camp still hinted a possible choice for Hillary for veep established resentment among her supporters. She felt hard done after all the Clintons have done for the Party. Biden rushed to appease Hillary's supporters: "Make no mistake about this, Hillary Clinton is as qualified or more qualified than I am to be vice president of the United States of America. Let's get that straight. She's a truly close personal friend, she is qualified to be president of the United States of America, she's easily qualified to be vice president of the United States of America, and quite frankly, it might have been a better pick than me. But she's first rate, I mean that sincerely, she's first rate, so let's get that straight." "Be careful what you wish for, Rush," Hillary Clinton said briefly to Rush Limbaugh. Rush's launch of Operation Chaos to prolonged the Democratic 2008 primaries led to Hillary Clinton being appointed Secretary of State. Senator Hillary Clinton, being New York junior senator to Senator Charles Schumer, weighed heavily in her decision to take the State secretary diplomacy job. Hillary Clinton literally knows the difference between the air she breathes in Washington D.C and the air she breathed in New York or any other place she lived. She has lived in D.C. all her political life.

Obama was elected president primarily because of his hope and rhetoric but after eleven months, he has been found wanting. His supporters are peeling away from him.

Eleven months as secretary of state hasn't been an easy ride for Hillary. She has been ignored and left out of the loop by Obama. And as a result, there is a battle brewing between the two. Political strategist and former Clinton adviser Dick Morris led us to believe that if Obama becomes radioactive, Hillary will switch and oppose Obama during the 2012 presidential election primaries.

Considering the way the drive-by media treated Hillary Clinton during the latter stage of the 08 Democratic primaries and the unbelievable smear Sarah Palin received during her vice president campaign, it is logical to say Americans clearly aren't ready for a woman to become Commander-in-Chief.

Democratic Party: Congressional Elections

In 2006, the Democratic Party swept into power with tremendous efforts from Rahm Emanuel and Charles Schumer. And in 2008, their momentum continued especially with Obama's historical campaign. They will face an uphill battle to win over the Republicans in the imminent 2010 midterm elections. Obama has gotten his fellow Democrats into a whole heap of trouble with their constituents back in their various counties. Some of these Democratic members up for reelection have already broken ranks with the party leadership and criticized their president. Obama knows that they will be content as long as he keeps throwing them a bone. Acorn and other Democratic criminal racketeering groups would definitely gear up to support the Democratic Party.[1]

The Left Agenda

Obama's Stimulus package

The first stimulus package was treated like monopoly money. The day of reckoning has been due on the Obama's stimulus bill that failed to stimulate the economy. Rush addressed the day of reckoning daily on his radio program while Obama ran from it. Democrats will always run from the truth.

What has the stimulus actually done for the country at large? How many jobs did the stimulus actually create? What qualified an entity to receive the stimulus money? What factors will be taken into account in measuring the success of the stimulus package? The devil is in the details. Obama keeps postponing the day of reckoning, but the fact that businesses keep going out of business is addressing the issues we face.

The Housing Crisis

Greenspan blamed the free market for the housing bubble

Greenspan, former Chairman of the Federal Reserve of the United States, condemned and blamed capitalism for the subprime mortgages. Rush defended Capitalism. Rush dismissed the notion that the free market collapsed. Rush said the free market was not free. The government was all over the subprime mortgage and, as such, it wasn't free. The coercion from the government forced the market to break down. The subprime mortgages, Rush said from the inception, "Were worthless paper." Securities and derivatives were just a cover.

Rush thoroughly assessed the housing crisis

Rush asked, why would banks lend money to people who can't afford to pay them back? Rush said they did it because of greed. But how do you define greed when your client can't pay back what you lend to them?

Rush defined the mortgage crisis as banks giving loans to a bunch of people with low income to buy houses. Rush said when we couldn't afford to buy a house, we had to rent. Rush asked, what happened to renting? Liberals called for people to stop renting and get into home ownership. From then on, living and paying a mortgage was a struggle which eventually led to the crisis. Rush said the mortgage crisis debacle can be "laid at the feet" of Liberals like Barney Frank, Barack Obama, Jimmy Carter, Bill Clinton, Janet Reno, Chris Dodd, Nancy Pelosi, Harry Reid and Fannie and Freddie 's Jamie Gorelick, Franklin Raines and Jim Johnson.

Main problems of the foreclose housing

Without beating around the bush, Rush said loaning money to poor minorities who couldn't pay back is the problem. It was engineered by a bunch of Marxists. "This was affirmative action via mortgage." No one had the guts to say it, save Rush.

Bernanke failed to blame low income earners for the mortgage crisis

Rush was irritated at Bernanke's, the Chairman of the Federal Reserve of the United States, assessment of the mortgage crisis. Rush rebuked Bernanke for saying the subprime mortgages were "peachy keen" until the housing boom collapsed.

Rush talked about retarding the progress of capitalism. Rush said the government paying for people's mortgage was "delaying the inevitable," because paying for people's mortgages would end one day: it can't be done forever. Rush said that delaying the process will only worsen the problem because the free market won't be corrected.

The seers: those who saw it coming

Rush believed the Bush administration saw the housing crisis coming, but they were beaten to a bloody pulp by Democrats who didn't want to lose the block of voters in that category. Rush asked, how inspiring is it that the people that caused the crisis, for example Bernanke and others, are in charge of fixing it? Rush said it took only a handful of corrupt Democratic politicians to cause the housing boom. The party of Clinton, Al Gore and Barney Frank is "inherently flawed by virtue of its ideology."

In conclusion, Rush said: "Again I say: If there were a Republican that this could be blamed on, we would know his name. He would be at Guantanamo Bay in isolation." The Democratic led government causes the sublime crisis. They forced banks to make risky loans. The Democrats can't exonerate themselves from the housing crisis. Republicans were not on the crime scene. If the tables were turned, if Republicans' fingerprints were found, there would have been calls for investigations and convictions. They would have been subpoenaed by Congress.

Rush's Prod to Stall the Democratic Healthcare Bill

Nitty Gritty Details: the truth about Obama's Health Care Plan
The expense of the healthcare reform will put a stranglehold on the already knife- edge economy. The Democrats want little or no liberty and freedom for Americans, so their healthcare bill suits them to the ground. The healthcare bill is not about healthcare. It's about remaking America in their own likeness. Rush said Obama's number one "signature issue" shouldn't be about healthcare, it should be creating jobs. But because Obama wants as many people as possible dependent on the government, the more people lose their jobs, the more they lose their health insurance. Rush said the world comes to America for their healthcare because America has the best healthcare system in the world. Rush said insurance and catastrophic problems in our healthcare system don't call for a total overhaul of the system. Obama's plan is to have absolute control over the lives of the American people, and this healthcare bill is a vehicle to make that happen. Conservatives say healthcare is a privilege, while Liberals say healthcare is a right. "But anything the government can take away from you is not a right."

Rush took the Party's onus onto himself

Obama and the Democrats were determined to pass the heath care bill by hook or by crook. "The question," Senator Sanders, the self-proclaimed socialist senator from Vermont, said while chastising Rush, "We should be talking about is not the end-of-life phony discussion of Rush Limbaugh, et cetera. What we should be talking about is how it can be that this nation spends almost twice as much per capita on health care as any other nation. That is the kind of debate that we should be having, not the issue of, "Does Barack Obama want to kill off the old people or the disabled?" That is insane."

Rush reacted. "It's not insane. It's going to happen!" On healthcare spending, Rush said we don't spend money on those that are healthy. Rush asked, does a healthy person goes in for a heart surgery? We only spend healthcare funds on the sick, not the healthy. Rush said if you cut healthcare spending and no money is spent on those that are healthy, the only alternative is to cut spending on the sick. Cutting spending on the sick is the only way to cut healthcare spending, because you can't cut spending on the healthy.

Rush Limbaugh remains civil as Bob Dole awaits Healthcare signing ceremony

The Democrats blame the Republicans for treading water on the healthcare bill. But vast majorities of the American people were against enacting the healthcare bill. The Democratic Party moved heaven and earth to pass a monstrosity and an unmitigated healthcare reform bill. The Democratic senate was in a pickle because their counterpart used every preliminary proposal at their disposal to stall their counterpart's progress.

Dole is a prominent American. He was the Vice President nominee in 1976 and he was the Republican nominee for president in 1996. During the 2008 primaries, Bob Dole, a former Senate Majority Leader, wrote a letter to Rush Limbaugh on behalf of John McCain. He urged Rush to simmer down his attacks on Senator McCain. Dole's letter was an endorsement for John McCain. And what happened in the general election? McCain lost to Obama by a landslide. And Bob Dole, in 2009, wanted Rush to turn it down and let Obama have his way with the healthcare reform. The Democratic healthcare reform bill is an absolute unmitigated disaster. Where is Bob Dole's credibility? He wants the healthcare bill passed by any means necessary.

Senator Dole and three of his colleagues urged Congress to work speedily in a bipartisan way and enact healthcare reform. But at the same time, Dole opposed a public option of the bill.

Talking about passing the Healthcare bill, Bob Dole said, "We're already hearing from some high-ranking Republicans that we shouldn't do that. That's helping the president." Taking an indirect swipe at Rush, Dole added, "Sometimes people fight you just to fight you...they don't want Obama to get it, so we've got to kill it. Health care is one of those things. Now we've got to do something." Dole said convincingly, "There will be a signing ceremony" on the horizon. Rush was tempted to respond to Bob Dole's remarks: "I am convinced Dole has no clue what's going on. I don't think Dole has the slightest idea. I'm giving him the benefit of the doubt, by the way, holding that view."

Mooting over Healthcare continued

Rush's push for the Republican senators to put a blockage on the senate healthcare bill had the desired effect. As the year 2009 came to an end three Democratic senators, including Harry Reid, took to the senate floor to defame and denigrate Rush Limbaugh. These authoritarian statists voiced their opposition over Rush's intimidation of Senate Republican leader Mitch McConnell.

Democratic Senators lined up to attack Rush Limbaugh. Senator Sanders' attacks on Rush were just a dress rehearsal. Majority Leader Harry Reid said. "Rush Limbaugh, Glenn Beck, they're upset at Senator McConnell (Republican senate leader) because he's not opposing the health care bill enough, there are no efforts made to improve this bill, only to kill this bill."

Senator Whitehouse from Rhode Island said, "This is about creating a political defeat for the president of the United States on their side, nothing to do with health care, entirely about creating a defeat for this new president, when in the face of all the obstruction that the distinguished Senator from Michigan described so eloquently, this record-breaking, unprecedented in the history of the Senate obstruction that we're seeing, the person who I think right now seems to characterize the leadership of

Ndyfreke Nenty

the radicalized right wing that is running the Republican Party, Rush Limbaugh, is telling the other side that they haven't been obstructive enough."

Rush reacted: "in response to my name being besmirched on the Senate floor by Sheldon Whitehouse and Dingy Harry Reid, I have confirmed I want to hand Obama a defeat."

The fact that Senator Whitehouse accused Rush of conspiring with the public against President Obama didn't sit well with Rush. Rush claimed that for the Democrats, it's all about power. They put Obama's wishes first over the American people's wishes. The majority of people that were against the bill weren't clamoring for Obama to lose; they out-rightly opposed healthcare run by the government.

Rush asked Senator Sheldon Whitehouse, "who died and named you chief of doctors?" Who gave you the sole authority to decide Americans' healthcare choices? Rush said Democratic lawmakers craved to pit Obama's likability against him.

Final Notes

New Jersey's Senator Menendez had the last word from the Democratic Party: "It is our solemn duty to put aside our ideology, to turn off Rush Limbaugh and leave politics in the cloakroom." Rush's final words on the healthcare bill: "The illusion of success has to be maintained until he (Obama) gets this health care bill through."

The Senate version of the healthcare bill finally came to a boil after months of being put on ice. But Rush's effort to stall the bill wasn't in vain. Time will tell. Concerned Americans will call for heads to roll after the severe aftermath of what has been perpetrated on them.[2]

The cornerstone of liberalism

Liberalism 201
What is liberalism?

According to Rush, liberalism is a "series of myths." And chief of those myths about Liberals is that people believe they have real compassion and care for others. They have great compassion for the downtrodden and the have-nots. But Rush said the exact opposite is true. Contempt is what they have for people.

"Liberalism cannot stand or cannot deal with the light of truth being shined on it."

Spreading misery is a primary element of liberalism. In liberalism, there is only one way that all Americans can be equal. That is if all American are equally miserable. Rush said Liberals try to equalize things by lowering the achievers, the wealthy and those at the top, rather than raising those at the bottom.

Liberalism is an unadulterated lie

Liberalism is a promulgation of lies and the biggest stranger to the truth. "Liberalism is a lie from top to bottom," from the local level to the federal level. By and large, everything about liberalism is an outright lie. Rush said the lie must be good and must be rooted in caring, fairness, equality and nondiscrimination, etc. Rush said what lurks behind that good lie is disastrous, hideous, egregious and insidious.

Rush exposed Liberals' real agenda

Democrats and Liberals don't want to solve the problems Americans are facing. Rush said the solution entails creating jobs, happiness and prosperity. And Liberals are against all that because they can't stand for people to be independent. They yearn for "insecurity and dependency."

Liberalism wants a Statist America
Rush said people are the problem in a "statist, centralized" nation. That is why Liberals are against individual liberty. They claim, from their leftist standpoint, that people are not able to do the right thing, so they shouldn't be given freedom.

Hate encapsulated in liberalism
Sponsoring and promoting hate is an "exclusive of the left." A Statist society thrives in promoting unrest, chaos, turmoil, contempt, foment and angst in order to accomplish their objectives. They want discord between the American people.

Talk about the good intentions: ignore the failures
Rush claimed that the war on poverty and the Great Society were liberal programs. And we are not supposed to analyze those Liberal programs because none of them worked. We are only "supposed to look at the good intentions."

Rush claimed that we must "give them credit for their good intentions." But we are not supposed to criticize the result of their good intentions.

Contempt from liberals
Liberals think Americans are just a bunch of cockeyed sheep looking for direction. They think of Americans with contempt. Rush asserted that Liberals don't care what the American people think. If you disagree with them, they will have contempt for you. "Democratic and liberalism cancel each other out. They conflict."

Depth of Liberalism
Liberals always "side with the minorities." They look at the White Republican majority, as corrupt, unjust and immoral. And as such, they feel they must pay. They look at the law to level the playing field, rather than searching for "legal adjudications."

Political correctness

Rush highlighted how liberals try to censor Americans. Rush noted that political correctness is liberal censorship in the form of silencing people's outcries. Political correctness is also turning a deaf ear on the public. And people like Rush, who never conform to political correctness in what they say, are being called extremists, bigots, homophobes and of course racists. Rush said truth is the "greatest casualty in political correctness." Political correctness erodes freedom.

Liberalism over the decades has expanded. It is now an umbrella that includes some components of Fascism, anti-Semitism, Communism, Stalinism, collectivism, authoritarianism, totalitarianism, Statism, Marxism, Radicalism, Socialism, Nationalization and Redistribution. Nazism is certainly also on its way.

Rush draws various conclusions

Elements of liberalism are prescriptions for disaster. And it's a shame that so many American are prescribing. Liberalism is an ideology that must be constantly fought. Rush continued: "Liberals do not look at inequality and try to raise those at the bottom. They punish those at the top." Liberals don't want optimism to win out. They want pessimism to be the end result.

Liberals and the Democratic Party continued to break down Americans into sex, race, gender and class. Democrats are dissenters of the truth. They are anti-American exceptionalists. Why liberals hate American exceptionalism is an issue conservatives can't wrap their heads around.

There is no possible way a self -proclaimed liberal can be a faithful believer of Jesus Christ. Liberalism is an ideology predicated on lies. Those (Christ's believers) in that category are just ignorant.

Moderates

2008 Election Fallout: Moderates have the best interests at heart for the Republican Party

Rush said the wizards of smarts' strategy was for McCain to seek "rock-ribbed independents." They did that, but at the end of the day, McCain lost moderates and independents 60 t0 39%.

Morton Kondracke, syndicated columnist, made headlines when he wrote, "How can the Republican Party rebound? The first step would be to quit letting Rush Limbaugh, Sean Hannity and Laura Ingraham set its agenda."

Rush asserted that it's a "stretch of the facts" to blame him for McCain's lost. Rush said Morton Kondracke, Arnold Schwarzenegger and many GOPs got what they deserved. They believed McCain was able to win moderates better than a true conservative candidate. Balkanizing the electorate is not the way to win elections. Segregating voters is not the way to win elections. Rush said regardless of people's religion, race or gender, conservatism ideas lift everybody. Rush claimed that instead of adapting the blueprint to win elections, we are trying to go moderate. Rush asked, why should we compete with the Democrats in expanding the government?

Rush Limbaugh /Sean Hannity talked about the different coalition in the GOP

Hannity's dialogue with Rush: "You see all the contortions they've been going through about who their head is and whether or not Reagan conservatism needs to be, you know, pushed in the past and this new modern version of a watered-down conservatism or watered-down Republican Party. I think Reagan spelled it out pretty well in March of '75 when he said, you know, "No pale pastels. Bold colors, bold differences." If they can't distinguish themselves now from Barack Obama and socialism and Jimmy Carter national security…" Rush in responding said in precise words, the problem that the Republican Party has it that it is run by the establishment; it is run by the Rockefeller, old guard, country club, blueblood types. The Party should be run by conservatives. Rush said a time will come when a true conservative lawmaker will emerge and lead the Party, like in 1995 with Newt Gingrich. The truth has to be told, and it's up to Rush, Hannity and Palin to toe the line for their Party.

Rush forecasted a battle with Republican moderates
Rush begged Moderate Republicans who have thrown in with Obama to "Leave us alone. Don't try to reform our party." Rush said there would be an "epic battle" between the elites and the people the elites think are hicks. Rush sides with the hicks and said the elites, the people who think they are smarter than everyone, would always blame any election loss on the hicks, the common people.

Big Tents: Not Grounded in Reality
The moderates talk about big tents, but their thinking is narrow. They have no connection whatsoever with reality. Moderates "seek the path of least resistance." Rush said Powell and McCain should go and form their own party instead of trying to hijack the GOP from their glory days.

No Alternative, No Reason to Vote
Rush stated that if a conservative or Republican candidate is not campaigning on the party's core platform by explaining and promoting capitalism, there is no reason to vote Republican because there has to be an alternative to liberalism. There has to be an alternative to voting Democratic.

Moved GOP to the Center
"In the midst of having the party's clock cleaned, the architects of the clock cleaning (eg Rep. Shays)" were saying that the GOP didn't do enough of what got them defeated. And that would be moving the Party to the center.

Republicans gag their principles because of Moderates

Rush believes that at any "sign of contretemps" and strident rhetoric from the GOP, the moderates will run back to the Democratic Party. Rush said if we are to believe that moderates are nonpartisans who are not guided by ideology, then why do they run to the "meanest extremism" Democratic Party once a Republican unleashes a harsh rhetoric? You won't succeed if you go through life appeasing and yielding to critics. The moment you do that, you surely "cease from being who you are." Rush said because of the squishy moderates in the GOP, we can't really tell what the GOP stands for. Conservative rhetoric is the truth, and that is why many are offended and would rather run back to the Democratic Party.

Liberalism lurking around for unsettled, on the Fence Conservatives

With the everyday possibility of being ambush, Rush talked about unsettled conservatives: "Once a conservative's a conservative, you've got 'em. But if you let go of them before they fully understand it, bammo! Because liberalism is gutless. It's so easy. It's the most gutless choice you can make."

Rush Summarized Moderates /Independents in General

Moderates and independents can't stand partisanship or mean-spiritedness and they can't handle the truth. As such, they would rather throw their lot in with the Liberals. Rush said the notion of Republicans chasing after independents is a total farce.

Independents are Liberals

Moderates are liberals

Liberals have no guiding principles. Moderates, by definition, can't be "governed by principles." One that has principles would either be a liberal or a conservative. Rush said they think they are a cut above those who are governed by ideologies. They think they are not narrow-minded. Rush said moderates are hero worshipers; where you find power, you will find moderates.

At the time of the 08 campaign, Obama was the number one most liberal United States senator in Congress. Joe Biden, his running mate, was the third most liberal senator in Congress. Doesn't it speak volumes about the 2008 Democratic presidential ticket? So who is sandwiched in between Obama and Biden? Senator Sanders, the junior senator from Vermont. Senator Sanders is registered as an Independent, not as a Democrat. So you have a registered Independent senator as the most liberal senator at Congress since Biden and Obama are in the White House. It proves that Independents are full-fledged liberals.

Rush uttered, "The great moderates, the great independents. Moderates are no such thing. They are linguine-spined liberals in waiting."

We can collectively put Marxism, redistributionism, appeasement, collectivism, and socialism all in the hand basket of liberalism. Conservatism is just freedom, liberty and the pursuit of happiness. A moderate, an Independent or a centrist are all categories of liberalism. Republican moderates, Mavericks, Centrist Republicans, Washingtonians, pacifists, limousine liberals, "Undeciders." At the end of the day, they all culminate to liberalism. They all stem from liberal premises. They are all part of the hard left. Rush said: "It's still a scarlet letter to be called a liberal," and by the same token, it's definitely a scarlet letter to be called an independent.

Centrist are liberals
Rush said the GOP moving to the center means a modernization of the party. "Centrism" is a left-wing code word, like "bipartisanship" is a left-wing code word. "Centrism" just means agreeing with Democrats, just moving in their direction." It is amazing that Moderate Republicans

like Maine's senators Collins and Snowe still have R (Republican) after their names.

Progressives are liberals

Because the word "liberal" is a dirty word in politics, they have adapted the term progressive. It's just a shell in which to hide their political identity. Rush said progressives are nothing but Socialists, Maoists and Marxists.

Other than a populist and a libertarian platform, conservatism is extremely diametric to liberalism.

Representative Ron Paul and talk host Neal Boortz are not proud to call themselves conservatives. They are supposed to be breaking bread with conservatism, but they would rather branch out and form populism and libertarianism as a third party. As such, they are independent. And what is independent at the end of the day? Liberalism. It is what it is. Ralph Nader's Green Party and Ross Perot's Reform Party also suffered the same fate.

Blue dog Democrats, Rockefeller Republicans, Reagan Democrats, conservative Democrats, and neo-conservatives. At the end of the long day, they are all moderates. And what is a moderate? Moderates are liberals. Rush said, "'Moderate' is just a code word for "liberal."

They will all fail the litmus test for being a true conservative. "Take the word Blue Dog out of it because at the end of the day they're still Democrats," Rush said.

It has gotten so intensely scrutinized that even a fiscal conservative is in jeopardy and on the brink of being labeled as an independent. One might then ask, who is saved? Who is a true conservative? Only a Reagan conservative and a social conservative are saved. A so-called conservative with liberal views is a liberal, and a liberal with conservative views is a liberal. Any third party that is not conservative is liberal. Borderline conservatives are not accepted. They are in league with liberals.

A prescription and a remedy wouldn't be able to save these "at the end of the day" liberals, because moderates have no principles.

The bottom line is that Americans are either conservative or liberal. You can't claim to love Jesus Christ but still harbor and embrace the tenets of Satan. It's either good or evil, God or the Devil, heaven or hell. There is no crossroads.

Conclusion

Putting lipstick on a pig doesn't in any way, shape, manner or form mean that the pig isn't still a pig. Labeling hardcore left liberals as progressive, moderate or independent doesn't mean they are not still liberals.

Liberalism is like the number zero when multiplied with other numbers including itself, it remains zero. Any philosophy or ideology that is in league with liberalism will succumb to liberalism.[3]

Rush's heir: Sean Hannity's Biography

Sean is a deeply religious social conservative. He originated the yearly "Freedom Concerts." The Freedom Concerts is a momentous charity program that affords scholarship funds to children of the US Military.

It's not relaxing to say Sean Hannity is Rush Limbaugh's heir. Sean Hannity is a well- established household name in the country and a colossal voice for the conservative movement. Sean is only surpassed by Rush Limbaugh and Newt Gingrich within the conservative hierarchy in America.

In another perspective, viewing Sean as Rush's heir is not an understatement because once Rush retires, all the brutal criticism, scorn, ridicule and hatred that Rush has received from the Democrats would be rendered onto Sean.

It remains to be seen if Sean Hannity will be more influential than Rush Limbaugh. Take, for instance, Prophet Elijah and Prophet Elisha in the Bible. Rush is the Elijah of today and Hannity is the Elisha of today. When Elijah was about to depart up to heaven, Elisha asked for a double portion of Elijah's power. However, though Elisha had double the blessing of Elijah, at the end of their lives, Elijah was still acclaimed as the greatest prophet in the world.

Hannity is a principal Reagan conservative who often stresses what it means to be a conservative. Sean's conservative influence on the American people waxes day by day. Sean gives nothing but unvarnished advice to his audience.

There are lots of question marks surrounding Sean's allegiance to the Republican Party. Sean often claims that he is a conservative, not a Republican.

Although he personally repudiated himself from the Republican Party, he still stands up for their causes and concerns. He proved this by releasing his top ten items for victory.

In the back of two consecutive congressional election defeats, Republicans will be hard pressed to be victorious in the 2010 election. Having closely witnessed the 2008 elections' smashing defeats, Hannity has turned his focus on grooming GOP Senate and House candidates running in 2010.

US House Republicans have been at sixes and sevens with the departure of Tom DeLay, so Hannity's items for victory will be of paramount importance for GOP lawmakers. In late December of 2008, Hannity thoroughly devoted his time to galvanizing a GOP victory in a senatorial runoff race in Georgia. That result was a dry run to test the magnitude of conservatism ascendancy. The dry run continued in November 09, where Americans witnessed an upset in the governor race in the very blue State of New Jersey. Again, Hannity was at the heart of it all. Hannity, time and time again, hosted the Republican victor, who before his stunning gubernatorial victory was a mere local politician. Hannity, just as he has done for most GOP politicians at Congress, brought the victor to the spotlight. Hannity's item for victory will be re-enforced in the 2010 midterm congressional election. Political strategist Dick Morris is another workaholic that is fighting to labor a successful 2010 year for the Republican Party. He foresees a sweeping 2010 Senate and House triumph. He foresees an event reminiscent of the 1994 GOP House revolution.

Sean Hannity roundly castigated

While Rush Limbaugh might think that Sean Hannity is the essence of innocence, liberals were fit to be tied with Hannity because he unearthed all of Obama's radical associations. The Democratic Party apparatus have viciously attacked Sean for his relentless opposition to Obama's radical policies. They reprove Sean on every single thing he has said about Obama and his associates.

CBS's 60 Minutes host Morley Safer conspired with actor, Alec Baldwin, and introduced Sean Hannnity as a dog. Baldwin said, "Not all Republicans are insane as these extremist conservatives." Mr. Safer responded, "an easy target for conservative junkyard dogs like Sean Hannity."

An interruption: Breaking News

Joy Behar said: "Rush Limbaugh is a terrorist" Joy Behar, co-host of ABC's View said on national TV that Rush is not a Republican. "He's a terrorist. Rush Limbaugh is a terrorist. You heard it here ladies and gentlemen," Behar said. And the other co hosts, Hasselbeck, Walters and Goldberg, didn't counter her statement as they applauded.

Rush is the last person on earth to be a terrorist.

Before calling Rush Limbaugh a terrorist, Joy Behar laid the curtain raiser for a vicious broadside on Rush by attacking Sean Hannity. Behar, in a dialogue with the other hosts, said: "And Sean Hannity, who I really think he is a dangerous, dangerous force in America." Sean is a dangerous force compared to the likes of Bill Ayers and Reverend Wright?

Hannity's top ten items for victory

A national security candidate
"Fully support NSA, Patriot act, tough interrogations, and keeping Gitmo open."
"A candidate that promises to ensure that our veterans can live out their lives in dignity."

An anti appeasement candidate
"The candidate will oppose any and all efforts to negotiate with dictators of the world in places like Iran, Syria, N.Korea, Cuba, and Venezuela without "pre-conditions."

A tax cuts and fiscal responsibility supporting candidate
"The candidate who pledges to eliminate and vote against all Earmarks."
"The candidate pledges to balance the budget."

A supporter of "Energy Independence"
"Supports immediate drilling in Anwar and the 48 states."
"Began building and using Nuclear Facilities."
"Expand coal mining."

A candidate that supports borders control
"Use all available technology to help and support agents at the border."
"Build all necessary fences."

A candidate that opposes the government-run healthcare system
"The candidate will look for Free-Market solutions to the problems facing the Healthcare industry, and will vigorously oppose any efforts to nationalize healthcare."
"The candidate will fight for individual health savings accounts, that includes catastrophic insurance for every American, so people can control their own healthcare choices."

A candidate for upgrading our education system
"The candidate pledges to save American children from the failing educational system."
"The candidate will fight to break the unholy alliance of the Democratic Party and teachers unions, which at best has institutionalized mediocrity, and has failed children across the country."
"Fight for choice in education and let the parents decide."

A candidate that will salvage Social Security and Medicare from going under
"The candidate will save social security and Medicare from bankruptcy."
"Options will include private retirement funds so people can control their own destiny."

A candidate that will vote to nominate judges that will interpret the Constitution
"The candidate vows to support only judges who recognize that their job is to interpret the Constitution, and not legislate from the bench."

A candidate that recognizes American Exceptionalism and the American Dream

"The candidate accepts as their duty and responsibility to educate, inform, and remind people that with the blessings of Freedom comes a Great responsibility. That Government's primary goal is to preserve, protect and defend our God given gift of freedom. That Government's do not have the ability to solve all our problems, and to take away all our fears and concerns. We need their pledge that we will be the candidate that promotes individual liberty, Capitalism, a strong national defense and will support policies that encourage such. It's our fundamental belief that limited Government, and Greater individual responsibility will insure the continued prosperity and success for future generations. We the people who believe in the words of Ronald Reagan, that we are 'the best last hope for man on this earth,' a 'shining city on a hill,' and our best days are before us if our Government will simply trust the American people," Hannity concluded.

Sean's heart and soul

Being conservative is all about life, liberty and pursuit of happiness. Being conservative is all about freedom of religion. Sean said: "We enjoy the fruit of our labor, we love our God. We are principle in our position." Sean said life is about "Finding what your God-giving gifts are and bringing them to fruition. We are endowed by our creator"

Conservatism, liberty, capitalism, free markets, property rights, and national security, are broad principles that define American greatness.

Sir Winston Churchill fought for civilization during World War 2: "Civilization will not last, freedom will not survive, peace will not be kept, unless a very large majority of mankind unite together to defend them and show themselves possessed of a constabulary power before which barbaric and atavistic forces will."

Sean's views on God

Sean argued that the reason the world puts human beings like Michael Jackson on a very high pedestal is: "Human being are flawed, there is only one King that is God in Heaven. The truth is the truth. Jesus was the only sinless man that walked on this Earth," "You have to find your inner peace, and your inner happiness from within, there is something greater than yourself and that is GOD," Sean said

Chronicling Obama and his acolytes lambasting Hannity

Democrats beyond the Obama orbit have tried to make mincemeat of Sean Hannity. They can't afford two powerful conservative voices on the radio waves. They have already claimed that the Republican Party is the party of conservative talk radio.

Democratic senator Harry Reid said about the Republican Party: 'They're taking their cues from talk show hosts, it's a party being run by a talk show host."

Sean has been effective since the latter part of Bill Clinton's presidency. Obama, the next Democratic president after Clinton, tried to apprehend Sean Hannity.

Throughout the 08 campaign, Obama and his surrogates reproved and tried to mire Sean Hannity as being anti-American. Obama was the leading marksman, with five direct attacks on Sean.

Sean never expected all the personal and gratuitous attacks from Obama and his acquaintances. Regardless, he still wouldn't have preempted them.

First strike

Obama was enthused by a supporter saying: "If this is our next president, he will, in fact, lead not only the Democratic Party, but this entire country from a culture of criticism to a culture of recognition." Obama then vented how he felt about Hannity, "I might have to put Mr. Burgess on Fox News. You know, I'll bet-I'll put Mr. Burgess up against Sean Hannity. They'll tear him {Hannity} up."

Hannity responded on Obama's metaphorical threat to rip him up: "Tear me up. All right. Let's get this straight, You won't come on this program to answer questions yourself, but you're willing to send this guy? Now I know you're used to the media fawning and falling all over themselves to give you five-to get five minutes with you, but if you can't answer questions from people who don't faint in your presence, then how do you expect to be the leader of the free world?"

Second Strike

On Bill O'Reilly's show, Obama stressed "If you were watching Sean Hannity consistently," After being interrupted by the host he continued, "Hold on a second. All I'm saying is these guys; they've given me a hard time."

Third Strike

Obama tried to stifle Sean's influence again when he talked about his own wife and kids: "Michelle has worked on keeping their lives as normal as possible back home in Chicago. They seem to be thriving mainly watching Nickelodeon. They aren't listening to Sean Hannity. Hannity isn't on Nickelodeon."

Fourth Strike

When asked "Whoever gets elected president, somehow, has to put their arm around the whole country and say, 'we're in this together.' Can you do that?" Obama's knee-jerk response was, "I can." Obama continued,

"And I think that's the tone that we've set from the beginning of the campaign. I mean, look. Is Sean Hannity suddenly going to get on the air waves and say 'You know, I was wrong about this Obama guy, he's my man.' No, that's not going to happen."

Final Strike

During the latter part of his campaign, Obama, then the preemptive 2008 Democratic nominee, was excited to render his last attack on Hannity. Jon Stewart interviewed Obama and claimed that Obama's rival had referred to him as a "celebrity, an elitist, a Muslim terrorist sympathizer, a socialist, a Marxist, and a witch." Obama responded: "There's a certain segment of hardcore Sean Hannity fans that probably wouldn't want to go have a beer with me. There's no doubt about that."

In Obama's first strike, why couldn't he think of a more acceptable word or phrase to use? Unless words do lie, Obama probably wished violence against Hannity. In Obama's third strike, Obama would probably wish Hannity was on Nickelodeon and vice versa. In Obama's fourth strike, Hannity would be wrong about this Obama guy if Obama ends up governing this country as a centrist like Bill Clinton did. Since Obama was the most liberal senator at the US Congress, it's a far cry from anticipating a centrist governing president. Only time, two or six years, will tell. In Obama's final strike, Obama insinuated that Hannity had catapulted all of the name calling.[4]

Spreading and redistributing wealth

Obama's main ideology: spreading the wealth

Before the general election, Obama said, in his own words, "It's not that I want to punish your success. I just want to make sure that everybody who is behind you, that they've got a chance at success, too. I think when we spread the wealth around, it's good for everybody." Rush defined Obama's remark: "Welcome to the objective of Barack Obama and the Democrat Party: spreading misery equally."

Rush rebuked New York Post's comparison of Obama to Hood

Rush warned media pundits not to malign and impugn Robin Hood. Rush said Hood "took from the sheriff of Nottingham." He took back what the state had stolen from the people and gave back to the "citizens of Sherwood Forest." Rush said what Obama is doing is not equivalent to what Robin Hood did.

Spreading of wealth replaced the pursuit of wealth

According to Rush, the pursuit of wealth is one of the primary factors that led to America's greatness. Rush said class envy and demolishing the wealthy in America has always been debated but until Obama surfaced, there had never been policies being pushed that prevented the pursuit of wealth.

What Founders had to say about redistribution

Thomas Jefferson, April 6, 1816: "To take from one because it is thought that his own industry and that of his father's has acquired too much, in order to spare to others, who, or whose fathers have not exercised equal industry and skill, is to violate arbitrarily the first principle of association -- the guarantee to every one of a free exercise of his industry and the fruits acquired by it." Rush said briefly, "Here's a Founding Father who wanted nothing to do with redistribution." Thomas Jefferson, in his first inaugural address, March 4, 1801: "A wise and frugal government ... shall restrain men from injuring one another, shall leave them otherwise free to regulate their own pursuits of industry and improvement, and shall not take from the mouth of labor the bread it has earned. This is the sum of good government." Rush weighed in "Under this administration, our pursuit of happiness is grounded with complete halt and it's been replaced with a pursuit of survival."

Rush warned that productivity will be destroyed once the golden goose is taxed. The golden goose is what creates the wealth, but Obama wants the government to be perceived as the only source of wealth. Rush debunked the liberal notion that government creates wealth. Rush said the government can't create wealth; the government can only confiscate wealth. Obama is a pure, unadulterated socialist. There are no degrees or grades when evaluating a socialist; they are all the same.

Governor Arnold Schwarzenegger's experience

The governor recalled: "I tell you something, I left Europe four decades ago because socialism has killed opportunities there, and many... and many, many, many entrepreneurs and business leaders all left and have taken jobs with them. And I tell you, in recent years Europe has realized its mistakes and begun rolling back some of its spread-the-wealth policies. And I tell you something. I tell you something. I am so fortunate that I have the chance of coming to the greatest country in the world, the United States of America."

Spreading the wealth: an agenda for the Democratic Party; the crux of Obama's 08 campaign

Spreading the wealth agenda has found its way prominently in the Democratic Party. When it comes to equalizing society, Rush said Liberals are not interested in elevating those at the bottom. They are only interested in taking from those at the top of the economic ladder.

Rush warned that harping on wealthy Americans is class envy at its finest. It's "designed to appeal to the lowest common denominator of American voter," and those voters are the ones who are unemployed.

Obama and his administration is about being the arbiters to those wealthy and achieving Americans. They want to be the ones to dictate how much one can make. Rush said Liberals preach a fair game. To the Liberals, it is only fair for everybody, those at the bottom and those at the top of the ladder to me happy but in the expense of taxing those at the top.

In conclusion, Rush said spreading the wealth is "full-fledged, undiluted, raw liberalism" agenda. Rush said these Liberals were thwarted during the Reagan presidency but with Obama at the helm, it's an opportunity to accomplish their mission. And Obama is the right vehicle for their jihad.

Obama stood firm in his spreading the wealth comment. He didn't back down. That is who he is: a Karl Marx like politician. "You can't rob Peter to pay Paul," Dr. Ukonne, a New Jersey professor, stressed. "That is the change we need. That is the change they need," Obama said.

Karl Marx's most famous quote was: "From each according to his ability, to each according to his need (or needs)."

Sean said: "Obama moves toward collectivism and socialism. His record is a record of uninterrupted liberalism." Slowly but surely, "America will be driven to a socialist redistribution Left," Sean warned. Informed Americans are witnessing "The endorsement of socialism. Socialisms will destroy investments, progress, jobs, expansion, property rights, individual rights, our entire economic system," Sean concluded.[5]

Change we need

Rush's warning

Rush pleaded for Americans not to let a Liberal demagogue diminish the greatest country in the world. Rush said Obama has "thrown down the gauntlet." He's running against American history and against our freedom and liberty.

Rush's sanctioned tears

Because of the foreseeable doom and gloom Obama is taking the country to, Rush spoke of the possibility of leaving America. Rush feels that as long as he's behind the golden EIB microphone, leadership will be provided to millions of Americans. "When you need to worry is when I tell you one day, "Folks, live from New Zealand, it's the Rush Limbaugh program." Yeah, that would be a day that I would sanction tears."

Obama's change strange to Americans

Rush said the hope and change Obama talked about was change but Obama wants to change the American system to a foreign system. And it's definitely not the change Americans need. He wants to change America to the likeness of Rev Wright and Bill Ayers.

In Conclusion

John F Kennedy said in 1960: "Ask not what your country can do for you; ask what you can do for your country." Rush said in 2008: "Ask not what your country can do for you; demand what your country can do for you."

"I will be at the forefront of opposition to everything he does," Sean Hannity said about Obama's radicalism. American voters have been bamboozled and hoodwinked into believing Obama's hope and change rhetoric. So far, all of Obama's rosy expectations have not manifested themselves. That is the opposite that we are witnessing.

Hannity then added: "I will be the fierce voice of opposition if Obama turns the greatest best country God gave man to a socialist utopia nation." Obama has this attitude that the United States solely needs to change from the status quo of the previous administration to his ideas of change and vision. That is why Obama has appointed 33 Czars within 11 months of his presidency. Yes, that is the change we need. How many Czars did Bush appoint compared to Obama? And what is an Obama's pay Czar? Compared to Bush's AIDs czar? Obama appointed a pay czar to dictate CEOs' pay and bonus packages. How could Obama not be considered a radical? "Change is good, but not change for change," said Sean Hannity. Not socialism for capitalism. America was built on the grounds of capitalism. And in 2009, just one president wanted to change the country's system. Stanley Howse said: "Give me all my change" because Obama wants to redistribute our wealth.

Challenging the whole concept of change

Why do we urgently need a drastic change? Are the people of the 21st century better than the people who lived in the days of the Stone Age? Are we better than our forefathers from the 19th century? What makes people in the 21st century better than the people from the previous centuries and generations? Why the sudden rush for change? The change we need is to worship God more. What is the result of the reading of polls on how many Americans believe in God? Believing in God is the change we really need. We live in an era of the most advanced technology. People of the 21st century are way more sophisticated than any previous era.

This also implies that sin has multiplied. And this generation is more evil than the generations of old. Jesus Christ said that it will be more tolerable for Sodom and Gomorrah than the days of the Pharisees: "I tell you the truth, it will be more bearable for Sodom and Gomorrah on the day of judgment than for that town," that don't believe in God —Matthew 10: 14/15.

America is a conservative and capitalist nation. But Obama and his supporters want to turn America into a liberal, socialist, redistributionist and fascist nation. This is not a matter of throwing words around; Obama's agenda includes a substantial component of socialism, fascism and collectivism. The latter is the hope and change Obama was talking about in his Acorn campaign for president.

America was built on the philosophy of capitalism. Capitalism is predicated on risk. Socialism is predicated on entitlement. Obama want Americans to be dependent on him. He wants them to be rewarded with welfare, Medicare and food stamps.

Change you can believe in: Change we need vs. Change we don't need

A change we don't need is Obama deluging the American people with unparalleled promises. Newt Gingrich said Obama uses rhetoric to hide from reality, unlike Reagan. Gingrich's daughter, Jackie G. Cushman, said we went from "Change we can believe in" to "trying to change what we believe. I think this is an administration dedicated to creating a very different America."

Gov. Rick Perry of Texas followed Gov. Stanford in rejecting Obama's stimulus funds. When you have this type of division between the federal and the state government and when you have people in America calling their various states their country, aren't we looking at USSR as a benchmark? Sean Hannity asked a young girl during the 2009 Freedom Concert in Dallas/Fort Worth: "What country are you from?" She said, "Texas!" When a superpower like the USSR gets decimated, then we know anything is possible. The girl's response to Hannity's question is nothing to sneeze at. It shouldn't be taken lightly.

Obama's policies encourage dependence. They will create a cradle to grave society. America is heading to new territories. Socialist utopianism is what the rest of the world practices and America, under the leadership of Obama, is taking us there. It's the antithesis of Moses leading the children of Israel out of Egypt. Democrats believe the State, rather than the family, is more qualified to raise children. They want to see more Americans depending on welfare. They want people to believe in entitlement, contentment and utopia. They want to wipe away the concepts of liberty, freedom, and responsibility from the American people. Just as in Europe, they want to create wards of the state. The beloved Moses didn't make it to the promise land. Will Obama lead America to become a socialist country? Time is no longer of the essence. Conservatism and God in heaven is of the essence.

The change we badly need is to finally get that monkey off our backs and unequivocally believe that there is an Almighty God in heaven. We have to put to rest any doubt that God doesn't exist so that we can focus on worshipping Him.

But the most important change we need is to believe wholeheartedly is that the God we believe is in heaven. If we can believe in Jesus Christ more than we believe that the physical existence of a fellow friend that we see daily is really human, then that would be the real change we need.[6]

Bush's third term

Compare and contrast: Obama/Biden and Bush/Cheney

Obama's first year as president is simply a Bush's third term without Bush in the Oval Office. It's unthinkable to compare an Obama/ Biden presidency with a Bush/Cheney presidency. Bush might not have had foreign affairs experience, but neither does Obama. Cheney is well-versed in foreign affairs, as he was once the US Secretary of Defense. Foreign affairs experience wasn't Bush best teacher: Cheney was that teacher. Joe Biden, who said Iraq should be divided into three regions, has mediocre experience in the foreign affairs arena. He was the Chairman of the Senate Committee on Foreign Relations. Bush and Cheney were much more invested in fighting to protect this country than worrying about their approval ratings. Cheney most especially didn't lose any sleep, regardless of his low approval rating. But Cheney did lose some sleep caring about the protection of the country.

Jesus Christ said: "let them alone: they be blind leaders of the blind. And if the blind lead the blind, both shall fall into the ditch," –Matthew 15 verse 14.

Bryon McCane claimed: "There is no way in hell that the blind can lead the blind; unless somebody plays the dog." Biden, not Obama has the vast experience, so he will definitely play the dog.

Blame Bush

Rush said right after Obama's presidential election victory: "I think the Democrats are going to be able to get a lot of mileage out of blaming Bush for all kinds of things for the next foreseeable future."

Rush predictions

Rush predicted weeks before Obama's inauguration that everything that goes wrong in the Obama administration, from the wars in Iraq and Afghanistan to the economy, will be "laid at the feet of" his predecessor George Bush.

Sean said, "They could have let 9/11 be a prelude to something worse, but they didn't. Bush administration will be defined as keeping this great country saved."

Bush and Cheney's formidable partnership prevented another terrorist attack on American soil. We could also acknowledge the fact that 9/11 was provoked by Bill Clinton. The 9/11 planners didn't use eight months to scheme their attacks on America. Bush was only in power eight months before the attacks. 9/11 was a leftover from Clinton's administration. Unfortunately for Bush, when al-Qaeda finally settled, Bush was president.

Obama chose Biden as his veep in an attempt to emulate Cheney. Biden was supposed to be the Cheney for Obama, but his ineffectiveness has reduced him to strictly funeral ceremonies. For eleven months, the Obama administration has been unsettled and unhinged. It's the reason they have sent out numerous trial balloons.

You can under promise and you can over deliver but Obama, unlike George Bush, did quite the opposite: "That's the change we need," Obama reiterated. "He's created this utopia in people's minds that he cannot deliver," Rush said about Obama.

The pure impugning of characters and the underlined hatred for Bush and Cheney wasn't only nationwide, it was worldwide.

When addressing the United Nations, Hugo Chavez, the Venezuelan President, said of an eight year Bush tenure: "It doesn't smell of sulfur here anymore. It smells of something else. It smells of hope."

When and where actually will the buck stop? Since when President Truman died in 1972, the passing of the buck hasn't stopped. But the Bush administration has been projected to inherit it the longest. Rush already said the first four years of an Obama's failed presidency will be blamed on the last four years of Bush/Cheney tenure: "They've got four years to blame Bush for everything that goes wrong during the Obama four years," Rush confirmed. Based on Rush's statement, Obama is a stop-gap president.

Electing Obama as president of America is like playing Russian roulette, especially with KGB Vladimir Putin on the horizon. After Putin completed his term as President of Russia, he picked one of his puppets, Dmitry Medvedev, to run for the presidency. With Putin's popularity among Russians, Dmitry Medvedev won the presidency by a landslide. And in an unprecedented maneuver, Putin appointed himself as prime minister of Russia. Imagine if Bush appointed himself or Cheney Prime Minister before his administration was done and dusted? But Bush was an astute president. The United States, unlike Russia, leads and others follow. Obama wants to change that. Obama wants America to be a follower like socialist European countries. Obama's mandate for change is to transform America to a "European socialist authoritarianism."

Bush, Cheney and Donald Rumsfeld's mentality was to capture any 9/11 operatives, radical jihadists, by and large, terrorists around the world. They were to be Guantanamo, trial and jailed until they assumed room temperature. Obama's anti-terrorism policies are quite the opposite. Obama and his administration neglected to use the phrase "terrorist" to label these despicable suicidal extreme terrorists.

Underlying hatred for Bush
Bush had been criticized to shreds by the Democrats. Hate is a sole property of the Democratic Party. "Eight years of unadulterated drivel, outraged hate aimed at George W. Bush." Books were written and films were produced about the assassination of George Bush.

Bush never responded to all the invective remarks hurled against him by the Democrats. Bush stayed above the fray, in regards to all his critics. Bush was busy planting intelligence officials in foreign countries to keep their ear to the ground to find out what would prevent this country from another 9/11 attack.

Obama's plummeting poll numbers
Rush said, "Every dime of it, every ounce of the problem -- is George Bush. So go back to blaming Bush for everything, 'cause the numbers are down." There is a huge groundswell of opposition to Obama's policies. His policies are unpopular. When his polls plummet, he rehashes his 2008 campaign rhetoric. When his job performance and his presidential approval crater, he regurgitates and cites the same old platitudes and

bomber stickers. When his unfavorable views skyrocket and his approval
rating is teetering above and below 50, he blames Bush.

President 44
A Welcome distraction

The Obama administration has been blessed with a number of
welcome distractions. The Obama administration yearns for welcome
distractions. Governor Sanford's immoral behavior, the sudden death of
Michael Jackson, the mouthy Professor Gates (a distraction that Obama
catapulted) and the Bernard Madoff sentencing are a few of the worthy
welcome distractions Rush said of Sanford's dereliction of duty: the
real crime Sanford committed was refusing to accept Obama's Stimulus
money for the state of South Carolina.

Governor Palin's resignation, Bill Clinton's hand in releasing two of
Al Gore's prisoners, the bickering over the nomination of Obama's
pick for Supreme Court, the failed Chicago Olympics bid (an Obama-
made distraction), the Nobel Peace Prize being awarded to Obama,
the controversial fallout of Limbaugh's bid to purchase the NFL's St.
Louis Rams, the 2009 Democratic gubernatorial election loss and the
terrorist related massacre at Ford Hood are more wanted distractions
that have occurred within the first eleven months of an Obama's
administration.

Unwelcome distraction

Rush's "I hope he (Obama policies) fails" comment was the most
unwelcome distraction for Obama and the Democratic Party. A remark
from Jim DeMint was another major unwanted distraction. Senator
DeMint's comment was greeted with disdain, he said, "It {health care
reform} will be his Waterloo, it will break him {Obama}." Congressman
Joe Wilson calling Obama a liar live on national TV rounded up the

unwanted distractions. Compared to welcome distractions, unwanted distractions are few and far between.

Vice President Joe Biden attacked Rush Limbaugh

Rush has pleaded for a paramount security for Obama because of Biden's utter incompetence. Rush was hesitant to say: "I don't want anything to ever happen to Barack Obama, but especially because Biden is number two." Vice President Joe Biden, while delivering a stump speech at New York for a congressional candidate, was relieved to attack Rush Limbaugh: "I know what Rush Limbaugh is against. I know what Dick Armey is against. I know what all these folks are against. I'm not being a wise guy. But I don't know what they're for." "He knows exactly what we're for. Scares him to death," Rush responded to Biden's remark. Rush said because conservatism is genuine, we are "unapologetic about our ideals." Conservatism believes in limited government, capitalism and national security. Individual liberty, a colorblind society, faith and the rule of law are essential to conservatism.[7]

Tea Party/Town hall

Conservatism on the Ascendancy

Who is mobilizing conservative grassroots?

The concerned Americans, who attended their local town hall meetings with a view to question their congressional representatives, were called mobsters by the Democratic media. They were described as rabid and fanatic. The Democratic media said the tea party attendees or the "tea baggers" were incandescent with rage. And the town hall attendees' inflammatory responses to their various congresspersons were premeditated.

Rush's radio program is an on air town hall meeting. Rush was livid with Speaker Nancy Pelosi and Senator Barbara Boxer's comments. The latter said the town hall attendees were paid lobbyists because they were too well-dressed to be average citizens. Senator Boxer talked about the so-called unruly mobs attending the town hall meetings: "And by the way, I saw some of the clips of people storming these town hall meetings. The last time I saw well-dressed people doing this was when Al Gore asked me to go down to Florida when they were recounting the ballots, and I was confronted with the same type of people." "It is ground zero in a battle to stop the government taking over our life," Sean Hannity stressed.

"You can't sit on the sidelines. It's not the time to lean back and recline on our seats. "You have to be involved," Sean said.

DeLay, Armey and Rush blamed for orchestrating tea parties rallies

Dick Armey, Tom DeLay and Rush Limbaugh were being fingered as the caused of the tea party rallies. Rush said the tea parties represent the "outpouring of genuine sentiment" that is sparked by love and devotion for this country and its founding. And no one GOP leader is responsible for the tea party rallies.

Rep. Waxman, a Democratic Congressman from California, said about the rallies: "That's not spontaneous. People show up in an organized way often sponsored by the Republican Party or Rush Limbaugh or some other group." Rush denied arming up the tea baggers: "But I haven't told anybody to go to any of these rallies." Because I knew I didn't have to. I've never asked you to make phone calls to Congress. Well, I did it once to demo what would happen if I did, I shut down the switchboard. -- You don't need a charismatic leader to get you out of the house and to spend money to drive or fly to Washington."

Rush gainsaid having anything to do with the rallies. "I'm too famous to go to one of these things. I can't overshadow these things." But Rush applauded the attendees for making the tea parties happen.

The media have no problem misreporting heartfelt rallies as manufactured un-American rallies. But Cindy Sheehan's picketing during Bush's presidency was genuine.

Rush against third party

Rush said he's only objective against the tea parties will be if it leads to a third party movement. Rush said a third party candidate only succeeds in "electing their alternatives." He cited John Anderson in 1980 and Perot in 1992. Rush said Reagan and Goldwater successfully took the Party back from the blue -blood country club Rockefeller types. And they didn't do it by advocating for a third party.

Rush supported his nemesis John McCain after the Senator won the 08 Republican nomination. But what was the alternative? Obama or a third party candidate? There wasn't much difference between the liberal Obama and the Maverick McCain. That could explain why Rush didn't rent his clothes when McCain lost the presidential election. Rush would support a Republican candidate over a third party candidate, even if the third party were conservative. Rush is against any third party candidacy. After Palin delivered her gubernatorial resignation speech, Rush was bewildered because Palin didn't mention her support for the Republican Party. Rush is hoping against hope that Palin isn't mulling over a third party movement.[8]

I Hope He Fails

Days before Obama's inauguration, Rush famously declared that he wanted Obama to fail.

Limbaugh was begged to offer a 400-word statement on what he hopes for the Obama administration. Rush responded automatically. He didn't need to ruminate over the question.

Rush maintained that if he wanted Barack Obama to succeed, he would have encouraged the Republican Party to support Obama. But because Obama wants the government to be in charge of the banking business, the automobile business, the mortgage industry, and the healthcare system, he would not just sit idly by and let Obama have his way. "Okay, I'll send you a response, but I don't need 400 words, I need four: I hope he fails." Somebody's gotta say it."

Hoped Bush failed when he got inaugurated. But their hoping for Bush to fail wasn't on substance. But hoping for Obama to fail is totally on substance. Obama wants to decapitate the private sector, he wants to take away individual freedom and he wants to reconstruct and remake America in his own image.

"I'm not giving him the benefit of the doubt, because I have no doubt." Rush said he has no doubt about what Obama's plans and intentions are. Rush said it is sad that many Americans believe change means immediate improvement. Rush reiterated: "I am ontologically certain" that Obama's policies won't work for America.

Pros
For over 2 decades, Rush has politically been a person of interest for the Democratic Party. There has been no shortage of controversy and scathing criticism against Rush coming from Liberals and Democrats.

But Rush's "I hope he {Obama} fails" comment was over the top for the opposition party and even a hatful of Republican members.

Ultra conservative Senator Rick Santorum said: "Absolutely we hope that his policies fail. I believe his policies will fail, I don't know, but I hope they fail. But I believe they will fail." "I'm willing to say it. Every Republican in this country wants Obama to fail, but none of them have the guts to say so." And that is a "dirty little secret," –Rush said.

Senator Vitter extolled Rush and also agreed he hoped Obama "Fails in advancing leftist policy."

Rep. Mike Pence went on the record and upheld Rush's shocking comment. Other GOPs on Capitol Hill claimed to agree with Rush but did not want to go on record with their statements.

Tom DeLay was asked to weigh in: "Well, exactly right. I don't want this for our nation. That's for sure. I tagged him as a Marxist months ago," because Obama is an "old school Marxist, radical liberal failed ideology."

Cons
Governor Mark Sanford said: "Anyone who wants him to fail is an idiot," yet Sanford was very hypocritical as he went on the record refusing Obama's stimulus package for the state of South Carolina. Sanford sent his top aides to apologize to Rush on his behalf.

Rep. Phil Gingrey
Phil Gingrey, a congressman from Georgia, said all Rush and co. could do was: "Stand back and throw bricks" and they aren't affording any "real leadership." The Congressman later profusely apologized to Rush: "I want to express to you and all your listeners my very sincere regret for those comments I made. I clearly ended up putting my foot in my mouth on some of those comments. I regret those stupid comments."

Rush responded: "Look at me as taking the heat. Look at me as taking the fire, directing it away from you so that you guys (Congressional Republicans) can go stealthily and do what you're doing here in building an opposition to this (bailout)." Eventually and predictably, the majority of the cons who disagreed with Rush turned to pros. The cons had rushed to judgment.

Rush Delivered a Detailed Explanation of his "I hope he (Obama) fails" Comment

Rush Stands up for the Private Sector

Rush said the duty of the American president is not to be the CEO of the private sector entities. Rush said he loves the United States and doesn't want the country to fail. However; Obama succeeding in decapitating the private sector means America will fail.

Knee-jerk Reaction

Rush told Americans to "stop and think" about what his "I hope he fails" comment means before they jump to conclusions. Rush said because Obama is a "cult leader" to many Americans, Rush's comment is being taken emotionally. And as such, those Americans are being insulted. Rush said Obama has to fail in order for personal liberty to be preserved.

Rush's "I Hope he Fails" Comment: purposely misquoted and taken out of context

Rush said he doesn't care if he is being taken out of context. The bottom line is that he loves America. Rush said since Bush is no longer heading the GOP, the opposition Party must find a villain. "I'm the proud receptacle, I'm the proud target. I don't want Obama to fail as a human being."

Republicans out of Cowardice and Fear say: "We want Obama to Succeed"

Some gutless wonders from the Republican Party distanced themselves from Rush's comment. They didn't want to incur the wrath of the liberals.

Rush said they would rather throw their beliefs and their principles out the window than be called racists just so as to not be criticized.

After Rush Addressed Republicans Cowering in Dark Corners Rush said he doesn't want Obama to fail; he want his policies to fail. He wants America to succeed. Rush said a "dirty little secret" considering his I hope Obama fails comment is that every Republican lawmaker in Congress wants Obama to fail but they don't have to guts to say it publicly.

Rush Identifies Two Sets of Obama Followers

Devoted leftists and those that are "emotionally invested" in Obama are the two groups Rush identifies. The former are intent on destroying capitalism; they are intent on destroying America's greatness. They are clones of Rev Wright and Bill Ayers. The latter internalize Rush's comment, twisting his words and claiming he means he hopes America as a county fails. Rush said they are "in denial about Obama the president and Obama's policies." Rush said those that are emotionally attached to Obama, instead of thinking their way through life, feel their way through life. And so Rush saying "I hope he fails" is perceived by those invested in Obama as Rush wanting the same fate for them too. Thus, Rush's comment had hit them where it hurt. Rush said it is quite the opposite. Rush wants all Americans to succeed, but the pursuit of happiness and the benefits of freedom and liberty are being stymied by their cult figure, Obama. On the other hand, Rush said Obama and the Democratic Party wants him to fail. And that has been evident with all the daily and withering attacks on Rush. Rush said that, unlike Obama, his audience is not emotionally attached to him. Obama craves for his followers to be emotionally attached to him. And as a consequence, they are uninformed. They believe all the drivel that Obama utters. And because they are uniformed, Obama would be able to swiftly pass his radical agenda without any outcry from his followers. Rush said many people are susceptible to "emotional manipulation." And Rush said "being taught how to feel" is political correctness and is the sole property of Liberals. Rush said demagoguery emotional manipulation is key. You first identify what the masses want. Then you promise to give them what they want, though in the back of your mind, you plan to do the exact opposite. Rush said Obama's worst nightmare would be if his followers ignored Obama's words and started actually thinking about what Obama is doing to America.

Rush further expounded on the emotionally attached and radical leftist types

Rush asked, what is the meaning of Obama saying "We gotta get rid of the failed ideologies of the past; we gotta get rid of the failed ways of thinking in the past and move on?" Rush said Obama's rhetoric has made his followers hope to "trump reality." Rush said because these emotionally attached people are obsessed with the way Obama speaks, they are not really interested in why Rush said he hopes Obama fails. They believe that Rush also wants them to fail and as such, Rush is an enemy to them.

Rush will support Obama if

Rush claimed that if Obama governs like Reagan by cutting taxes and not eliminating the Bush tax cuts, he would called his reign a success. "I would hope he would succeed if he acts like Reagan."

Limbaugh's I hope he fails comment was first perceived to be a disservice and only added insult to injury to the Republican Party amid the erosion of the congressional elections defeats they suffered in November 2008. But few months later, Rush's comment reinvigorated the Republican Party.

Presidential nominee John McCain opted to let the sleeping dogs lie when he was asked to comment on Rush's supposedly outrageous comment. McCain said: "I can't really analyze Mr. Limbaugh's remarks particularly since I don't know the context. I think most Americans want this president and this country to get out of this ditch we're in. He doesn't agree with his philosophy, I understand that."

Conclusion

Rush, when interviewed by Sean Hannity, said he defines the United States "succeeding by virtue of Obama failing." Rush said he wants all Americans to succeed.

Rush's statement, "I hope he fails" single-handedly dampened Obama's first year in office. Rush bailed out the Republican Party that was on the verge of foreclosing.

Grading Obama
Obama, after three months in office as president

Rush was asked to rate Obama's first three months in office. Surprisingly, Rush didn't jump to condemn Obama. "But you can't grade him an F," Rush said about grading Obama. "I was asked this last night on the panel in Beverly Hills that I appeared. I gave him a D, because you gotta allow room for more failure. If you give him an F now, you're saying it can't get any worse, and believe me, it can, and it will. So you gotta leave room for failure here."

Rush gave Obama a D. Most Republican pundits gave Obama's performance an F, but Rush has given Obama more rope to tie himself with and more opportunities for Americans to agree that Rush's "I hope Obama fails" comment wasn't a practical joke.

Obama, after six months in office as president

Rush provided an analogy on the US's destructive economy

Rush feels that in terms of fulfilling his "stated objectives," Obama has failed miserably. Rush said Obama's "stated objectives are not his real objectives." Rush outlined an analogy of Obama's "purposeful destruction" of the American economy: A large airplane that housed thousands of messengers has taken off. The plan is piloted by Obama and Biden, his copilot. And the flight attendants are the secretaries of Obama's administration. Obama's people are ordering the messengers to jump off the plane without wearing parachutes. They are saying to the messengers: "you will be fine, just hope, just be patient." The routine of ordering people to jump off the plane without parachutes continues. Rush said we all know that jumping out of a plane without parachutes will result in death. In reality, Obama's policies, which have been implemented to stimulate the United States economy, are not accomplishing the desired effect. Coming back to the analogy, Rush said that Obama is forcing messengers out of the flying planes without a parachutes. And in subsequence trip, he does the same practice of forcing more messengers out without parachutes. Obama just "keeps promising" that it will work. "It's gonna work if you just have faith. Just trust me. It's gonna work." Rush said the upshot to the analogy is that the more people are pushed out of the plane without parachutes, the closer we get to realizing that the practice wouldn't result in fatality.

Obama, after nine months in office as president

Rush reiterated, "I started the year (2009) by saying, 'I hope Obama fails.' But now (nine months later) I'm actually asking myself, 'Is it possible that Obama wants America to fail?'"

Not fair to judge Obama in three month increments

Either America is Failing or Obama is Succeeding

Rush asserted that every sane person in America knows that his comment "I hope he fails" was not said in the context of America falling. After twenty-one months, more Americans are dependent on the state and on the government. Rush said Obama has succeeded "in impoverishing and enslaving" them.

Obama's twenty- one months disastrous reign in the Oval Office is a microcosm of what will befall America in his remaining time in office.

Obama's campaign was predicated on remaking America. He banked on the fact that the country was facing an economic plight. Obama said, "America is – is no longer what it could be, what it once was." He made us believe that he was the talisman and he acted like a messiah that had the power to do the unimaginable. Millions of Americans were enthused and excited about Obama. They accepted Obama instantly without scrutiny. Millions of others raised their eyebrows with skepticism but still opted to join the bandwagon. They let their emotions get the better of them. However, Obama's opposition believed from the conception that Obama was running a smoke and mirrors campaign.

Obama is determined to transform America in his own vision, not in the vision of the majority of Americans. He believes that America's best days are behind her. And as such, America needs to undergo a massive sea change, a change of momentous proportions. Obama wants to create his own significant change that would go down in history and eclipse that of 1776 (United States Declaration of Independence.) He wants to create his own change that would eclipse when blacks were allowed to vote. And Obama holds the blueprint for change.

Obama's whole campaign was a fraudulent dog and pony show. On Election Day, November 4, 2008, 69 million Americans voted for Obama. They were at the show to cast their lots with Obama. The show will go on for the next two or six years. So it's fair for Obama's critics to update the country on how the dog and pony show is fairing every 3 months or less.

Millions of Americans are still watching the show. They are still being fooled by a charismatic, egotistical ideologue. However; after twenty-one months, some of the 69 millions that voted to watch the show have been hit by reality. They've realized that Obama was putting up a smoke screen to gets their votes.

The future of America is bleak, not looking promising by any stretch of the imagination. We have two or more years to deal with Obama.

The die-hard Obama supporters will be at the show until Obama's reign as president is over. They were transformed from being brainwashed to being brain-dead. Some of them are bordering on ignorance, and some of them are suffering from abject ignorance. Even when push comes to shove, even when all else fails, they prefer to be at the dog and pony show. They are placing their hopes on a man, not on God.

In Conclusion

Rush's widely criticized remark reaped the most dividends for the GOP in 2009. "I hope he fails" begot the tea parties. "I hope he fails" begot Palin's bestselling book sales. "I hope he fails" begot the 2009 New Jersey and Virginia gubernatorial victories. Rush received volumes of cut-throat criticism after his blockbuster remarks.

The most popular 2009 statement against Obama was uttered by Rush. Rush's popularity was overwhelmingly increased around the world. Rush became known by the unknowns just because of the statement he made. He didn't anticipate the degree to which his unscripted and unprepared comment would echo worldwide. After twenty- one months of an Obama presidency, Limbaugh and those in agreement who hope Obama's radical policies fail had the last laugh while the dissenters with nothing to say went off with their tails between their legs.[9]

Vast Differences between Republicans and Democrats

"For as much then as we are the offspring of God, we ought not to think that the God head is like unto gold, or silver, or stone graven by art and man's device. And the times of this ignorance God winked at; but now commanded all men everywhere to repent" (Acts 17 verse 29-30). The moral of this verse is that God winks at man's ignorance.

Republicans are all about substance, core belief and principles. On the other hand, Democrats are all about just words, just speeches, platitudes, crusades, rhetoric, fairytales, false change and false hope – the list is endless. And it all culminates in a complete hoax. Example – manmade global warming.

Karl Rove, a former Bush top aide, claimed to Sean Hannity that he is not a high roller but hangs out with the high rollers. Republicans are the high rollers. Democrats are the elitists who show "antipathies towards people (the less fortune) who aren't like them," Obama confirmed the argument during his historical campaign.

Republicans ostracize those without core conservative principles because our beliefs are short and simple: you either accept it and live with it or you will be vocally pushed out of the party. There is no fulsome praises towards our constituents coming from our leaders. Our sincerity has erased one of William Shakespeare's quotes: "There are no daggers when we smile." Democrats have no core beliefs.

Democrats will do anything to stay in power. For example in 2002, a year and a half after Bush took office and months after the wounds of the 9/11 tragedy were still fresh, US House Democrats led by Richard Gephardt rested their hopes of gaining more seats in Congress on the sinking stock market. Any point drop in the stock market was gladly anticipated as another seat gain by the Democrats. Minority leader Gephardt said about the Bush administration: "So far, the administration's approach has been a familiar strategy: Use harsh rhetoric to condemn wrongdoers while delaying and watering down whatever reforms might come out of congress." He then boldly alluded that the ailing stock market was not going to be an opportunity gone begging in the possibilities of gaining as many as 50 seats in the looming 2002 midterm election.

Republicans are not power hungry. For example, Speaker Gingrich, Speaker-elect Livingston and Majority Leader DeLay foretold their resignation from Congress after their misconducts surfaced. They weren't greedy for power, even though their misdemeanors were like chump change compared to the impeached President Bill Clinton and Governor Blagojevich.

Liberals want to redefine marriage. They want to legalize same sex marriage despite the fact that the Holy Bible says marriage is between a man and a woman. If liberals reject the words in the bible, the bible will also reject them. "Whosoever shall fall upon that stone shall be broken; but on whomsoever it shall fall, it will grind him to powder,"-said Jesus Christ. {Luke 20 v 18}

Liberals are the Pharisees of old, while conservatives are the Sinners and Publicans of old. True conservatives are on the right track to make it to the kingdom of God. With that said, here is an advisory warning for conservatives: they shouldn't take their eyes off the prize and they shouldn't get too comfortable because no man is guaranteed the kingdom of God.

Rush underlined the significant difference between Liberalism and Conservatism

Rush jumpstarted and talked about crocodile tears and real compassion: Conservatives have everybody's best interests at heart. Real compassion is conservatism. Liberalism holds the notion of caring for people, but that notion is a complete hoax.

Rush said any person who is not a conservative will surely become a liberal. Liberalism is easy and seductive; whereas conservatism is a "thought process." Rush said it requires "intellectual application" to live your life as a conservative, but there is no thought process required in living as a liberal; all there is to it is feelings.

Rush stated that Liberals don't believe people are competent enough to overcome obstacles in life. They look at people with contempt and condescension. These obstacles are placed by these same Liberals. They are schooled to work in government; they are trained to control government. Conservatives are the antithesis; they want to work in the private sector and reduce the size of government. Rush said Liberalism is "built around government," while conservatism is built around avoiding government.

The Democratic Party created miseries and sorrows that the downtrodden face. Rush said Liberals act like they care for the poor, whereas they actually loathe them. Rush said genuine compassion is sole property of conservatism because conservatism cares for every individual. Conservatism wants people to be the best they can be. The only way that can happen is if governmental obstacles aren't put in their way. Rush said Liberals have cemented in people's mind that they are the "caring party."

Rush noted that conservatives are always labeled as "mean-spirited" and "cold-hearted," but they are the ones that contribute to charities etc privately. Rush said conservatives are "focused on good works." Republicans don't long for public relations. Liberals are viewed as angels with a compassionate heart, but they give away money that is not theirs.

"We conservatives define compassion not by how many people are receiving government assistance. We instead define compassion by counting the number of people who no longer need it."

Rush said about liberals always talking the talk. "Liberalism is the most gutless choice you can make." Liberalism seeks a cult figure and a demagogue as their leader. They talk the talk, but they don't walk the walk. They feel sympathy for the less fortunate, but they don't do anything to solve their problems. They make you feel like they care. Rush defines a liberal as someone who see abjectly homeless people on the corner and thinks, "I am a great American" because I care about them. "What did you do for them? Well nothing, but I care."_But conservatives see these homeless people's situation as unpalatable and unaccepted. And they enact legislations to solve the situation?

Class envy is the sole property of the left. "Equality of outcome," falls under class envy. For liberals, it is not fair that some people are wealthier than others. It's not fair that some live in good neighborhoods while others live in abjectly poor neighborhoods. Rush said Liberals believe that every American must be the same before the United States is considered a just country. Inequalities must be corrected. Not taking into account physical appearance, Rush said: "no two Americans are the same." Rush said psychologically, there are differences in desire, ambition and abilities. America was founded on the concept of individual freedom.

Quality Conservatives Pit against Quantity Liberals

Conservatism is all about quality not quantity, and when Republicans chased after quantity, they failed. We saw McCain trying to reach out for moderates in the 2008 election. There is a fine line between being a liberal and being a conservative. With that said, many that cross over to the conservative side of the aisle will find out that becoming a conservative comes with lots of convictions and determinations. They will either be foursquare to the conservative core principle or kicked right back to where they originally belong.

The Democratic Party is all about quantity. They angled to get votes, for example, Acorn.

Conservative views are in stark contrast to any other ideology. The conservative belief is in a league of its own. And it can never be watered down.

Conservatism is based on nothing but the truth while liberalism is based on everything but the truth.

Obama vs Palin

Rush's assessment of Palin and Obama

Rush contrasted, "Obama is Washington, but Palin is American." Rush asserted that Palin is a genuine American and a "real story of accomplishment." Rush said that hundreds of Americans can vouch for Palin's story. On the other hand, Obama's original story had to be hidden and must be rewritten in order for it to be vouched for. Rush chronicled Palin's resume, including her being on the city council, a mayor and a governor. And she didn't have the privilege of Republican hierarchies supporting her during her gubernatorial race. Rush said Palin fought against corruption in Alaskan politics, and she is a far cry from the Washington DC political cesspool. Rush said that although she has the fame, she thinks and lives like we common Americans do. There is no elitist blood in Palin. Palin disdains the perspective of those who advocate for government taking over liberty.

America will be heading to a real lost decade if Obama should win reelection in 2012. The crux of the 2012 election will be: is America ready to elect a woman as president? The piece de resistance for the GOP in 2008 was when McCain announced his running mate. Policy wise, McCain skirted the advice of Rush. He didn't heed what Rush said during the election.

However, McCain did send Palin to seek Rush out for an interview. Palin started mirroring McCain's policies, and that made a Republican victory more arduous. McCain, not Palin, was the underbelly of the GOP 2008 ticket in terms of substance. But Palin was more susceptible to criticism than McCain was.

Democrats like ex presidential nominee John Kerry have derided Palin for being a social conservative. Palin was severely peppered by the media. Attacks against Palin ratcheted up throughout her campaign for Veep. Palin found herself in the middle of a Democratic and Republican sandwiched attack. It was beyond condescending and offensively patronizing the way they attacked Palin.

After her shocking resignation, Palin walked her supporters through all of the events that led to her decision to relinquish her seat, but she stopped short from admitting that she was determined to run for the Oval Office.

The narratives changed on Obama throughout the 2008 campaign. And Rush said: "Her (Palin) story can be vouched for by hundreds. Obama's story must be hidden. Obama's story must be rewritten. Obama has no one vouching for his story."

Chambliss, the Georgian senator, was on the ropes until Palin came and campaigned for him. Palin's impact was a major national victory for Chambliss.

The amount of money donated for Obama's campaign was inconceivable. Obama might have the upper hand in the 2012 election like any other incumbent president, but that could be obviated by who we nominate. Remember what happened in 1992? Walker Bush lost his reelection status to Bill Clinton.

When Palin resigned, everybody came up out of the woods to denounce her decision. They basically said she is unable to finish serving a full term as a governor, so how could she serve as president? Sean gave an insight: "Becoming a governor or a senator is not a prison sentence. 18 months Obama was running for president and still took home a paycheck. Hold everybody to a standard not just a Palin." The level of dedication for Obama's senatorial duties ebbed because he was totally focused on his presidential campaign.

There have been numerous senators and governors that opted to resign from office just to take a pay increase for an executive cabinet position. Palin, on the other hand, resigned to private life without any offers on the horizon.

The whole bottom line is that Palin and Obama both terminated their respective offices. Although one resigned her position because she was a lame duck governor, why didn't the other step down upon announcing that he was running for Commander-in-Chief? Palin stopped receiving tax payers' dollars while Obama continued receiving tax payers' dollars until once he became the 44 president.

After the 2008 elections, Palin has unquestionably increased in stature. She's risen to such unprecedented heights that she would be demoting herself should she make a run for the US Senate. The presidency is the only office she is esteemed to run for. Palin didn't disavow being a Republican despite all the attacks from stuffed shirt Republicans. She showed unwavering support for the GOP candidates that ran for office in November of 2009.

There was a blackout in the media on Obama's unpopular deeds. Obama was vulnerable on multiple fronts during the 2008 election, yet McCain couldn't capitalize on them. 2012 will be a different ball game. If Palin gets the nod, she will definitely capitalize on all of Obama's vulnerabilities. The bottom has fallen out on Obama's hope and change rhetoric, so Obama would be forced to resort to the cornerstone of his 2008 campaign.[10]

The Republican Party: The GOP Establishment and the Conservative Movement

Rush Limbaugh leads the Republican Party as a whole. George Bush's expired presidency and Senator John McCain's failure to win the 2008 presidential election left former Speaker Newt Gingrich to head the GOP establishment.

The Future of Republicanism

We can talk about the seven spirits of God, we can talk about the seven continents and we can talk about the seven individuals that control the Republican Party. The Party revolves around these powerful and influential figures.

By virtue of being the 43rd US president, **George Bush**'s influence on the GOP is far from being stifled. The former governor of Texas is spending most of his time with his extended family, something he couldn't effectively do as president.

George Bush will be exhumed to give his support to GOP candidates once election time approaches.

Karl Rove is a constant fixture for the GOP and a political wizard of the highest caliber. Rove owes President Bush a debt of gratitude for putting him in the limelight. Since Rove became President George Bush's deputy Chief of Staff, Rove has been a handful for the opposition party. Rove was viewed by many Democratic senators as the advisor behind Bush's successful reign as president. He was the man behind the curtain in Bush's White House. His relationship with George Bush dates back to when Bush was governor of Texas.

Sean Hannity remains high in the GOP's pecking order. His radio and cable programs are vital for the Republican Party. Although Sarah Palin is a bona fide Republican star and is significantly growing in leaps and bounds, she is a far cry from being as influential as Hannity. Sean ignored the spate of criticism that was ranted against him when he unmarked Obama's radical friends. Sean Hannity is positioned perfectly to become one of the greatest American conservatives we have ever witnessed.

The House GOP would never in this generation have a leader like **Tom DeLay**. Dennis Hastert was sandwiched between Newt Gingrich and Nancy Pelosi as the Speaker of the House. Newt Gingrich is extremely popular among Americans, and Nancy Pelosi is well-renowned as America's first female House Speaker. With that said, no one knew Dennis Hastert because he was completely overshadowed by Tom DeLay, then the Majority leader. DeLay was an ultra conservative legislator in the House, just as Barry Goldwater was in the Senate. DeLay is on a par with Barry Goldwater. The big shot from Sugar Land, Texas, is working under the radar for the conservative causes.

We hear of presidents balancing the federal government budget. However, on a rare occasion, Speaker **Newt Gingrich** balanced the budget in 1995. In the mid nineties, Newt Gingrich matched Clinton's popularity. Bill Clinton lost a lot of sleep wondering if Gingrich was going to run for president in 1996.

However, Newt put off a presidential run till 2000. In 1997, Newt fell prey to the House rules and subsequently handed in his resignation. The sudden and devastating scandal dashed his presidential aspirations. It was political suicide for the closest thing to a Reagan.

Nine years later, Newt was back on the national scene. Rumors flared up again in 2008 that Newt Gingrich was on the brink of running for president. Bill Clinton had his work cut out for him to work in a bipartisan way with Newt Gingrich. The Georgian statesman was a pain in the neck for Clinton until he resigned from Congress. Gingrich is constantly involved with the GOP establishment. Candidates running for federal offices are waiting patiently for his endorsement.

The opposition party might consider **Richard Cheney** as damaged goods, but the Republican Party knows Cheney is one of a kind. Cheney hangs around to give advice to Republicans and to the country's national security officials. Regardless of having no future political ambitions, Richard Cheney still remains high in the GOP's pecking order. He is still a looming presence in everything the GOP does.

Rush Limbaugh is on top of the food chain. Rush has been saddled with much of the party's responsibility. On numerous occasions, Rush has thrown himself under the bus for the Republican Party in order for them to block horrendous Democratic legislations and to pass legislations that are supportive of the American people.

At the end of the day, members of the Republican Party constantly reprehend Rush on many fronts. Rush has come to realize that being assailed by members from his party comes with the territory of being the GOP leader. The constant pestering by conservatives Rush received to run for president has finally subsided.

As a United States president juggling his radio program, Rush Limbaugh would be under-employing himself. He won't be able to give his utmost best to his listeners. Rush would be hankering and itching to give his all, but inevitably he would be hindered. He would be conflicted with too many executive agendas. The pay cut that Rush would have to be subjected to would be disastrous for Rush.

Even if he prefers to go full-time as president, thereby suspending his radio program, he would still be under-employed. In the first place, Rush is overqualified to be a United States president. Unlike you know who, Rush wouldn't have any dialogue whatsoever with world dictators. Rush would move the United Nations away from the United States so that the likes of Mahmoud Ahmadinejad, Hugo Chávez and Moammar Gadhafi would not have any reason to step foot in America. Rush would be completely open and forthright with Americans in regards to his policies and agendas.

Talking about bipartisanship, Rush would be the most partisan president America would ever witness. If Rush were to govern as a centrist, he would be contradicting himself. Rush believes that centrists, moderates and independents are all liberals. So in that context, Rush would be hypocritical. The last thing Rush would want is to be mistaken as a liberal Republican.

The GOP Before Rush's "I hope he fails" comment

House GOP leadership was dwindling. Boehner, the US House Minority leader, wasn't effective enough especially in galvanizing GOP grassroots support. House GOPs wished they were yonder from touching distance of the remarkable mid-nineties of Newt Gingrich and the early new millennium when Tom DeLay was in command. How much do we salivate for those days? Roy Blunt off as Minority Whip and Eric Cantor as his replacement are fresh blood, and they provide an opportunity for the GOP House to turn things around. Mike Pence is another optimistic representative that is trying to rebuild the GOP House. Rush's political executions were the meal ticket for GOP's congressional and presidential election victories from 1995 to mid 2004. And many GOP statesmen have been grateful for Rush's unerring leadership.

In 2006, the GOP chances of retaining the House they held since 1994 receded when Tom DeLay resigned. Republicans in Congress still haven't recovered from their 2006 midterm loss, where they were utterly decimated. House GOPs are behind enemy lines. They need a DeLay to come and roll call incompetent House GOP members of Congress. After the 2006 sweeping defeat, they were still unable to resume normal service. And in 2008, another damaging comprehensive defeat was inflicted by the Democrats. If the Republican Party ignores Rush in 2010 or in 2012, they will be looking down the barrel of yet another loss.

The GOP senate is a joke. They need more than a Hail Mary. Since November 2006, they have lost 15 senators in their reelection/election bids. They have been reduced to a bloody pulp. The Republican Party has not been the same since Senators Bill Frist, Rick Santorum and George Allen left Capitol Hill in 2006. A year after that, Trent Lott also vacated his leadership position and Congress as a whole. All those departures left the Republican senate in turmoil. To make matter worse, you have 1980's politicians, McConnell and Alexander, heading the GOP senate. They need to hand over the reins of the party to Senator Jim De Mint. Maybe then we could see a light at the end of the tunnel for the senatorial representatives on Capitol Hill.

Rush is about done picking up the pieces of the 2006 midterm and the 2008 congressional loss. He is still being blamed within the party's hierarchy. He's been blamed for not asking Tom DeLay to relinquish his leadership post upon the unraveling of a scandal. Rush struggled to come to terms after the egregious 2006 GOP election loss.

Republicans are waiting in anticipation for the forthcoming 2010 midterm elections with unbridled optimism. It is vital, is of the essence that Republicans come hell or high water retakes at least the upper or lower chambers of Congress in 2010. They have to be anchored in conservatism. They need to recapture the House or the Senate so as to stop Obama from prevailing socialist leftwing radical agendas and policies.

The looming 2010 midterm congressional elections have the makings of being a successful year for the GOP. Republicans should be adamant in espousing conservative principles instead of resting on their laurels. Rush, Palin, Sean and other conservative cocks that crow unadulterated conservatism have urged Republican politicians to take a bold stand in articulating core conservative values. Reagan did it, Gingrich did it and DeLay did it.

Americans are witnessing the beginning of a political tsunami. Before 2010 eludes us, they will transpire to be political earthquakes. Just to name a few: a political earthquake in the form of Senator Harry Reid, the leader of the Democratic senate losing his seat is anticipated. Reid's reelection bid is under threat. Reid is on the brink of surrendering his impregnable Nevada Senate seat. Senator Boxer of California is facing an uphill battle with a well-versed conservative candidate. The GOP is confident he will gain back one of the chambers of Congress.

In only eleven months, Obama suffered a stunning repudiation in the 2009 gubernatorial elections' fallout. Many Democratic members had lost their confidence in him. Anger percolated over the loss of two gubernatorial races. Anger also percolated over the loss of the so called "Kennedy's seat." John Corzine's gubernatorial reelection loss in the state of New Jersey and Virginia's gubernatorial candidate, Creigh Deeds' landslide defeat were just a curtain raiser for what is at stake for Obama and the Democratic Party. As the Democratic incumbent president, Obama will continue trying to keep his congressional colleagues' hopes alive in the slim hopes of retaining Congress after 2010. Democratic incumbents' future hinge on the 2010 midterm elections and as such, they are prepared to go the distance to continue supporting Obama's demands because they believe in Obama's popularity.

Obama knows that his opponents smell blood in the water. He also knows that he is the immense hurdle his party faces. Obama has left them in a precarious position. Obama is looking for some type of damage limitation, but it seems to be too late. From the GOP standpoint, nothing can be redeemed. Obama will definitely pull out all the stops to ensure that the GOPs aren't victorious. And if that means recalling Acorn, then he will do it.

Establishment

Newt Gingrich heads the establishment, and he is believed to be seeking a 2012 presidential run. Michael Steele runs the Republican National Committee (RNC). The RNC is nothing but a fundraising GOP organization. The RNC will be going into administration trying to compete with their counterpart, the Democratic National Committee {DNC}. How much money was donated to Obama during the 08 presidential campaign as compared to McCain? It was unmatchable and incomparable. The DNC is like Hollywood in terms of political donations. The DNC consists of billionaires like George Soros, Oprah Winfrey, Michael Bloomberg and Warren Buffett in terms of philanthropists and major donors. The DNC consists of big corporations and "fat cat" CEOs in terms of funding from corporations. Where are the concentrations of wealth in the Republican Party? Who does the RNC have? Rupert Murdoch?

John McCain was the Republican establishment's ideal candidate for 2008. The establishment overwhelmingly endorsed him. They chose Sarah Palin from the conservative movement in an attempt to balance the equation. But the GOP ticket wasn't balanced. If the same script is repeated in 2012, if they nominate a moderate in 2012, the Party will go down in flames. It might be time to go back to the drawing board time for GOP. They will be on pins and needles, especially with the possibility of a third party, which would mean the loss of Rush Limbaugh and conservative voters.

The conservatives have had it with Colin Powell's lip service, but the establishment has gladly accepted him back to the Party. Sean Hannity, having interviewed Powell when he was State secretary, came out and trashed Powell for attacking Rush Limbaugh. Sean said: "Powell is without principle, he is expedient, he is seemingly without anchored, his views are shallow and don't represent Republican views. We need a convicted politician like Reagan not a convenience politician like Powell."

The GOP establishment didn't criticize Powell when he voted against McCain in the 2008 presidential elections because they didn't want to be dismissed as racists. But thank God for Rush, who didn't need to have the guts to call it as he saw it.

According to Rush, the politicians running the GOP have a "defeatist inferiority complex" because they crave to be accepted and liked by the hard left.

The GOP establishment, instead of aiding Palin after the 2008 election, hung her out to dry. Rush has leaped to Palin's defense on numerous occasions and has reprehended the GOP for attacking Palin. Rush said it's a shame that "The Republican Party's been just as mean-spirited to her as the Democrats have."

Rush asked: "Why do people in our party allow themselves to be defined, manipulated, flaked, formed, shaped, whatever, by these Democrats?"

Republican Leadership Remains Void

In the electoral politics arena, Rush acknowledged: "There's no real political leadership, and everybody is scared of me in the Republican Party." Rush said Republican lawmakers are scared of disagreeing with him.

Schwarzenegger's take on Rush Limbaugh

The governor of California was asked about his take on who leads the Republican Party and his crystal ball prediction for the future of the GOP. Gov. Schwarzenegger said: "They say that Rush Limbaugh is the 800-pound gorilla in the Republican Party. But I think that's mean-spirited to say that, because I think he's down to 650 pounds, so I think one should be fair to him about this whole thing. No, I think that, in all seriousness, the key thing is to keep that large tent."

Rush's unvarnished advice to Republican Politicians

Conservative candidates should espouse the founding documents. They should be confident in talking about freedom, liberty and the pursuit of happiness, because that is what makes Americans exceptional. Rush said conservatives don't see Americans as victims, but as the "greatest collection of human beings" in one given and blessed nation. Freedom results in the disparity of different outcomes.

Liberals advocate for sameness. The outcome in equality leads to the liberal fairness jihad. Instead of trying to elevate those at the bottom of the ladder, they condemn those at the top. They are hell-bent on equalizing society, and they do this by "making everybody equally miserable."

Why Republicans hate Rush

There is no mileage for a so-called conservative to try to undermine another conservative, especially if the argument is slanted towards rejecting liberalism. Fox News' Van Susteren asked Rush: "I was going to ask you about the Republican Party. Why don't they like you? Rush said there has been infighting occurring in the GOP for who is leading the Party since Bush is longer the president. And there is an identical struggle too. Rush said the friction that we faced is primarily about social issues, specifically abortion. Rush said the Rockefeller blue -blood country club types and the quasi-conservative " inside-the-Beltway" media are profoundly embarrassed to have pro-lifers in the same Party with them. Rush said that on many occasions, he has been accosted by blue- blood hierarchies at ceremonies poking him in the chest and asking him what he would do about the evangelical Christians and pro-life voters. Rush said they believe pro-lifers are destroying the Party and are hindering the Party from winning elections. Rush said the only time the GOP are victorious in elections is when a conservative is nominated. "Am not an elite. I'm not a country club, blue-blood Rockefeller type. I'm considered unsophisticated and, you know, sort of, "We don't want Limbaugh. We don't want to be associated with Limbaugh, that radicalness and so forth. "

The Conservative Movement

Rush Jumpstarted Conservatism after the 2008 Election Lost

Days before the 2008 general election, Rush's sleeves were rolled up and he was ready for the rebuilding of the conservative movement. A day after the Republican loss of the 2008 presidential election, Rush said right off the jump that the conservative movement needs no overhaul. Rush said those people who abandoned the conservative movement must "stay abandoned."

The Rebuilding Commence

Rush admits the road to recovery and rebuilding the conservative movement will be steep. Furthermore, we have to oppose liberal premises like redistribution of wealth in the canopy of fairness. Liberals believed that "Confiscatory taxation" will grow the economy, and the expanding of government will lead to America's greatness.

Rush Limbaugh has been leading the conservative movement since the early nineties. Rush and Sean Hannity have dovetailed conservatives in America better than any other pairing Americans have ever witnessed. They are the indefatigable leaders for the conservative movement. The messages that they have articulated have been vital and priceless.

New Emerging Vicious Opponents for the Conservative Movement

With the election of Obama, the conservative movement has their hands full with Eurosocialists joining the conservative movement's opponents. With the election of Obama, multiculturalists are in league with liberalists to dismantle conservatism. The conservative movement will be in a constant battle against liberalism and its allies for the preservation of this nation. "Buckley/Goldwater/Reagan/Gingrich conservative movement, I will try to lend my hand. I certainly will do what I can to make it a big-tent conservative movement."

Sarah Palin is fresh blood for conservative causes and ideas. Gov. Huckebee is a genuine conservative, but he is not moving the conservative movement. Sanford's career is on thin ice and his influence to the movement has been stopped dead in its tracks. On the other hand, his fellow countryman Jim de Mint, the Senator who triggered a firestorm because off his analysis of Obama, is booming as a major figurehead for the Movement. Jim De Mint picked up the flag that was dropped by Sanford. Newt Gingrich has been tame. He is focusing on leading the GOP establishment, and that is a colossal distraction.

Senator Chambliss, who was on pins and needles throughout his reelection and his runoff campaign until Sarah Palin showed up, pledged to the conservatives that they wouldn't have to worry about revisiting his moderate voting days.

Powell and the GOP establishment want to decimate and render the movement powerless and dilapidated. For those who have abandoned the conservative movement, Rush knows that their departures are not a cry over spilled milk because once a conservative, always a conservative.

Hillary Clinton's liberal slant might overwhelm her conservative slant, but she was originally a conservative. She is the main reason why Bill Clinton, when he was president, tilted towards the right on some issues. Rush's goal is to use his radio program as a window to convert contentious moderates and liberal zealots who have been shielded and deceived by the Democratic Party.

Conservative ascendancy actually began in Georgia

Rush claimed Obama threw everything in that campaign except himself and "Plaxico Burress and a loaded gun." Obama sent African American rappers Jay-Z and Ludacris to campaign against Chambliss. The Republican Party only sent Sarah Palin to campaign for Senator Chambliss, and Chambliss was victorious.

Chambliss said after his election victory: "Smaller government, fiscal responsibility...more individual rights and freedoms, and lower taxes. And we've gotta get back to those fundamentals. That's what we talked about on the campaign trail, and obviously it resonated with our constituents here."

Jesus Christ said, "No man, having put his hand to the plough, and looking back, is fit for the kingdom of God." Luke 9 verse 62. Conservatives that know what conservatism is all about but still opt to align themselves with liberalism are not worth their salt. And Christ said afterwards: "Remember Lot's wife,"-Luke 17 verse 32. We should remember what befell Lot's wife: "But his {Lot} wife looked back from behind him, and she became a pillar of salt,"-Genesis 19 verse 26.

The tea parties rallies, town halls melees, Mark Levin's surprise book sales, the continuous blackening of Rush Limbaugh and Sarah Palin, the 2009 GOP gubernatorial victory in the bluest of blue states of New Jersey and the early 2010 senate victory in the state of Massachusetts are all forerunners that indicate that there is a genuine conservative politician on the horizon. It's only out of the conservative movement that the Republican Party can beget a presidential candidate that can put Reagan's achievements in the shade. Governors Sarah Palin and Mark Levin's books were the two bestselling books of 2009. The gubernatorial victories and Levin/Palin's book sales, coupled with Rush's "I hope he fails" comment, vindicated the rise of the conservative ascendency.

Scott Brown won the so-called "Kennedy seat" in Massachusetts, of all places. That victory was a miracle. A Republican winning a US Senate seat in the bluest of blue states of Massachusetts is unheard of. Even more astonishing was Scott Brown winning over a seat held by the godfather of the Democratic Party, Ted Kennedy. Ted might not have been the longest serving US Democratic senator, but he was certainly the most influential Democratic senator for years. Brown might have run on the conservative platform, but he's no different from RINO Republicans.

GOP Candidates for Senate/House

Rush's advice for Incumbents and Future Republicans running for office

Conservatives need to put the euphoria of the 2009 gubernatorial victories behind them and concentrate on the forthcoming elections.

A GOP 2010 electoral landslide has been predicted. The GOP can't afford to let their guards down because the Democrats are probing for weaknesses. The Democratic Party has pegged the GOP back from regaining the House and the Senate for four years. If they lost in 2010, they would have to wait for two more years if they were to regain back control of Congress. It could be a long, blistering road that can never be recovered for the Republicans if the party ignores Rush in subsequent elections to come.

Since Tom DeLay left the House GOP in Congress, Republicans have been left powerless. The GOP would really be left in the doldrums should they fail to heed to Rush advice.

Rush believes that candidates should "stand up for the institutions and the traditions" that define American's greatness. Rush said their electability and reelectability resides from the concept that led to the greatness of this nation.

It's imperative for GOP politicians seeking federal office to amplify the conservative message preached by Rush, Newt and other pamphleteers. The GOP politicians in Capitol Hill up for reelection have to avoid throwing caution to the wind. Like in 2006, they were a handful of Congressmen that were involved in scandals. The Democratic Party, with a battle cry, capitalized on their scandals. GOP leaders understand that there should be no margin for error.

In the grand scheme of things, the first twenty- one months of Obama's presidency didn't matter because of the effectiveness of Rush's "I hope he fails" comment, but two or six years of Obama at the reins of government will certainly be a matter of grave concern. Rush's brilliant and improvised schemes coupled with an anticipated Republican 2010 Congressional midterm victory would reduce the severity of Obama's radical policies.

The last House on the Left

A repeat of the 1994 GOP House takeover is predicted in the beckoning midterm elections of 2010. Dick Morris calculated a major scale victory for Republicans. Dick Morris is on top of it all. He is following closely each and every House and Senate race in the country. What is forecasted to happen in November of 2010 would be a political earthquake, a midterm sweeping victory that would eclipse that of 1994. Republican leaders are on the watch for potential pitfalls on the horizon that would hinder their 2010 success.

Democrats are in a critical situation, where just about every Democratic seat in the House is in play. The vulnerable Democratic lawmakers are prepared to face the music as November 2010 approaches. They are adamant and forthright in supporting their beloved Speaker of the House.

1994 was the year of the House revolution led by Newt Gingrich and a few members of Congress. 2010 would be the House apocalypse led by tea baggers. It would be the last House on the left for Democrats and liberals.

The tea baggers know that an alternative to a liberal candidate must be chosen and supported come 2010. If the alternative is not much philosophically different from the liberal candidate, then the tea baggers must apply the lesser of the two evils approach.

It would be a tragedy for Speaker Nancy Pelosi to, upon losing her position as Speaker of the House, be demoted to an ordinary Representative from California 8th district. Food for thought for Nancy Pelosi is to resign from office a few months before the election or suffer a wholesale repudiation. Dennis Hastert, Nancy Pelosi's predecessor, announced his retirement from Congress after the Republican loss the House in 2006. Trepidation surrounds Nancy Pelosi. Nancy Pelosi is searching for a glimmer of hope.

The more her fellow Democrats resign from office, the more sleep she loses. The more the crunch time (November of 2010) inches closer, the more reality hits her. Pelosi would have to pull a rabbit out of her hat to ensure her Party continues to control Congress after the 2010 elections. At least she made history as the first woman Speaker of the House.

Is Reaganism over?

Reaganism 001
The Reagan era represents "conservatism 101." Reagananism believes everybody can be the best they can be. In order for that to happen, the best can only be achieved "if people embark upon the quest themselves." Reagananism doesn't look at people and group them into race, gender or class; it looks at people as individuals.

Republicanism before Reagan
Rush recalled the GOP's days before Reagan were blighted by poor leadership. Rush noted that before Reagan, big tent politicians were losing elections left and right.

The country club blue- blood Republicans, under the leadership of Bob Michel, were never able to win over 135 US House seats. "Nelson Rockefeller {former Vice President} getting drunk at the '76 convention in Kansas City, falling off his chair is about as far as they ever took us." But Reagan came up with two landslides in the 1980's to significantly thwarted Rockefeller and Michel's achievements. And in 1994, the Republican House takeover, led by Newt Gingrich, took back the House after 40 years of Democratic control.

Conservatism is the blueprint for victory
Rush referenced Reagan's two landslide presidential victories and the Gingrich-led Republican Revolution: "The blueprint for Republican Party success is all the way back in the 1980s and in 1994."

Republicanism after Reagan

Rush said both Reagan and George Bush were pro-life GOP nominees for president, yet they both won their elections and reelections for the presidency. Rush said he is "sick and tired" of hearing that the only way Republicans can win elections is if "pro-life Christians" are driven out of the Party. Rush said in 1980, when Reagan ran against Gerald Ford, he was running against the entire GOP establishment. That pit conservatism against republicanism. And although conservatism wasn't victorious, republicanism was beaten by liberalism. Reagan brought in moderates to the Republican Party, but "they came in as conservatives," not as moderates. Rush said Reagan did this by not changing who he was. Rush said conservatism isn't holding Reagan as a cult leader.

The Battle over the Heart and soul of the Republican Party: GOP Turf War

Powell's Republican intro

Rush claimed that Republican presidents made Powell a household name. Reagan made Powell a four- star general. HW Bush appointed Powell as chairman of the Joint Chiefs. George Bush appointed him as secretary of state. "Powell owes his name and his ascension to various heights to Republicans."

Powell endorsed Obama: "In a strategic moment of timing," Rush said.

Before Powell surfaced, the jaws of defeat were looming for the GOP. After Powell endorsed Obama, it was difficult for the GOP to snatch a victory.

Rush knew it was too big a gap to bridge. Powell's endorsement to Obama wasn't Powell's "finest hour." Rush labeled the logic Powell used in endorsing Obama as "Swiss cheese." Rush said the fact that Powell waited until late October to endorse Obama caused "maximum impact for Obama, maximum damage to McCain." At that time in late October, Obama's poll numbers were plummeting because of deleterious news about Obama. So Powell's timing in endorsement Obama was purposeful. Rush said Powell's endorsement of Obama was totally about race. Powell has always been called the Liberals' favorite Republican. If Powell endorsed McCain over Obama he would have been rejected, just as the Rice and the Thomas and the like are being rejected. And he would have been bashed to kingdom come if he didn't support the first real African American candidate for president.

Rush feels the GOP nominee for president was the quintessential candidate Powell advocated for. Yet Powell ignored McCain and chose to announce his endorsement for Obama at the time that would "inflict the most harm" on McCain. Rush asked, how could it not be about race? What would have happened to Powell, a prominent African American, if he didn't vote for the first black nominee in a major Party running for president?

Powell mad at Rush

Rush's memory is far from fading. Rush stated that in 1996, Powell stopped short from announcing which party he belongs to. He wouldn't be open on what his beliefs and principles were. At that time, his approval numbers were in the seventies. Rush said he was one of the political figures urging Powell to choose which party he belongs to. From that moment on, Powell hated Rush. Powell wasn't open about his beliefs because he knew his poll numbers would plummet. Rush said Republicans, including him, wanted Powell to run against Clinton. Rush said that at that time, Powell was the "precursor to Obama." Everybody was pleading for him to run for president. And when Rush said race was the underlying reason that led Powell to endorse Obama, the hatred Powell had for Rush only intensified. Rush said nobody had the guts to openly say that Powell's endorsement was purely about race.

Powell waited for too long to decide whether or not he would run for president in 1996.

Rush said on August 16, 1995, He's (Powell) playing it very coyly. He's done a very good job of keeping everything he believes on every issue totally secret. He doesn't know -- and that's why he's so high in the polls. He's acting like he doesn't want it, but he'll make every speech he has a chance to make and the situation is psychological. "Please, Mr. Powell, General Powell. Please run," and what can be a better situation than that?"

Powell was moved to declare himself a Republican

Powell formally declared himself a Republican. He said: "I became a Republican because I believe, like you, that the federal government has become too large and too intrusive in our lives. We can no longer... We can no longer afford solutions to our problems that result in more entitlements, higher taxes to pay for them, more bureaucracy to run them, and fewer results to show for it."

In 2008, Powell's set of principles changed

Powell claimed that: "Americans do want to pay taxes for services. Americans are looking for more government in their life, not less." Rush reacted to the so-called archetypical Republican. According to Rush, Powell totally "reversed himself" from his speech at the 1996 Republican convention. Rush said, between him and Powell, Powell was the one that had change but everyone felt Rush was the one that should be kicked out of the Party. Powell, not Rush, was the one that called against lower taxes, against small government. Rush said it is people like McCain and Powell that have obliterated the party's identity, yet he is the one on which all of the blame has been placed.

Powell's broadside on Rush

Powell directly attacked Rush in an interview. Powell said: "When you have nonelected officials such as we have in our party -- who immediately shout racism or somebody who is quite prominent in the media says that the only basis upon which I could possibly have supported Obama was because he was black and I was black, even though I laid out my judgment on the candidates, then we still have a problem." The interviewer then said: "The guy who used the term reverse racism, that's Rush Limbaugh, and he has said some not so favorable things about you." Powell responded: "Mr. Limbaugh of course, is entitled to his opinion, but he's not on any membership committee, he doesn't decide who I am or what I am no more than I decide who he is or what he is. So we've had this running debate, let's call it that, and he's entitled to his opinion and I'm entitled to mine."

To stop listening to Rush is to stop listening to the truth

Powell's outspoken criticisms of Rush continued. He said on December of 2008 that Republicans should stop listening to Rush Limbaugh: "Can we continue to listen to Rush Limbaugh? Is this really the kind of party that we want to be when these kinds of spokespersons seem to appeal to our lesser instincts rather than our better instincts."

Rush responded: "So Powell is talking to Republican leaders about tossing me out of the party, and people should stop listening to me and helping Democrats with any legislation that might be aimed at taming talk radio."

Six month later, Powell, speaking to corporate executives at a conference, said: "I think what Rush does as an entertainer diminishes the party and intrudes or inserts into our public life a kind of nastiness that we would be better to do without."

Rush or Powell: a supporter or a traitor?

Rush asked, how is it that Powell, who sabotaged McCain's chance of winning the presidency, should remain in the Party and be a major player, whereas Rush, who supported McCain, should be the one discarded from the Party? "The turncoat, General Powell, is the one who the party is gonna listen to? McCain's a moderate. I supported McCain. Powell, who wants a moderate, did not support McCain. It's unreal. It's just incredible."

The reason why Powell threw Republicanism under the bus: Powell Epitomizes RINO {Republican in Name Only}

In precise words, Rush said after Powell went before the United Nations Security Council to plead his case on why Iraq harbors WMD, he was deemed a sellout. Powell lost his credibility in Washington DC. Therefore, the opportunity to endorse Obama was crucial, Rush said Powell's reputation needed to be brought back from the brink; it badly needed to be resuscitated. Rush said Powell wouldn't have let the opportunity to endorse Obama go begging.

Rush asserted that Powell's standing among elite Washingtonians was threatened because of his United Nations presentation. So in order to get back into good standing with his fellow Washingtonians, he endorsed Obama. According to Rush, Powell's intent was to get even with the Bush administration because he felt embarrassed that Bush sent him to the United Nations Security Council. So the endorsement by Powell was meant to even the score with the Bush administration.

McCain the scapegoat: Why Powell didn't support McCain

McCain didn't feel that he was sold down the river by Powell's endorsement of Obama. Rush stated it was a "dead giveaway" for Powell to say that the reason he voted against McCain was because the GOP is becoming a narrow Party. Rush said McCain is known for always currying favors with Democrats. Rush said McCain had to cross the aisle to legislate the McCain-Feingold and the McCain-Kennedy acts.

Powell said after being reprehended by Rush and Cheney, "I may be out of their version of the Republican Party, but there's another version of the Republican Party waiting to emerge once again,"

Rush believes the version of the GOP that Powell is "waiting to emerge" is not the conservative wing of the party. It's a version that is for more government spending and higher taxes. It's a version for illegal amnesty. "The only thing emerging here is Colin Powell's ego. Colin Powell represents the stale, the old, the worn out GOP that never won anything." Rush said Powell represents the Party of the likes of President Gerald Ford, Nelson Rockefeller and Arnold Schwarzenegger.

Opinionated Republican leaders Claimed: "Colin Powell is the model Republican"

Rush can't for the life of him understand why Powell, who strategically endorsed Obama in such a way that he eventually ruined the Republican nominee's chances of winning, is considered a model Republican. Add to that the fact that McCain was Powell's ideal Republican moderate. Rush asked, how can the Party's base be built with moderates? Rush advised everyone to let General Powell and whichever GOP politicians who think they are "the piece de resistance," go and create their own Party. Rush said moderates "don't have an opinion 'til they decide where the consensus is, the majority is, and go with it."

Colin stopped beating around the bush

Rush said point blank that Powell should stop running around claiming to be a Republican who wants to reform the party. Instead, he should "close the loop and become a Democrat." The endorsement of Obama proved that he's a full-fledged liberal Democrat.

Rush's final writing on Powell's wall

Powell knows that for the rest of his political career, he will have to deal with the harsh reality of being frozen out by the conservatives. Rush clinched the argument: "The political impact of the Powell endorsement will be mostly irrelevant, but his betrayal will be forever. It's totally about race."

McCain vexed Rush

Rush was livid at John McCain's refusal to attack Obama with any substance during the 2008 election. McCain was afraid of being call a racist, so as Obama launched attacks on him, he turned the other cheek. And then McCain fell on his sword when he condemned his own people for calling out Obama's full Muslim name (Barack Hussein Obama,) which then gave room for more trashing from the Obama camp. Rush observed Palin mirroring McCain's policies and he knew the chances of McCain pulling an upset were bleak.

However, Rush's glass was half fill. As a leader he remained optimistic, so that millions of conservatives would also keep the faith that McCain was going to win the presidency. Rush called into action: "We're going to have to be the ones to secure victory for him {McCain}. We're going to drag him across the finish line and then take on the other challenges that that presents."

But after Sec. Colin Powell, Gov. William Weld and other Republicans defected to throw their support to Obama, Rush knew that the scales had been tipped. Rush resigned himself to rearranging the deckchairs on the Titanic. As an icon with 30 million audience members, Rush's glass was now half empty, and he said one week about the general election: "We're going to drag McCain across the finish line -- then we start rebuilding the conservative movement. It's going to happen whether he wins or loses, but especially if he wins too."

At this point, Rush knew an Obama victory was a foregone conclusion. He knew that McCain was not going to the Oval Office, but back to the upper chamber of Congress. What did Rush really mean by "drag McCain across the finish line"? Rush meant dragging McCain to the finish line to give his concession speech. Rush finished rearranging the deckchairs as soon as McCain was done delivering his speech. The next day after McCain's defeat and after Obama was pronounced victorious, Rush announced the rebuilding of the conservative movement. Rush also announced ridding all the Republicans that voted against McCain and those who believed the GOP had fallen into the abysmal depths of despair.

Newt Gingrich, the Greatest Republican Politician Pitched Against Rush Limbaugh, the Greatest Republican Legend

Speaker Newt Gingrich acted as a peacemaker when asked to comment on the Cheney/Limbaugh versus Powell/Moderate Republican political tug of war. CBS's Harry Smith asked Newt Gingrich: "Is there room for moderates in the Republican Party?"

Speaker Gingrich responded: "Yes. I am a -- I am a Reagan Republican. Reagan believed in very broad base, he always talked about "my fellow Republicans" and those independents and Democrats who want a better future. A third of his votes were Democrats." Harry Smith followed up: "Well, but you also have a voice of ideological purity out there that unless people kowtow to," Gingrich's second response: "You just shrug them off!" Harry Smith followed up: "So your advice to other Republicans is shrug off Rush Limbaugh?" Gingrich concluded: "My advice is that -- that Colin Powell is a great American, I'm proud that he's Republican, and, you know, Dick Cheney is a great American. I'm proud he's Republican. I'm glad both of them are Republican."

Newt Gingrich, plain as day, got caught up in the Limbaugh versus Powell crossfire, and Rush asserted that he's a conservative, not a purist.

Conservative Republicans "don't always agree with each other." Rush said Reagan got Moderates by not pretending to be like them. Rush said Powell rejected McCain and voted for Obama. Rush asked, how proud can Newt be of Powell, who strategically endorsed Obama a few days before the General Election, a move that all but ended the slim chances for McCain to win? Rush doesn't care if Powell tarried with the GOP, but for Newt to herald Powell as an ideal Republican didn't sit well with Rush. "If Colin Powell is the model for the Republican Party, there's no reason to ever vote Republican again."

Rush brought Newt to Reality

Rush Limbaugh took a brief swipe at Newt Gingrich. Rush pointed out that he didn't, like Newt, sit with Nancy Pelosi on a global warming TV ad. Rush said he didn't, like Newt, promote Hillary's healthcare plan. Rush boldly said of the 2009 House and Senate congressional campaign committees: "The bottom line is that at least half the people in that room, maybe more, wish I weren't on the radio." And these prominent Republicans wished Rush didn't say all the things he said. "And Newt is one of them."

From a GOP Lawmaker's standpoint

When asked about his take on the leading articulators of conservatism, Rush Limbaugh and Newt Gingrich, calling Sotomayor's {Obama's Supreme Court appointee) comment racist, Senator Cornyn from Texas attacked both icons: "I think it's terrible. This is not the kind of tone that any of us want to set when it comes to performing our constitutional responsibilities of advice and consent. Neither one of these, uh, men are elected Republican officials. I just don't think it's appropriate. I certainly don't endorse it. I -- I think it's wrong." Back in the day, Rush Limbaugh thoroughly fundraised and supported Cornyn's senate candidacy. Newt Gingrich was once the second in line to the presidency, but Cornyn is only a mere junior senator from Texas.

From a Pseudo-intellectual's Standpoint

EJ Dionne, a veteran columnist for the Washington Post, took that honor. He said: "If you doubt that there is a conservative inclination in the media, consider which arguments you hear regularly and which you don't. When Rush Limbaugh sneezes or Newt Gingrich tweets, their views ricochet from the Internet to cable television and into the traditional media. It is remarkable how successful they are in setting what passes for the news agenda. The power of the Limbaugh-Gingrich axis means that Obama is regularly cast as somewhere on the far left end of a truncated political spectrum."

Infighting GOP Internecine: It Goes Down to the Wire

Rush talked about the GOP Infighting between the country club blue-blood Republicans and the rock-ribbed conservatives. Rush proclaimed that a battle for the "hearts and soul" of the GOP is brewing. The conservative wing of the GOP is in a tug of war with the elite country club blue- blood Republicans.

Infighting Primary caused by Social Issues

"They're called country club or blue-blood Republican, liberal Republicans," Rush said about moderate Republicans. Rush said the country club or blue- blood Republicans are nothing but liberal Republicans. These blue bloods are not conservatives. Rush said social issues are what had caused a fracture between the blue blooded country club types and the prolife conservatives. The social issue, in this case, is abortion. The blue bloods are hell-bent on getting rid of the social issues on the Party's platform because they believe that is what is destroying the party. They believe pro-life conservative voters are the "death knell" of the Republican Party.

The political warfare within the Republican Party has been narrowed down to the Cheney/Limbaugh wing vs. the Powell/Ridge wing, with

Newt Gingrich as the chief mediator. The mediators are those who are cowards, those who don't want to be criticized, those who want their political reputation to be as clean as the wind driven snow.

Rush versus RINO Republicans

Rush's response to criticism from Senator Hagel

Hagel attacked Rush: "Every country out there has their know-nothing party. And of course we're much educated by the great entertainers like Rush Limbaugh and others. I wish those people would run for office. They have so much to contribute and so much leadership, and they have an answer for everything, and they'd be elected overwhelmingly if Rush would run for anything or any of those people. They love just to rip everybody else down and try to make fools of everybody, and they always have the answer."

Rush was unfazed by Hagel's criticism: "Senator Hagel, as I have said countless times, I will not endure the pay cut to run for office. You ought to try doing talk radio, Senator, if you think handling criticism is such a tough thing." Rush asked, what does Hagel, a Republican, expect to happen to him if he often supports the Democratic Party agenda?

Rush didn't wait for the pendulum to swing back his way. He asserted that one of Hagel's major problems as a senator weren't caused by the mean-spirited Democrats, but he's biggest problem or enemy was Rush Limbaugh. "But man, oh, man, take on the leader of the conservative movement like this" Rush uttered. Rush said never once did he rip Republican lawmakers for the fun of it. Rush said he can't make a fool of Hagel; Hagel is the one that makes a fool of himself by allying himself with the Democrats. Rush says he preaches how to improve the life of Americans.

Final words to Hagel on his way out of Congress

Rush said politicians like Hagel need to expect to be subjected to criticism if they uphold liberal agendas. "At times it was difficult to recognize you as even a Republican. What are we supposed to do here? It was certainly difficult to recognize you as a conservative." Rush dismissed Hagel's notion that the only way to make a meaningful difference is to run for political office. Rush said that as the conservative leader behind the EIB microphone, it is impossible to measure the number of criticisms he receives every day compared to those that Hagel received as a senator. Rush claimed Hagel epitomized all the past and present RINO Republicans in Congress.[12]

United States versus the rest of the World Liberty versus Tyranny

What is American exceptionalism?

Rush stated that the history of the world is tyranny, torture, totalitarianism, dictatorship and dungeons. But America is and as always been the exception. And that is what American exceptionalism is all about. Rush said the history of the world is also poverty, starvation and famine. Rush said America is the only place in all of humanity that didn't emerge from tyranny, dictatorship, etc.

Rush could not for the life of him understand why people around the world would wage an endless battle to destroy America despite the fact that America had liberated them. Rush said Americans are surrounded by people who want the absolute power to control their citizens and to limit freedom. Rush said they are in the Middle East, in Africa, in Europe, everywhere. They hate and fear America because we are their only opposition. We opposed dictatorship and tyrannical government.

Rush said the 44th American president is trying to replicate the rest of the world; he wants America to lose its individual liberty. This quest to transform America to be like the rest of the world is something that has been going on for over 50 years. It has been perpetuated by the Liberals.

American exceptionalism is what separates America from the rest of the world. After learning about American exceptionalism, is implausible that Democrats are tearing the history of this country to shreds.

Domestically, Rush said not everybody has the same ambition, ability, desire, devotion, intelligence, commitment and educational opportunity. Rush said only in oppressive and authoritarian nations are outcomes guaranteed to it citizens. Rush said the United States' "enshrined documents" is what laid the foundation for America to be an exception to dictatorship, torture and, by and large, human history.

Rush's Message to socialist third world countries' leaders

Rush said dictators and tyrants are jealous of American exceptionalism. They want what America has achieved. They don't want to free their people because they don't want to "create mini-United States in their various countries." They want to have total control over their people; they want to keep them in perpetual bondage.

Where cometh poverty?

Rush believes the end product of liberalism and socialism is poverty. Furthermore, the only antidote of poverty is capitalism.

America's unsung heroes

Rush claimed that the reason the United States has outdone the rest of the world in just about "everything that raises" the living standard is not because "our DNA is different," but because of freedom and liberty. The founding document is the key.

America liberated the world

Rush asserted that the freedom recognized by our Founders is the reason the United States is the most powerful, the wealthiest and the most industrious country ever created. The United States is the most technologically advanced and most productive county in human history. We have liberated Europe, Asia, Africa and by and large the entire world from oppression. Germany and the rest of Europe were rebuilt by America after World War II. We even rebuilt and enhanced the economy of the Imperial Japan that attacked us. The United States' objective has always been to "improve the quality of life" for people all around the world. During a natural disaster, the world turns to United States, not the United Nations, for relief efforts. Freedom is a major part of the creation of the United States. Our Creator, God, endowed us with certain inalienable rights: life, liberty and pursuit of happiness. Rush said every human being is born with a "yearning spirit," but not every human being is allowed to "exercise it." Thus, we have statist and authoritarian countries. Our Founders were able to exercise their yearning spirit and, as such, the greatest nation in the history of civilization was created. Rush said the United States is not without fault, because of our past discrimination and those who were denied certain rights and opportunities. However, denying of rights to the minorities in the past decades is water under the bridge.

Americanism in a Grave Jeopardy
President Reagan's warning

In 1961, Ronald Reagan alerted Americans about the consequences of having a socialized medicine system. He said "Behind it will come other federal programs that will invade every area of freedom as we have known it in this country until one day, as Norman Thomas said, we will awake to find that we have socialism, and if you don't do this and if I don't do it, one of these days you and I are going to spend our sunset years telling our children and our children's children what it once was like in America when men were free."

215

Rush said that although they have been "beaten back for 50 years," they never cease from trying to take over this country. The war against the destruction of America will never end. The history of mankind is socialism, communisim, statism and totalitarianism. Rush said there are thousands of Norman Thomases around today. "They call themselves progressives" because socialist and liberal are dirty words in American politics. Rush said people like Norman Thomas want to take away the freedom that distinguishes America from the rest of mankind. And in 2008, with the election of one of their own, they will try in every waking moment to snuff away our liberty. Rush said they are in the US Congress. They own all the levels of government and they will, in due time, own our individual freedom. That was the message that Regan was trying to relate.

Conclusion
Rush begged Americans to be awake and aware of stiff-necked social extremists. Rush painfully admitted: "United States of America. Home of the free, land of the brave -- but not for long." Socialism has made great inroads in America. Therefore, conservatism and capitalism have to continue to be a formidable obstacle to socialism. Rush concluded, "They've accepted it {socialism} in Europe, we've gotta learn to accept it here. We are Europeanizing ourselves right before our very eyes."

Are you American?

1-Whosoever doesn't believe that Jesus Christ is the Son of God is not American.
2- Whosoever detests Rush Limbaugh, speaks evil of him, wishes him dead and has said despicable things about Rush is not American.
3- Whosoever doesn't believe "that all men are created equal, that they are endowed by their Creator with certain unalienable Rights, that among these are Life, Liberty and the pursuit of Happiness" is not American.

4-Whosoever doesn't share the social conservative views of Sean Hannity, but would rather resort to chastising him, is not American.

5- Whosoever agrees with Rush Limbaugh that Obama's policies (socialist, appeasement, Marxist, redistributionist, nationalization, etcetera) should fail is American.

6- Whosoever has impugned and maligned US Military personnel and remarked that our brave men and women are "air-raiding villages and killing civilians," have "killed innocent civilians in cold blood," are "in the dead of night, terrorizing kids and children" and have called our troops Nazis is not American.

7-Whosover personally hates Barack Obama and wants him to end up like JFK is not American.

8- Whosoever abhors George Bush and Dick Cheney, character assassinates them, schemes evil intentions for them and calls Bush a devil is not American.

9-Whosoever is against American exceptionalism, feels that the country is "a down-right mean country and said "goddamn America" after America single-handedly liberated the world from dictatorship rule and built and transformed developing countries into first world countries is not American.

10- Whosoever wants the government to take over the private sector, the healthcare industry and wants government to turn the United States into a cradle to the grave-nanny state society is not American.

11- Whosoever believes that there is only one true God and He is the Almighty God in heaven is American.[13]

End.

CHAPTER FOUR

A Fight against Racism

Racism lives on

"Hating is a birth defect" Bryon McCane said. Racism is also a birth defect, but it can be suppressed. You can curb the feeling of racism if you're determined to do so.

In Philadelphia, Obama said this about Reverend Wright: "I can no more disown him than I can disown my white grandmother, a woman who helped raise me, a woman who sacrificed again and again for me, a woman who loves me as much as she loves anything in this world, but a woman who once confessed her fear of black men who passed her by on the street and who, on more than one occasion, has uttered racial or ethnic stereotypes that made me cringe." Rush asserted that in this matter, Obama disowned his white half. Obama "has thrown his white grandmother under the bus."

Three days later, Obama then said about his grandmother: "She is a typical white person who, if she sees somebody on the street that she doesn't know, you know, there's a reaction that's been bred into our experiences that -- that don't go away and that sometimes come out in the wrong way."

Three days after Obama's comment about Wright, Obama referred to his white grandmother as a "typical white woman," and Rush then said Obama "drove the bus backwards and ran over her, where he threw her under the bus."

A "Typical white person?" Rush said that Obama's statement proved that Obama is a black American first, and an American second therefore he is not transcendent on race. But the problem, Rush said, is opening "race wounds." Obama is trying to undo America's racial progress.

White Democrats and liberals in America are the typical white people to whom Obama was alluding. White conservative Republicans are not typical White Americans.

Obama's election victory is God's making

Before 2008, there was a belief that racial prejudice would hinder Obama or any African American from winning the White House. However, the country's blistering racial past didn't come back to haunt Obama.

God put Obama out there for His purpose and to let the world know that God is still in command. God did it to let people know that he is still on the throne and this is still God's world. But that doesn't mean that Obama is sent from God. There have always been just and unjust kings that reign in Israel and Judah.

Ratcheting up Racism

Rush on why racism won't ebb because of the first black president
Rush claimed that, being that Obama is the first black president, Al Sharpton and Rev. Jackson will level racism on any substantial criticism of Obama. Their race business will be "more prominent." Rush has

discounted the notion that electing the first black president will all but certainly end the race problem. Rush said it will only get exacerbated. In order for guilty Americans to finally get the "legacy of sin due to slavery" out of the country's system, they voted for Obama. Rush said some voted out of pure unadulterated guilt because they thought racism in America would finally end. Casting their votes for the first black president "makes them feel better." Talking about original sin, Rush said America will never be able to get rid of it.

At a tender young age, African Americans youths are predisposed to discriminate against a white person. Racial favoritism has been shown exceedingly toward African Americans, especially in the political field. They have been pampered for way too long. They trade on that fact and they cry racism, bigotry or discrimination if they sense they are being maltreated. Rush said thousands of Americans "lived in a cocoon." They have been taught by liberal politicians that they are privileged and special. They have also been taught that they are victims. Rush said because they live in a cocoon, which "protects them from the real world," they are contended with their comfort level. If you blew up their cocoon with the truth, they would get aggravated and lash out at you. Rush feels that they have been taught that the Republican Party is the Party of the white man. They have an emotional attachment to the Democratic Party.

When 21st century African American leaders make divisive and race baiting comments, when they tend to divide along racial lines, where do the African American people turn to for guidance?

The more they evoke racial utterances, the more they get discriminated against. Those who live in glass houses shouldn't throw stones. Racial discrimination can never end. It could cease or ebb, but it can never be vanish. Fighting discrimination is a spiritual battle, not a physical battle.

Rush recalled: "Jesse Jackson once said that African-Americans cannot possibly be racist because even if they are they don't have the power to implement their racism or to wield it over anybody."

Who Cares?

Kanye West said about Bush: "George Bush doesn't care about black people." West's statement is not about Bush; his statement is about the white man.

West is predominately speaking for the majority of African Americans. He's one of their spokespeople. There is that widespread mentality that whites don't care about blacks. Why should a white man care about you? Why are they so special that you whine, jeremiad, lament, complain and moan if you feel they don't care about you? All men are created equal. There is nothing special about a white man or a black man. We are all adulterated sinners, sinners of the darkest characters.

Do African Americans want God with his infinite love to care for them, or do they want a white man to care for them? God's fondness is what they should be vying for.

In September of 2009, Kanye West embarrassed and humiliated a white teenage singer for an award she received live on national TV. His disgraceful actions proved that it isn't just Bush he's irritated with. President Obama had to call Kanye West a "Jackass" for his actions.

In reverse, do African Americans care about a white man? How can they possibly have a tender heart for a white man when every time something out of the ordinary happens, it is always headlined as racism? "Therefore all things whatsoever ye would that men should do to you, do ye even so to them," Jesus Christ said. African Americans should do unto others as they want done to them.

The bible said that we are entitled to be concerned for one another. But in the real world, are we practicing what the bible preaches? Christ said love your neighbor just as you love yourself. Not a single word that God uttered will go in vain. God's words will be used to judge every human being created.

Christ said, "Thou shalt love thy neighbour as thyself,"-Matthew 22 v 39b To sum it all up, human care ends up in vain, while care from above is everlasting.

Racism on display

Radio host Don Imus uttered a radically disparaging statement about the Rutgers' woman's basketball team. Imus said: "That's some rough girls from Rutgers. Man, they got tattoos and…That's some nappy-headed hos there. I'm gonna tell you that now."

The reaction to Imus's statement was nationwide. Imus was chided for his racist remarks. He faced a flood of calls for his firing prominently from Rev. Sharpton and Jesse Jackson. Al Sharpton said about Don Imus: "I have no idea whether he is a good man or not. This is about the use of public airwaves for bigoted, racist speech." Barack Obama also weighed in: "He didn't just cross the line. He fed into some of the worst stereotypes that my two young daughters are having to deal with today in America." William Bennett, Reagan's education secretary and Bush's drug czar, also made shocking remarks: "If you wanted to reduce crime, you could, if that were your sole purpose; you could abort every black baby in this country, and your crime rate would go down," After his racial slur, there were widening calls for Bennett to lose his radio show.[1]

Prominent African Americans

Martin Luther King said: "I have a dream that my four little children will one day live in a nation where they will not be judged by the color of their skin but by the content of their character."

Quanell X and other black activists in Houston had a fit when a billboard claimed that human right leader Martin Luther King was a Republican. An overwhelming majority of African American voters, registered for the Democratic Party, motivated the organizers of the billboard to stake their claim about Martin Luther King. Kamau-Imani, the individual responsible for the billboard, said of African American voters: "Your blackness, your street cred is tied up with whether you are a Democrat or not."

"Dr. Martin Luther King Jr. would not be with the party of Newt Gingrich, he would not be with the party of Sarah Palin, he would not be with the party of Rush Limbaugh, Michael Savage or Sean Hannity," Quanell X said. Quanell X reiterated his comment: "The party of Tom DeLay, the party of Rush Limbaugh, the party of Sean Hannity would not be the party of Dr. Martin Luther King, Junior!"

These civil right activists that rallied against the billboard epitomized the same African American leaders that were reprehensible towards Sec. Condoleezza Rice and the same leaders that claimed that Barack Obama isn't the first real African American President. These leaders, starting with renowned activists like Al Sharpon and Jackson all the way to local activists like Quanell X, are nothing but segregationists and seperationists. Was Martin Luther King a Democrat or a Republican? Judging people by the "content of their character" was one of King's beliefs. Some of these activists agreed that human rights activist Martin Luther King's dream came to reality when Obama became the first black president.

Kamau-imani is on a quest for the Democratic Party to stop corralling African American voters.

Racisms in America have been catapulted by Eric Bishop (Jamie Foxx: and Rev. Al Sharpton. Foxx said about the late Michael Jackson: "No need to be sad. We want to celebrate this black man's — this black man. He belongs to us, and we shared him with everybody else. They talking about what he looks like in the media. It don't make a difference what he looked like. Am I right? It was all about what he sounded like."

Jamie Foxx's comment on Michael Jackson was meant to be divisive.

We are all Americans, all citizens of the world, but the Foxx's, and the Sharpton's of the world are hell-bent on separating people. Foxx is still on probation after he crudely mocked a white teenage pop singer on his Sirius radio show. There was clearly a racial element that led to Foxx's disparaging tirade against the singer. Foxx later issued an apology.

Feminist anger

First Lady Michelle Obama was in total agreement with Sotomayor, the country's first Hispanic Supreme Court judge. Judge Sotomayor said she felt like "a visitor landing in an alien country," after she was admitted to Princeton University. Rush juxtaposed Michelle and Sotomayor's statements. Rush stated that because of racism, he understands the chip on their shoulder and the "lingering anger" of Michelle Obama and Sotomayor. Rush said what Michelle and Sotomayor want is retribution against the white people. They want to get even. And that is why they display their anger and rage.

Michelle Obama commented on the fear that Sotomayor, then a student, felt about being a minority at Princeton University. Rush said unlike homeless minorities, Michelle and Sotomayor should "get over it." Rush said there is no reason for them to bicker over the great injustice, since they are no longer under the hush. They are at the pinnacle of power. Rush said misery, rage and anger is the liberal's happiness.

Obama is classless

Professor Gates, a preeminent African American scholar, overreacted when apprehended by a white cop. The cop wrongfully arrested Gates for breaking into his own apartment. President Obama happened to be a colleague to Gates. A reporter asked Obama for his take on the incident and whether or not race had played a part in the event. Obama immediately jumped to conclusion without knowing the facts: "I don't know, not having been there and not seeing all the facts, what role race played in that, but I think it's fair to say, number one, any of us would be pretty angry; number two, that the Cambridge Police, uh, acted stupidly in arresting somebody when there was already proof that they were in their own home."

Rush said his first reaction would be the antithesis of Gates. First and foremost, he would be thankful to the neighbor. Rush said Obama, as well as most Americans, don't know what happened at Gates' house. It wasn't a profiling incident because recently; there have been numerous break-ins in Gates' neighborhood.

Rush differentiated between a presidential reaction and a community agitator's reaction

Rush claimed that Obama's reaction was far from presidential. Rush said of the presidential response: "I know Gates, he's a friend of mine. I don't know what happened. I'm going to leave this up to the local authorities." Rush said Obama's reaction was the reaction of a community organizer who succeeded in sending a message to Americans that police officers are stupid.

Rush's message to Obama

In terms of Obama's response, this was not a matter of stooping low. This was a matter of a classless community organizer in full effect. According to Rush, Obama has a "charmed life." But he is acting like he's a victim. Rush said the fact that Obama took the question about Gates meant Obama was acting stupidly. Rush said Obama's reaction was the reaction of a community organizer. Obama's reaction was that of a street agitator. Rush said Obama's response to the Gates incident was just to distract Americans from his political setback.

Police Officer was asked to Apologize

Cop Crowley said: "What I did was right. I have nothing to apologize for. That somebody of his level of intelligence could stoop to such a level and berate me, accuse me being a racist or racial profiling and then speaking about my mother, it's just... It's beyond words. I treat everybody the same."

Rush said because Gates is friends with Obama and Oprah, that gave him the ability to hurl insults at the cop. Gates thinks being a distinguish professor at Harvard gives him special privileges and, as such, the cops should kneel down and apologize for not knowing who Gates was.

Obama's teaching moment

After his reckless comment, Obama neglected to offer even a half-hearted apology. He instead conveniently doubled down by opting to make it a teaching moment. Let's hear it from the horse's mouth. Obama himself said: "There was indisputable evidence that blacks and Hispanics were being stopped disproportionately. Uh, and that is a sign, an example of how, you know, race remains a factor in the society. That doesn't lessen the incredible progress that has been made. I am standing here as testimony to the progress that's been made, and yet the fact of the matter is that, you know, this still haunts us."

"In some ways this is every black man's nightmare and a reality for many black men," Gov. Patrick of Massachusetts said of what befell Gates.

The cop was only trying to ascertain whether Gates was the rightful occupant of the supposed break in. Professor Gates snapped on the police officer. Belligerent conduct was evident. He was being too mouthy. He went as far as calling out the cop's mother: a typical African American attitude, if you will. His racial and uncouth tone got him arrested. "Gates didn't have hate speech hurled at him," Rush concluded.

The difference between a Rice and a Powell

Rice left the Democratic Party not because she was guaranteed to work for Bush senior. She left because of her principles and values. Her innate diplomacy is not hard-line by any means. Her decision to accept counsel by her advisers not to run for president was based on the fact that she had been lambasted for much of her government career by fellow African Americans. She was a Democrat but because of her disagreements with Carter's policies, she became a Republican.

Powell is only a Republican because he was appointed by Republican presidents to different ranking cabinet positions. He failed on the diplomacy front. He has never been attacked by prominent African Americans. His true nature was telling when he showed his repugnance for and denounced any more Republican appointed Supreme Court Judges. He seems to have underlined his commitment to the Republican establishment by claiming that a new version of the party should be created. The Democratic Party loves and admires Powell. He's their favorite Republican. Democrats hate noticing African Americans belonging to the Republican Party, but Powell is the exception. Republican conservatives are still waiting for Powell to renounce his place in the party, just has Rice did when she was a Democrat. He continues to be discarded by conservatives.

Take a tour of African American schools and look at the school walls. Yes, you would see President Obama and family, yes, you would see Colin Powell, but where is Condoleezza Rice? Where is Clarence Thomas? They have been profoundly rejected by their own people. Watch out for those who have been rejected. Jesus Christ was the prime example. "And he [Jesus Christ] beheld them and said, 'What is this then that is written, the stone which the builders rejected, the same is become the head of the corner.'" {Luke 20 v 17} [2]

A Real African American for President

African Americans, excluding Africans born in America, are looking for a true African American to be the first US President, since Obama is without slave blood. Obama is a Kenyan American. Obama wasn't down for the struggle. Obama has already broken the glass ceiling and have given them hope for a similar historical event. Obama is like a Nelson Mandela born in America. Comparing Mandela to Obama would be extremely disrespectful and degrading. Mandela spent more than two decades in prison actually fighting for the freedom of his country. Even if African Americans firmly disagree with this notion that Obama is not fully one of them, another dirty little secret is that Obama is half white. So as Americans are realistically waiting the first real African "slave" American to be president, so do the Jews await the first Jew in the Oval Office. Hillary Clinton would have been the first woman in the history of the nation to be Commander-in-Chief, but we have to still congratulate big sister, the United Kingdom's Margaret Thatcher, for being the first head of any major country.

Top of the pile

Rev. Wright

He attacked Richard Cheney and then said he was open to being Vice President. If he's open to being Vice President, why can't he go up a notch and be open to the United States presidency? Is he going to run as a Democrat or a Republican? Democrats do hold grudges unlike Republicans, but Wright hasn't really agitated the Democratic Party. Most importantly, Wright served the nation. He is in that category of the McCains, the John Kerrys and the Max Clelands who faithfully served America. His unacceptable "Goddamn America" comment could be swept under the rug by the drive-by media. Although he's not a pol by any stretch of the imagination, he could also follow the steps of both Reverend Al Sharpton and Jackson.

Wright certainly wouldn't be getting Jews' votes due to his statement: "Them Jews aren't going to let him talk to me. They will not let him (Obama) to talk to someone who calls a spade what it is." After 9/11, Wright led the America bashers by proclaiming that the chickens of militarism had come home to roost.

Deval Patrick. He is the Democratic governor of the Commonwealth of Massachusetts. Patrick made history as the second ever African American to win a gubernatorial race in America since the Reconstruction, but the third ever African American to be named governor. With all of his years ahead of him, we need a seer to anticipate any impediment that would prevent Deval Patrick from being a main challenger in subsequence elections to come, especially with Obama having opened the flood gates. Patrick is also a loyal acolyte of Bill Clinton. He once worked in Clinton's administration. Patrick is busy raising taxes in the turf of the Kennedy's, but opposition will wax against him if he continues. Gov. Patrick might be a strong presidential contender in the offing.

David Paterson. The stop gap appointment governor runs around trying to bulldoze Rush Limbaugh out of the state of New York. Paterson, the handicapped Governor of New York, might use his office popularity to one day test the waters. Officially a governor but actually an acting or unelected governor of New York, as of 2009, he is concurrently serving with Deval Patrick as one of the only two governors in the United States. Past governors of New York like Nelson Rockefeller and Franklin Roosevelt used the popularity of their office to be elected Vice President and President of the country respectively. Having said that, how popular is David Paterson? He had an approval rating of 30%. Even New Yorkers were begging for the return of the politician he succeeded, the disgraced client # 9 predecessor Eliot Spitzer, to come in and bail New Yorkers out of the slipshod hands of David Paterson. Meanwhile, Paterson would even let a future presidential election race bother him. He would be pondering and hoping that popular ex-Mayor of New York City, Rudy Giuliani, doesn't run for the New York governorship in a 2010. He might toss the idea of running for president on the backburner and eventually be a coward like ex-New York governors Mario Cuomo and George Pataki. The New York state senate should have announced a special election to replace the shamed and abashed governor Spitzer, rather than granting Paterson, the lieutenant governor, the job.

Spitzer, the former depraved governor, is ready to shrugged off the minor contretemps and jump back into the political arena. Obama literally requested Gov. Paterson to resign as soon as his acting term as governor is over. In terms of Paterson running for the governor election, that decision has already been made for him.

Paterson said about Obama's request:" If you look at it from their perspective, they (Obama's administration) haven't exactly been able to govern in the first year of their administration the way other administrations have where you would theoretically have a period in which the new administration is allowed to pass some of the needed pieces of legislation. From their perspective, losing any executive seats, losing any congressional seats, losing any seats in the United States Senate is very important to them."

Paterson consulted heavily with Senator Charles Schumer to appoint Kirsten Gillibrand. Schumer warned Gov. Paterson not to appoint Caroline Kennedy to the senate. Schumer knew that, like Clinton, he won't be able to control Kennedy.

Gillibrand was appointed by Gov. Paterson to seek out the remaining term of Secretary of State Hillary Clinton.

Paterson has seen the writing on the wall. He knows his party doesn't want him to run. He knows he will be a drag for Democrats running for statewide offices. But he wants to clinch onto power with the slightest of threads. There were even rumors in the pipeline that New York Democrats had a ploy to replace troubled congressman Charles Rangel with Paterson.

Ken Blackwell

One of George Bush's henchmen, Blackwell narrowly lost the 2006 gubernatorial race in Ohio. Former Ohio State Secretary, Blackwell still holds lots of power state-wide. It's only a matter of when he will release that power of his, especially when US Senator Voinovich's hints of retirement are in the air. Blackwell, an ideal African American presidential applicant, is understood to be working with Speaker Gingrich on grassroots organizing.

Sean Combs

It was not a good way for Sean Combs to start his political career, by uttering racial profanities against John McCain and Sarah Palin during the 2008 presidential elections: "Sarah Palin scares me...She is worse than the boogeyman." Gov. Palin scares Combs? All the rugged arties that Combs had worked with in his label since the early nineties haven't scared him as much as Palin did? What about the murder of his close associate, Christopher Wallace, that didn't scare him more? Combs continued uttering racial epithets: "John McCain is bugging the f--- out." "What is the reality in Alaska?" Comb asked. "There aren't even any crack heads in Alaska. There aren't no black people in Alaska." At least the good citizens of Alaska don't have to worry about crack pipes on their kid's playground, unlike Combs' neighborhood. There are many who doubt whether Combs, a highly successful business icon, could leave his immature lifestyle and be a gentleman.

Harold Ford

A suspect in the eyes of the Democrats, Ford narrowly lost the 2006 senate race in Tennessee. Throughout the 2006 campaign, his US senate race against Coker was in a dead heat. The substantial number of early votes seemed to be breaking his way. He had to wait until the final hour before conceding the senate race to Coker. With some Democratic heavy hitters campaigning for him and some refusing to endorse the former Congressman, his loss was quite predictable. Apart from giving speeches at various occasions, he is a Fox news contributor. Ford has many years ahead of him to rectify his senatorial lost. Coker's limping victory ended Ford's hopes of being one of the youngest ever senators in American history. In early 2010, Ford was on the verge of announcing his candidacy for the US senate in the state of New York running against Gillibrand, but his decision was halted by the protestations coming from Obama, Sharpton, Schumer and Reid. Ford is poised to be a potent force for the Democrats.

Michael Steele

The Republican national Committee (RNC) chairman, Steele has experience in the executive branch. He was the former lieutenant governor of Maryland. He is another possible presidential candidate that runs around attacking Rush Limbaugh on various fronts.

Rush's "I hope he fails," and the "reverse racism," comments have given Steele room to make headlines lambasting Limbaugh. Steele also used his capacity as RNC Chairman to launch an attack on Obama: "He's young. He's cool. He's hip…he's got all the qualities America likes in a celebrity, so of course he's going to be popular…but this is not American Idol." He ran for the US senate in 2006. He won the Maryland GOP primaries, but lost the general election. It was close, but no cigar for the Maryland politician. Steele's loss, which was by the narrowest of margins, raised hope for other Republican future candidates in the state of Maryland.

Representative Jesse Jackson Jr.

Junior is a prodigy of his father. His young political career might have already been tarnished by his father. He got involved in Barack Obama's senate seat scandal. Jackson was pinned against the wall by FBI agents. He was said to be the anonymous Senate Candidate #5 in the Blagojevich probe.

J.C. Watts

Watts is a close friend to conservative leading voice Sean Hannity. Once the 4th ranking House GOP congressman, Watts was under the watchful eye of Newt Gingrich and Tom DeLay. Once he retired from Congress, he virtually disappeared from public life. Watts knows he needs to resurrect his career; he needs to raise his national profile. Watts won't be drawn on what his targets are, but he's been groomed to replace either Tom Coburn or Jim Inhofe in the US Senate representing Oklahoma. Watts is also mulling over offers by constituents to make a gubernatorial run in his state of Oklahoma.

Roland Burris

Burris, a senator in default of an elected senator, for days was denied entrance to Capitol Hill. Burris was a former Illinois Attorney General. He was appointed by the former corrupt governor of Illinois, Rod

Blagojevich, to replace President Barack Obama. The Governor was accused of trying to sell Obama's senate seat to the highest bidder. Blagojevich, against whom charges of impeachment were leveled, brought the reputation of Illinois governor's office into disrepute and said: "Please don't allow the allegations against me to taint a good and honest man (Burris)." Burris ran for governor twice but never even got the party nominee ticket. He failed on every front of his political campaigns until he got the Attorney General position. According to Rush, Chicago mayor Richard Daley is actually the dictator of Illinois. He dictates who gets prominent congressional and gubernatorial jobs in the State. Daley was totally against Burris' appointment.

He "Would take the imprudent step of appointing someone (Burris) to the United States Senate who would serve under a shadow and be plagued by questions of impropriety," the US Democratic Caucus wrote about Blagojevich. Burris thought he had reached the pinnacle of his career when he was Illinois' Attorney General, until when he was elected by the former governor to the open senate seat. Even in the eye of the storm, Blagojevich had the audacity to appoint Burris. Integrity on the side of the impeached Governor would have been lauded if a special election to take Obama's seat was scheduled. But Blagojevich was pressured by African Americans in Illinois to appoint an African American to Obama's seat.

The legally appointed US Senator was initially rejected. He spoke of the situation: "We were not allowed to proceed to the (senate) floor for purposes of taking oath. We will consider our options." The Democratic senate leadership finally agreed to swear Burris in for the sole purpose of being the only African American in the senate. Burris, because of all the roadblocks that he went through, released a statement that he won't be running for his senate seat reelection, thereby assuming a lame duck position. Senator Burris went down in history as the fourth ever African American senator after the Reconstruction.

Reverend Jesse Jackson

He came decently close to winning his party's nomination for President in the 1988 elections. He posed more of a threat to Walker Bush than Michael Dukakis, who eventually got the nod over Jackson. Rev. Jackson is a civil rights activist by his own standard, though he takes the job in a moonlighting way. Jackson is a role model to thousands of African Americans.

Alan Keyes

He actually ran for President in the 2008 presidential elections, but without a legion of Republican heavyweight endorsements he was completely anonymous. There is a faint chance of that happening in 2012, especially since he got arrested for protesting Obama's commencement speech. Keyes, a political veteran, unsuccessfully ran against Obama in 2004 for a US senate seat in the state of Illinois.

Reverend Al Sharpton

What qualifies an individual to be named a Reverend? If it's a certain Al Sharpton, modifying the definition of Reverend would be healthy. Al Sharpton already knows what it means to run for the presidency. In 2004, he tried to achieve what his fellow Reverend Jackson couldn't accomplish in 1988, but he was way off the mark. Sharpton is the country's most forceful and foremost civil rights leader since Martin Luther King, Jr. The firebrand activist had once been on the IRS and the FBI radar for some personal dealings during his 2004 presidential run.

Colin Powell

Powell has been pleaded to stay over at the Democratic Party by conservative Republican heavyweights. Of course, Powell is itching to come back to the GOP after endorsing Obama over McCain. The Republican hierarchy might forgive him, but it will never be the same. Suspicions would always surround the US 65th State Secretary.

Powell is no doubt the most popular African American Republican figure in America. He might have double-crossed the GOP, but his influence on the party hasn't been stifled.

A potential presidential run might have to wait until Obama is out of office in 2012 or 2016. The diminution of Powell's profile wouldn't come from the Republican establishment, of which he is a major part. It would come from conservative Republicans, which he betrayed with pride.

Jim Clyburn

Jim Clyburn is the House Democratic Majority Whip and the fourth most powerful lawmaker in the US House of Representatives. During the 2008 presidential campaigns, Clyburn was trying to decipher between Hillary Clinton and Barack Obama. He stayed uncommitted until a friendly agreement was reached. And what transpired? Clyburn's daughter was elected for a top cabinet position in Obama's administration. That was nothing but a show of undiluted political cronyism by Obama to the Clyburns. As a superdelegate, his endorsement of Obama finally capitulated Hillary's presidential campaign. Not only was he able to sway delegates from his district to Obama, but because of his popularity in South Carolina, Congressman Clyburn was able to influence delegates from other districts in the State

Clyburn, the third ranking Democrats in the House and only the second African American to hold that prestigious position, is extremely popular in South Carolina. South Carolina plays an important role in the presidential election primaries.

John Lewis

John Lewis is a ranking Democratic US House member. Martin Luther King Jr. would have wished Rep. Lewis to be America's first black president instead of Obama, whose real country of birth is still being debated. Lewis was prominently present during King's "I have a dream" Washington March speech.

His activities and his longevity for the Civil Rights movement established Lewis to be the most prominent African American politician in the state of Georgia and a highly influential United States Congressman. Lewis was the second African American to represent Congress in Georgia since the Reconstruction.

When Obama announced his candidacy for the presidency, he was presenting to the American voters a resume enhancement with no chance of winning his party's nomination. But after the Iowa primary, his resume really got enhanced. Therefore, future African American Presidential hopefuls could learn from Obama.

Secretary Rice and Supreme Court Justice Clarence Thomson are excluded in this profiling.[3]

Political Timeline

Republicans in America are sheepishly viewed by the majority of Americans as white racists. In the sixties, the passage of the most sweeping Civil Rights Act for all Americans was only made possible by the Republican leadership, amid opposition from the opposing party.

How many African American State secretaries, Treasury secretaries, Defense secretaries, Attorney Generals and Supreme Court Judges did the last two Democratic presidents Jimmy Carter and Bill Clinton's administration appointed? None, zero, nada.

On the other hand, Republican President Walker Bush, (Bush 41) nominated and appointed Clarence Thomas as the second African American US Supreme Court Judge in the history of the country.

Richard Cheney, then Secretary of Defense under Walker Bush, was responsible for the appointment of Colin Powell as the Joint Chief of Staff Commander. By the way, the Joint Chief of Staff Chairmanship position is the highest ranking military officer position in United States.

Vice President Richard Cheney and President George Bush (Bush 43) pushed for the appointment of Colin Powell as the first minority to be appointed Secretary of State. By the way, the office of the Secretary of State is the highest ranking cabinet position in the executive branch or fourth in line to the presidency. Even Ronald Reagan was involved. Back in the eighties, he promoted Powell to a four star general. And Walker Bush then put the icing on Powell's cake by promoting him to a full five star general.

To decapitate this argument, Dr. Rice was first appointed to a top national security position before Rice was the first minority female to be elected as the Secretary of State under Republican president George Bush. To add insult to injury for the Democrats, Alberto Gonzalez was the first Hispanic to be appointed as the Attorney General in the Bush administration. He too is a minority.

To summarize this argument, Jimmy Carter and Bill Clinton intentionally overlooked an African American to be appointed to a high ranking position in their cabinet or in the highest court of the land. In their eyes, no African Americans were qualified. But Reagan, Bush 41 and Bush 43 recognized the substance that Powell, Thomas and Rice could bring to the table and that they could make America a better and racially free nation.

How much more proof is needed? Conservatives/Republicans are not racists. Liberals and Democrats are purveyors of racism. They are all in disguise. They are all playing masquerading politics. What they say in public is not what they say in private. For crying out loud, Obama proved that when he went to San Francisco. Because there were no media outlets allowed when he has giving a speech to his rich associates, he said: "Bitter people in Pennsylvania clinging to their guns and religion with antipathy towards those who are not like them" (Those who are not like his elite supporters).

"Just words just speeches" Obama regurgitated. Just word just speeches.

Judging through votes

The 2008 election results read:
Only about 55% of whites voted for McCain, but 95% African American voted for Obama, McCain's 21% haul of the Jews' vote was out-beaten by a wide margin of 78% of the votes for Obama.

The exit polls showed that 95% of African Americans voted for Obama, but less than 95% of white Americans voted for McCain. Who are the real racists, African Americans or white Americans? Only 55% of white Americans voted for the Republican nominee. Yet African Americans complained about being discriminated upon. Race was the major factor in the 2008 presidential election. The trend can't lie.

Rush said: "The Democrats have been mired in race for decades. Liberalism is perverted."

Liberal Democrats are the biggest racists in America because to them it's all about race. But for the Conservative Republicans, it's all about principles. Conservatism deplores racial discrimination and divisive statements. Liberalism is the opposite. The majority of liberals are the real racists in America.

Colin: Bush/Cheney not racist

Colin Powell confessed: "Never in the two years I worked with Ronald Reagan and George Bush did I detect the slightest trace of racial prejudice in their behavior. They led a party, however, whose principal message to black Americans seemed to be lift yourself up by your bootstraps. Some did not have boots, which is why they couldn't pull themselves up by bootstraps. I wish that Reagan and Bush had shown more sensitivity on this point."[4]

Racial Struggles

With all the historical struggles African Americans have gone through, Obama's presidential victory is probably one of the signs of Armageddon. The apocalypse is beckoning. We are living in the last days. Anthony Henderson said: "The last days are almost over."

African American should quit blaming the White man for all their years of struggle and discrimination.

Christ didn't convert all the Pharisees, scribes, elders and chief priests to believe in Him, to believe that He was the Son of God. He had the power but he didn't, because not everything is meant to happen. Racism, discrimination and bigotry between various races around the world will continue: it can never be completely stifled. It's all been in God's design since Lucifer, the Devil, fought for his own Kingdom. No man, soul or what have you can ever end discrimination. It's a part of human life that has been going on from generation to generation. African Americans should quit lamenting and finally put to rest the notion that one day the racism that they face will end.

Rush's message for African Americans

This notion that an Obama presidency will cease the struggles African Americans are going through is a complete myth. African Americans will continue to be the downtrodden racial minority group in America with or without a black man ruling the country. It's only the hand of God that can change that.

The struggles continue, especially amid the joy of having a black president. Rush asked, in terms of change in "economic circumstance," what difference does it make to have a black president, when black senators, governors and mayors had all been elected? Rush said as long as the less privileged minorities keep placing their hopes on Obama to improve their well-being, they will end up like those of Obama's relatives who are living in slums and huts.

Rush's personal true story

Rush recalled being relieved of his duties: "I've been fired seven times. I've been told "you can't" I can't tell you how many times, "Forget it, if you go through the rest of your life trying to show those people that they were wrong, you're never going to be happy because they're never going to admit it and you'll never know how they really feel." And that advice was some of the best advice I ever got." To paraphrase what Anthony Henderson said, "Armageddon will prove that struggling is not a legend."

Slavery

Slavery occurred all across the seven continents, but predominately in Africa. The concentration camps and the extermination camps that faithfully led to the holocaust were also a part of slavery. More than Six million Jews were killed. No white American alive in this 21st century ever harbored slaves in our country. All the slave masters are dead and gone. Their original injustice can't be punished. President Lincoln, a Republican, initially abolished slavery in the 19th century.

If the days of slavery were happening in the 21st century, Americans would be totally against it. It would be completely outlawed.

African Americans have come a long way. Israelites, after 40 years at the wilderness, came a long way. The revolutionary war to create this great county (USA) helped the founders come a long way. Human beings in general have all come a long way.

War against slavery

In the wake of dispatching 30, 000 American troops to Afghanistan, Obama, while accepting his Nobel Peace Prize, said: "No matter how justified, war promises human tragedy." Rush dissected Obama's claim: "Morally correct just wars end human tragedy." Rush said the United States is the only county to go to war against itself for the purpose of ending slavery. Rush said that war, the Civil war specifically, sought to end human tragedy. It was a just war. Ending slavery is a just reason to embark on a war. Rush said that is what Obama doesn't understand, but he should at least appreciate the fact that blood was sacrificed to outlaw slavery. Obama said "No matter how justified, war promises human tragedy." Rush then said "Just wars end human tragedy. For a country like the United States, that's why wars are fought, to liberate people."

In America, the State run Democratic media keeps bringing back the days of slavery just to poison African Americans minds once a major election is on the horizon. But it was certain chiefs and leaders in these poor African countries, during Colonialism and Imperialism, selling their own people to the White Europeans that eventually led to their independence. We all have to sacrifice. Africans sacrificed their own brothers and sisters for their country's independence.

Christ said: "And why beholdest thou the mole that is in thy brother's eye, but considerest not the beam that is in thine own eye? Or how wilt thou say to thy brother, let me pull out the mote out of thine eye; and behold, a beam is in thine own eye? Thou hypocrite, first cast out the beam out of thine own eye; and then shalt thou see clearly to cast out the mole out of thy brother's eye," Matthew 7 verses 3, 4 and 5.

Millions of Americans fought for the freedom of our country. They sacrificed their lives for this great country during the 1775 Revolutionary War (American War of Independence.) Human beings have always had to sacrifice in one way or another. World War 1 and World War 2 were also a part of this sacrificial notion. Personally, we don't have to sacrifice for the forgiveness of our sins: Jesus Christ was the last sacrifice.

Democrats used the history of Slavery to bash America

Rush feels the "never-ending guilt over slavery" is one of the left's characteristics and traits. They believe America hasn't done enough to expunge the slavery days in our history.

Discrimination

Apart from as clear as a bell racial discrimination that exists between blacks and whites, there is discrimination between African Americans and Africans. There is discrimination between the Jews and the Middle East. There is discrimination between Eastern Europe and Western Europe. There is discrimination among the various Hispanic countries. The comparisons are endless. And it goes deeper that just minorities verse majorities.

Igniting Racism

"You've got conservatives whites here, and I think there are some whites who are probably not ready to vote for an African-American candidate." Ed Rendell, Democratic governor of Pennsylvania, opined.

Former Democratic Congressman Murtha, who once maligned and impugned the character of our Marines, said: "There's still folks that have a problem voting for somebody 'cause they're black. This whole area years ago was -- was really redneck, particularly older people. They're hesitant, they want change but they don't want to see things go too far."

Obama's message to people of color

Obama declaimed: "Make no mistake, the pain of discrimination is still felt in America by African-American women paid less for doing the same work as colleagues of a different color and a different gender; by La-tin-os made to feel unwelcome in their own country; by Muslim Americans viewed with suspicion simply because they kneel down to pray to their god; by gay dead brothers and sisters still taunted, still attacked, still denied their rights."

"This is the original litmus test. This is the original list of sins." Rush believes Obama's message was meant to divide along racial lines and to stoke hatred among Americans.

An exasperated but concerned Obama pleaded: "If you're African-American the odds of growing up amid crime and gangs are high. Yes, if you live in a poor neighborhood you will face challenges that somebody in a wealthy suburb does not have to face. But that's not a reason to get bad grades. That's not a reason to cut class. That's not a reason to give up on education and drop out of school. No one has written your destiny for you. Your destiny is in your hands, you cannot forget that, that's why we have to teach all of our children! No excuses! No excuses."

Lifetime of apologies

Because of slavery, African Americans feel entitled to a
lifetime of apologies

African American leaders don't want bygones to be bygones. They don't
want to forgive and forget, even though none of them, from Sharpton
down, were born during the days of slavery.

Rush recalled what Jackson said: "Minorities are entitled to have racist
views in our country according to the Reverend Jackson because they
don't have any power. They don't have the power to implement their
racism." Slavery can't be rectified, it can only be outlawed. The original
perpetrators and culprits were not brought to justice, but the Republican
Party fought to end slavery. Lincoln abolished slavery. He was the
first Republican president. Sharpton and co. want compensation. They
want to be compensated forever. The days of slavery are long gone. The
pains and struggles that African Americans went through for years is
history. It's all water under the bridge. And that history of the days of
slavery can't repeat itself. Just as God repented himself from destroying
mankind with flood and the compromise was the rainbow. Let bygones
be bygones, let the hatchet be buried. But Al Shaprton, Jackson and
Harry Reid won let it happen.[5]

Depressed Minorities and Majorities
under the Democratic Party's Canopy

Since the 1960's, Democrats have been able to hog African American's
votes. Democrats will do anything to get votes. One of their ads coming
from the Missouri state Democratic Party read: "When you {minorities}
don't vote, you let another church explode. When you don't vote, you
allow another cross to burn. When you don't vote, you let another

245

assault wound a brother or sister. When you don't vote, you let the Republicans continue to cut school lunches and Head Start." The ads were aimed at tarnishing the Republican Party.

Result of being brainwashed by Democrats

Rush wondered why an overwhelming majority of African Americans have failed despite the vast prosperity that surrounds them. Rush said the educational opportunity is there, as is the opportunity to be prosperous, yet they are not seizing that opportunity. And those that have been highly successful, Shelby Steel, Clarence Thomas, Thomas Sowell and Condoleezza Rice, have been attacked by the Liberals and by their African American people. Rush said "it was almost as though the Democratic Party was content" with a vast majority of the African American population being angry, restless and agitated, as long as the Democratic Party could say that it was the Republican Party that put them in that state of mind.

African Americans have continued to be window dressed by elected Democratic politician for years. Liberal politicians espoused their views on the need for a complete overhaul on living conditions. Liberal politicians longed for waifs and for the homeless. They longed for their votes, and they longed to make them wards of the state. Making the less fortunate wards of the state meant voting for the Democratic Party.

African Americans are easily susceptible to the flawed Democratic policies. The homeless waifs become impressionable to the things they hear from the Democrats.

African Americans have been brainwashed and indoctrinated to liberalism. Rush said: "And it is the poor who habitually elect liberal democrats, yet they remain poor."

Rush asked, what has the Democratic Party substantively done for African Americans? Since the 1960's, before the Civil rights was enacted, they still gripe about the same old problems. They have been told by Democrats that the Republican Party hinders their progress. They have also been told that the Republican Party is a party of bigots, sexists, racists and homophobes, so as to get them to vote Democrats. But all the promises by the Democrats haven't come to fruition. Rush said definitely things have changed for Obama and his family, but what about the poor African American folks?

The Democratic Party, since the 1960's, lived to delude African Americans voters. They took advantage of MLK's impact and President Johnson's passage of the civil rights act. Why are liberals disgusted about an African American being a Republican voter? Two prime examples are the smearing of Supreme Court Judge, Clarence Thomas, and the smearing of the 66th Secretary of States, Condoleezza Rice, by Democratic congressional leaders and by prominent African Americans.

African American Anger: No end in sight

According to Rush, African Americans are "taught to be enraged" at the United States. They are taught to hate the United States because of slavery and discrimination. They are taught that discrimination will keep them at the bottom of the ladder.

You have Al Gore, Rush's archrival, of the Democratic Party misleading blacks into believing that Republicans are racist. "The Republicans know theirs is the wrong agenda for African Americans. They don't even want to count you in the Census," Al Gore said.

Look to yourself, don't look to Politicians

In precise words, Rush said African Americans should stop placing their hopes on the black leaders in government to improve their living conditions; instead they should look at themselves for improvement. Rush said that after 50 years, things are still miserable in the African American community. They were given affirmative action, but things haven't dramatically changed for the better.

The whole Democratic Party is a black-on black crime. Before Obama became president, Bill Clinton was regarded and accepted as the first black president. But once Obama assumed office as president, Clyburn and other African American leaders have abjured their praise of Bill Clinton.

You have the Congressional Black Caucus and the Congressional Hispanic Caucus, but you don't have Congressional White Caucus. Why do we have to segregate? Aren't we all Americans?

The Democratic Party views African Americans as inferior

The Democratic Party preys on low income earners, the homeless and blue collar workers. They prey on largely the minorities. The Democratic Party views black Americans "as inferior, incapable of success without the help of the Democrat Party." Without the government's help in the form of programs like "affirmative action." Rush said Liberals think that average Americans are incompetent. But with African Americans, the Democratic Party doesn't only think they are incompetent, they feel sympathy for African Americans because of slavery.

Reparation: The return of wealth to its rightful owners

In precise words, Rush said African American leaders want reparations and, as such, Obama's economic agenda, which included Obama's stimulus plan, constitutes reparations. The redistribution of wealth, taking from the rich and giving to the poor, also constitutes reparations.

Various Conclusions

To Americans

An African American United States president was a masterstroke for the African American community in America and in the world. With that said, after twenty- one months of inept leadership, one can conclude that Obama will be the first and only African American president unless a true African American conservative gears up and emerges, and there seems not to be a Condoleezza Rice on the horizon. Due to Obama's inability to govern at the highest level, questions will no longer be asked as to whether an African American or person of color can lead effectively.

To African American politicians

In all sincerity, a failed first term or second term of the Obama presidency will destroy the hopes of other potential African American who will wish to run for the office of the presidency. The "typical white" Democrats that voted for Obama would be reluctant to support another African American hopeful for president.

To the President's supporters

The majority of the poor Obama voters won't even have a pot to piss in by the time Obama's administration comes to an end.

To the African American community

African Americans should remember that racial bygones can never truly be bygones.[6]

Freedom Activist vs. Reparation/ accountability Activist

Post racial and post divisive activists like Rush and Sean are waging a blood, sweat and tears fight to make their country a decently colorblind nation so that other countries will follow. But antagonists like Jackson and Al Sharpton don't want a colorblind America. They have imprinted on African Americans' mind that the days of slavery still live with us – even though we finally elected a black president.

Because of slavery, in longevity, Jackson and co. have been looking for reparations and accountability from the white man. Meanwhile, Rush and Sean are trying to suppress the racial divide between Black and White. They are advocating racial harmony.

Since white people were involved in slavery, the ball is in their court to etch to the African Americans that America is not the America of the 1600's. Rush, an activist for privacy and freedom, has to prove again and again that the days of slavery are way behind us.

God doesn't look at people's skin color. God looks at our hearts. If slavery was the worst event that ever befell America, Rush Limbaugh is the best thing that God has given America.

Rush claimed that Democrats and Liberals believe racism is a "part of our heritage;" so they will continue to portray America as an inherently racist nation.

The Republican Party is the colorblind party. Rush Limbaugh has been fighting for America to be a colorblind society. Reverend Jackson and co. have been trying to undermine his efforts in exchange for fame and money. Sharpton, Van Jones, etcetera want African Americans to continue to be the oppressed minority in this country. They want them to be targeted.

Conclusion

Doing away with racial profiling and racial stereotyping is not on Sharpton's menu. They can't wrap their minds around the notion that America's racist past is history. Rush and Sean preach a post-racial America, while Jackson and Al Shapton preach the antithesis, thus making it difficult to improve racial relations.

Rush vs. the NFL

Congressman King stood up for Rush and demanded the NFL to explain why they opposed Rush's bid

The concerted effort by the media to impugn Rush was shown when fictional quotes were hurled at Rush. Rush was accused of uttering nine racially divisive quotes. Of all the quotes, it turned out that eight were fabricated quotes. Only one of the nine quotes (a quote directed to the sports media's extolled McNabb.) was uttered by Rush. It was almost a perfect script to finally destroy Rush, if only the quotes were genuine.

Rush Limbaugh's 2003 quote about quarterback Donovan McNabb. Rush said: "overrated ... what we have here is a little social concern in the NFL. The media has been very desirous that a black quarterback can do well—black coaches and black quarterbacks doing well. There's a little hope invested in McNabb, and he got a lot of credit for the performance of his team that he didn't deserve. The defense carried this team."

NFL commissioner Roger Goodell faced the US Congress

Because of the NFL's refusal to grant Rush's bid to buy the St. Louis Rams, Representative King wanted to know the qualifications needed to be an NFL team owner. The NFL deemed Rush's remarks unacceptable, thereby disqualifying Rush to participate in the purchase of the Rams. The Congressman flooded Goodell with questions.

Rep. King censured Goodell on the House Floor. He talked about the nine quotes: "And, by the way, of those, eight are complete fabrications. They're not based on anything. They're not a misquote. They're not a distortion. They're complete fabrication. And the one that remains stands true and shines the light against the media, not against Rush Limbaugh. And so if you're concerned about this, Mr. Goodell, then I'd ask you, you know, are you prepared to level the same charges against

Fergie and J.Lo, {Dolphins owners, who had made divisive statements }or are you prepared to apologize to Rush Limbaugh today?"

Rush was stunned to hear a Congressman standing up for him: "How about that? I mean that just doesn't happen to me. That just doesn't happen to me. And I had no idea this was going to happen. I'm just overwhelmed by it."

Roger Goodell said Rush's comments were "polarizing comments," but the NFL chairman refused to reveal whether he took into account all the eight fabricated quotes. Roger continued to prevaricate about the reason Rush was dropped. Congressman King continued inquiring: "Mr. Goodell, were you considering those other eight quotes that I referenced when you made your statement or were you considering the one that is true, (Rush 's quote on McNabb)the one that I've read to you and the one that doesn't shine a negative light on Rush Limbaugh but upon the media?"

After much interrogation, King concluded that there was only so much Goodell could take

Rep. Steven King from Iowa said: "I'll just close with this. Here are Rush Limbaugh's -- his position, and after 20 years on the radio, there's nothing there that would undermine this. He says, "My racial views? You mean, my belief in a colorblind society where every individual is treated as a precious human being without regard to his race?" And I'll close with that, Mr. Goodell, and I'd ask you to go back and take a look at the owners of the Dolphins and the language that's in the public venue, the songs that they recorded, review those lyrics and I'll provide some of those lyrics to you and I'll ask you to come back and respond to that question after the hearing as to whether you'll put the same scrutiny on those owners who have really signed a negative light on the NFL as opposed to somebody (Rush) that the NFL apparently just doesn't agree with his politics. I yield back."

The NFL vs. Rush: The Aftermath

The NFL is 75% African American, so it was only fitting to see Al Sharpton and Jesse Jackson leading the charge against Rush's St. Louis Rams bid. Rush was mystified by the extent the liberals would go in destroying his career. Rush addressed the tide of leftist opportunists that were out to denigrate him. He stated that the attacks on him are not actually about him, nor are they about the NFL or the St. Louis Rams. The attacks are about destroying conservatism. It's about the liberal media's quest to subdue prominent conservatives. Rush said it's about jeopardizing the future of America. The "august characters" of Reverends Al Sharpton and Jesse Jackson happened to spearhead the smear on Rush. Rush said the smear is "characterized by mischaracterization and lies." At the beginning of this smear, Rush said Sharpton wasn't involved, but as things got interesting, Sharpton perceived the benefits of chiefly involving himself in the smearing of Rush. Jackson followed suit and became prominent in the scam.

The media empowered Al Sharpton. He said this about Rush: "I think that he sells racial kind of, uh, statements. Whether in his heart he means it or not is really immaterial. You cannot sell that in the daytime and then go to the conference table later and go against what you sold as your personality. He has to be the same person." In response, Rush said Sharpton is known for running hoaxes to destroy people's lives. The only credibility left for the likes of Sharpton comes from the liberal media. In disguise, Liberals are about sympathizing with the poor and less privileged minorities, and Sharpton and Jackson are their major representatives. Rush said if he is a racist, as he's been portrayed to be, how come he wants to make African Americans millionaires? How come he wants to be involved in a business that is 70% African American?

Senator John McCain was asked to weigh in on the sheer double standard that the NFL exhibited toward Rush Limbaugh. Senator

McCain responded: "First of all, let me make it clear Rush Limbaugh never supported me, in fact was very critical of my efforts to secure the nomination of my party, so it's not as if -- I think I'm speaking objectively. I think it was wrong to exclude him from an ability to engage in the free enterprise system. I think that he had every right to make an investment and I don't think it was fair to keep him from -- put this kind of pressure on him because of his political views."

The Arizonian statesman didn't let his philosophical disagreement with Rush Limbaugh take precedence over the truth of the matter.

The Media's Waterloo

Rush's case with the NFL was further proof that the media live a lie. Rush said: "It's gotten to the point now if they can't do the hit piece with real quotes, they'll make 'em up or they'll report made-up quotes."

Scum smearing Rush

The media used slanderous, fabricated quotes to condemn Rush's bid. Rush believes the orchestrators of the smear campaign against him began with leftwing sportswriters. When the scam grew in leaps and bounds, the Democratic media got involved. The fabricated quotes that were attributed to Rush got repeated without "any fact-checking" by the orchestrators of the smear. Rush never uttered any of the reported quotes.

The liberal newscasters that reported these bizarre quotes fell all over themselves at the accusation that they didn't even bother checking the validation of the quotes. Rush noted that those who repeated the quotes did so to enhance their "prejudice and bigotry" agenda against him. Rush said this is not about race and it is not about a white prominent American buying an NFL's team. It is about ideology. It's about discrediting conservatism. Rush said: "The idea that somebody could reportedly say, {one of the fabricated quotes} 'Hey, slavery was great! You know what? Why, it kept the streets safer at night,' in 1998 and it is only now (2009) surfacing?" Rush said how can such a quote of that magnitude sit dormant for a decade and neither Bill Clinton nor Obama never use it against him?

The NFL's double standard

Rush noted: "We've got a guy, Snoop Dogg, a rap sheet longer than my leg, who's just been hired to do promo commercials for the NFL pregame show on ESPN. Yet I, El Rushbo, divisive, uncivil, coarsening American politics. I'm thinking I better go out and commit some crimes and do some time, and then the NFL will have me and maybe the Democrat Party as well."

Final notes

The deliberate attempt to stain, vilify and destroy Rush's reputation was unsuccessful. Rush said he loves the NFL and he is probably the "biggest nonpaid promoter" of the NFL. Rush said: "the hatred that I am able to mirror" for America to witness is evidence of the hatred against conservatism. Rush said he is more sad for America than about what the NFL did to him.[7]

Wards of the state

Power in perpetuity for Democratic Lawmakers

The Democratic Party is solely responsible for destroying African Americans' families. According to Rush, there is a strong "emotional connection" between the Democratic Party and African Americans. African Americans are immensely attached to the Democratic Party. Rush said for 50 years, the Democratic Party and Liberals have destroyed the black family.

Liberal programs

Rush asserted that trillions of dollars has been spent on programs like the Great Society over the last thirty years to solve the problems African American were facing. However, Rush noted, the problems haven't been solved. Rush said the involvement by the federal government "in the massive welfare state" has been detrimental to minorities' families because the federal government has taken over the role of the father. "The father no longer had to hang around because the government was there every week or month or however often the checks come."

One's party ascension to power

Rush always believed that the New Deal and Social Security enacted by Democratic president Franklin Delano Roosevelt was created to "establish the Democratic Party" as the Party of the disadvantaged, the Party of the have-nots, thereby making them wards of the state. In return, these liberal politicians get their votes during election time. Rush feels that by making them wards of the state, the Democratic Party has obstructed and suppressed minorities from "realizing their dreams." Rush said by making them wards of the state, they "owe their existence" to the Democratic Party.

Trillions of dollars treated like Monopoly money

An obscene amount of money has been spent on liberal oriented programs. Rush said anger, hopelessness and rage still percolate, despite the fact that trillions of dollars have been spent to salvage minority groups. Rush said they are still waiting for a mascot, a savior to finally solve the problems that have stemmed for many decades. Rush said: "There is no right way to do what" President Franklin Roosevelt did for the black family.

From millions to billions to trillions of dollars as far as the eye can see have been spent in the name of welfare programs by the Democrats to lock up African Americans votes.

Perpetual Power New Deal 2: FDR started, LBJ guided and Obama is to finish

Water is what the deer pants for. Power is what the Democrats yearn for. Power is the birthright for Democrats. Rush talked about a major repair project that is underway at the federal level. Obama is not fixing the US economy. Rather, he is fixing the Democratic Party. Rush said FDR's uninterrupted 16 years rule firmly solidified the Democratic Party as the majority party in America. But the stronghold was cracked by Nixon and broken by Reagan. In the legislative branch of government, the 1994 Republican revolution broke the Democratic Party's stronghold on power. Obama's Stimulus bill and healthcare bill are both oriented towards creating a second FDR and a second New Deal. By and large, Obama's bills represent an attempt to enhance the Democratic Party "so that it once again is restored to its rightful position of power by birthright for as far as the eye can see."

Rush stated that the US economy that is being broken has not been repaired. The economy has been ignored. The first thing for Obama and Democrats to fix is the Democratic Party that was dealt a blow by the eight years of the Reagan administration in the 1980's. And in 1993, after 40 years of Democratic House control, Newt Gingrich led House takeover. This also dealt a blow to the Democratic Party in Congress. Therefore, Obama wants to set up 50 more years of uninterrupted Democratic power.

It seems this generation of liberals, till hell freezes over, won't give up trying to control American's lives. Rush said Obama's healthcare bill is to entrenched Democrats power in Congress.

The obfuscation on health care continued, and Rush explained the scheme drawn out by the Democrats. Rush claimed that FDR and LBJ back-loaded the tax increases and front-loaded the benefits when Social Security, Great Society and the war on poverty were enacted. "So you got the goodies with apparently not having to pay for it." But Rush said Obama and the Reid led Democratic Party have run contrary to what FDR and LBJ did. The healthcare bill was front-loaded with taxes and the benefits were back-loaded. With their plan, the bill appeared to be "fiscally prudent."

Rush said the reason why the Obama/Reid plan is contrary to what the FDR/LBJ plan was is that there are no benefits absolutely. There only thing waiting for Americans in four years' time is government control of the American peoples' lives. And Rush said if these Democrats should implement their plan in 2009, no Democratic lawmakers in Congress running for reelection in 2010 will be reelected. Therefore, they will have to wait until 2012, after perhaps Obama has won reelection, before it's finally implemented. Rush said their idea is about perpetual power for the Democratic Party and about marshaling and ruling the American people's lives.

In conclusion, Rush said, the American left has "screwed up the Great Society" and the "War on Poverty." They have spent trillions of dollars, yet poverty hasn't been eradicated. "Poverty has won! It's time to declare a winner. "

The Democratic Party Destabilizes the African American Community

The primary agenda of the Democratic Party is to create wards of the state, those that will vote them (politicians) back into office. The Democratic Party will continue corralling African American votes. They will never give up the ghost.

The results of the New Deal caused gang violence. African Americans are heavily involved in street gangs. African Americans make up the majority of the infamous Crips and Bloods. These dangerous street gangs are involved in robberies, drug dealings and other atrocious crimes. African Americans have high drug addiction rates. African Americans make up the highest population of homeless Americans.

African Americans have record high percentages of children out of wedlock, teenage pregnancy and high school/college dropouts, all because of the Democratic Party. It's a black-on-black crime. Who occupies the vacuum in prisons/jails? African Americans have the highest rate of incarceration, despite being the minority. They have the highest criminal recidivism rate.

The Democratic Party sponsors African Americans with food stamps, welfare, Medicare, etcetera, in exchange for their votes. The healthcare bill is a stepping stone for the Democratic Party to take control of American's lives. They have already succeeded in taking over the responsibility of fathering the African American households. Taking over the role of parenting the African American community is a microcosm of what will befall America if this unmitigated disaster of a healthcare bill is passed.[8]

Programmed

Summarizing Sean's reaction to the worshipping of a man
The way Americans idolize any human being is wrong. Many disagree with the critics that wrote off Michael Jackson as a pedophile or a child molester. But he wasn't found guilty of the charges, so according to the Man's law, he wasn't a pedophile. There were lots of weird questionable behaviors about him. At times he was unrecognizable, especially with all of his reconstructive surgeries. While many live in the bubble of Michael Jackson mania as a king, many also concluded that his life was a tragedy.

Sean's partial take on Jackson
The overwhelming postmortem criticisms about Michael Jackson were both just and unjust. What went so radically wrong with him? Everybody put him on such a pedestal. Human beings are not meant to worship other human beings. There were broad spectrums of people that admire Michael Jackson. You can admit their talents, but idolizing and worshiping a human being is wrong.

Politics on Michael Jackson
In the political world, the media believes that Obama has transcended race. In the sports world, Eldrick Tont "Tiger: Woods has transcended race. In the world of Hollywood, Will Smith, is also in that category. In the music world, the late Michael Jackson was also in that category. Rush puts politics on Michael Jackson. Rush feels that Michael Jackson's biggest success paralleled the success America had under President Ronald Reagan. Rush talked about the 1980's hit singles "Billie Jean and Thriller" being the height of Jackson's success. Rush asserted that that "level of success," may never be surpassed in this generation. Rush said Jackson flourished in the Reagan era. He languished in both the Clinton and the Bush eras. "And sadly, Michael Jackson died" in the era of the first African American president.

Rush claimed that Jackson wasn't a member of a group. But he took weirdness to another degree. "Michael Jackson epitomized the individual."

The euphoric supporters who placed hope and trust in Obama
Obama's euphoric supporters are banking on Obama providing a free roof over their heads, brimming their automobile' gas tanks and more unrealistic hopes.

Rush said so many Americans really believe that Obama would take care of their personal needs. "For crying out loud! Can we be blunt? His aunt lives in a slum." Rush recalled what Obama's supporters said: "Obama is going to pay for my gas! Obama is going to keep me in my house!"

Obama Worship Syndrome

All the Obamamanians, his voters, the drive-by media and the Democratic voters's "mystical little guys" were being programmed by the so called "Messiah," which is wrong. We can't be programmed by a man. You must be programmed by the Almighty God in heaven. The One who can give and take life in a second. The One who resurrects the dead, even in this day and age. The One who nobody knows his ways. The One in front of whom everyone kneels, including Lucifer and all the angels. They all must bow down before him and must confess that Jesus Christ is the Lord and the Son of God.

Americans largely voted for Barack Obama because of his speeches. And they worshipped Obama's style of delivering speeches, they worship his lofty rhetoric. They have all forgotten that God in heaven is a jealous God.

Anthony Henderson said Obama surreal speeches sounds like "paradise, and if you just try close your eyes you can view it. But reality hits you soon as you open your eyes you find that you still live a 'depressing' life." Obama's hope and change and "yes we can" speeches were platitudes, bumper stickers, crusades and what have you. "Just words, just speeches," Obama echoed.

What in the atmosphere will make a human being hero worship another human being? Human beings are flawed; we are on the verge of being held captive by death. Worshiping a human being is worshipping death. But worshiping God in heaven is worshipping life.

Rush Limbaugh, time after time, rebukes hero worship and hates to be hero worshipped by his supporters. But the same can't be said about Obama. President Obama craves hero worship. Obama knew his voters were hero worshipping him during his 18 month campaign for president, yet he let it to continue. He didn't condemn their actions because that's what he salivated for. "The hubris, the ego, the arrogance, and the conceit of a guy," Rush said about Obama.

Rush addressed an insane pundit

The glorification of Obama by his supporters and the likes is just beyond the pale. They placed him instead of God as the last beacon of hope and change. Rush feels it was extremely offensive for a media pundit to refer to Obama as a god. Rush said it is sad that many Americans and people worldwide view Obama as a god. As such, whatever destruction befalls America, Obama will be blameless for it.

Made politicians

Extolled Democrats like President Obama, State Secretary Hillary Clinton and Senator Al Franken are all disciplined in political science or in politics. Commended Republicans like former State Secretary Rice, Vice President Cheney and Senator Rick Santorum also majored in political science.

All of the Congressional and State-governmental made politicians, who weren't political science majors, should be ashamed of themselves. They used money to buy a political seat. All users of a popular family name, the users of personal wealth, and the users of fame to vote themselves into office should also all be ashamed of themselves. They think their wealth makes them entitled to run for office. They are, in part, the causes of all the crises the country is going through. Journalists and military personnel are exempt, as are those who loathe the government.

Why is talk radio surplus to requirements?

Rush has two jobs, one paid and one unpaid. His radio program and his duties in leading the Republican Party: both involve politics. On the other hand, Al Franken became a comedian, a talk radio host and a politician. Jerry Springer took the same route as Franken. The more money, the more flawed talents they have. They are rich and wealthy and they have nothing but ample time, so they feed on the average Americans' talents by depriving and plagiarizing them. Their skills are manufactured and come with greed. It's not a talent from God. It is all for their own egos. They will do anything to satisfy their egos. They crave standing ovations.

Rush Limbaugh and Sean Hannity weren't talk radio hosts after being famous, unlike Montel Williams and al Sharpton. Talk radio was their goal, their drive and their ambition. What is Al Sharpton? He's a Reverend, a politician, a talk host, an activist.

What happened to the originators like Don Imus, Rush Limbaugh, Larry King and Randi Rhodes, in the days when talk radio was really talk radio? You have Al Sharpton infiltrating and polluting the American talk radio medium. Sharpton is a man that survives by feeding on any racial controversies. All these phony talk radio hosts are performing for the love of money and fame.[9]

Black-on-Black Crime

Rev. Jackson's indiscretion

Jackson proves what kind of a role model he is to African Americans. Before the commencement of an interview on Fox News, Rev. Jackson first used the so-called "n word" to refer to African Americans. Jackson wasn't satisfied; he was itching to get more worries off his chest. Jackson then threatened to remove Obama's testicles. Jackson said: "See, Barack been, um, talking down to black people, on this faith based, telling n----s how to behave. I want to cut his n- -s out…Barack…he's talking down to black people." Rev. Jesse Jackson said, while whispering aside to a fellow panelist.

Sharpton, who had fought in opposition of the "n word," gave a sound and honest response to the incident:

"I think this certainly does not reflect the Reverend Jackson that we all know and love. I think that we have to be consistent. We have denounced the N-word. I think clearly all of us must strive to do in private what we profess in public. Once we take this public position we have that responsibility. I've said and many of those in other groups, NAACP and others, that we've all used it in the past. And we've got to stop it as we challenge this nation. We can't challenge others without challenging ourselves. I still hold Reverend Jackson in high esteem, but certainly do not at all condone the use of the word by Reverend Jackson, myself or anyone else."

However, Sharpton refused to throw his friend to the wayside. He left that responsibility to Rev. Jackson's son As expected, Congressman Jackson Jr. threw his father under the bus by condemning his father's crude comment: "His divisive and demeaning comments about the presumptive Democratic nominee-and I believe the next president of the United States-contradict his inspiring and courageous career." Clearly, Junior's reprobating his father's conduct was for political expediency.

Imagine Rev Jackson, of all people, using the "n word" to refer to African Americans? His actions are forgiven but are not forgotten. We have to remind the world anytime he talks about race issues that he himself is an undiluted hypocrite. How low can he get? The only African American figure that we are waiting to use the "n word" in public is Al Sharpton. It is outrageous how many times Rev Jackson uses the "n word" while sitting on his porch. How many times does he curse at Obama when relaxing at his own backyard? The whole bottom line is all the years and service Jackson put in fighting discrimination for African Americans has all gone down the drain. All the times he has referred to African Americans as N---as and all the racial curses he has uttered while in his private dwelling all came home to roost when he made that comment on Fox News.

Black-on-Black advice

Obama reveals the truth about the African American community on Father's Day: "We know that more than half of all black children live in single-parent households, a number that has doubled-doubled-since we were children. We know the statistics-that children who grow up without a father are five times more likely to live in poverty and commit crime; nine times more likely to drop out of schools and 20 times more likely to end up in prison. They are more likely to have behavioral problems, or run away from home or become teenage parents themselves. And the foundations of our community are weaker because of it."

"There's a reason why our families are in disrepair," Obama's Father's Day speech. "And some of it has to do with a tragic history, but we can't keep on using that as an excuse. Too many fathers are AWOL, missing from too many lives and too many homes. They've abandoned their responsibilities. They're acting like boys instead of men."

Obama attacked Associate Justice of the US Supreme Court, Clarence Thomas

Rush fiercely defended a friend

Obama was asked during a Saturday forum which of the nine Supreme Court Judges he would not have nominated. In Obama's response, he went after the only African American Supreme Court Justice. Obama said: "I would not have nominated Clarence Thomas. I don't think that he ... was a strong enough jurist or legal thinker at the time for that elevation. {from the

265

lower Courts to the Supreme Court} Setting aside the fact that I profoundly disagree with his interpretation of a lot of the Constitution." Rush was poised to response, he said Clarence Thomas went to Yale university, was on the DC Circuit Court of Appeals and worked as an assistant attorney general with US Attorney General John Ashcroft. Compare him to Obama, a community organizer that served 140 days in Congress. Yet Obama had the audacity to belittle Clarence Thomas. Rush said Obama isn't fit or qualified to shine Clarence Thomas' shoes. Rush chronicled Thomas' poverty stricken past life. "Obama was born with a silver spoon in his mouth compared to Clarence Thomas." Rush said Clarence Thomas, unlike Obama, is a result of American exceptionalism.

Justice Thomas was nominated and appointed by Walker Bush. At that time, in 1991, Obama wasn't even a state senator. He was a community organizer. For crying out loud, what does a community organizer know about elevating a Court of Appeals jurist?[10]

An African American grudge

African Americans are peeved at white Americans for no logical reason. The majority of African Americans hold a generational grudge against the white man. Their ill will feeling towards the white man will last until they take their last breath. That means they won't die with God's instructions.

"He shall die without instruction; and in the greatness of his folly he shall go astray," –the last chapter of Proverbs 5. This is not a black man or a white man's world. This is God's world, and His design is what human being have gone through right from the existence of Man, right from Adam.

They accused the white man of racism, greed and slavery. If it's not one thing, it's another. If it's not bigotry, it's prejudice.

Holding a grudge because of greed

Why does the white man tend to be wealthier than the black man? African Americans are upset and envious about the notion.

Obama talked about the white man's greed" "It is this world, a world where cruise ships throw away more food in a day than most residents of Port-au-Prince see in a year, where white folks' greed runs a world in need, apartheid in one hemisphere, apathy in another hemisphere. That's the world! On which hope sits," Obama recounted from Wright's Audacity of Hope sermon.

Liberals blame Western civilization for the white man's greed.
Rush said "it is only white man's greed that keeps otherwise well-qualified people of race and color subjugated to inferiority."

They shouldn't be troubled about the white man's wealth. In the time of Moses, the Egyptians were much wealthier than the Israelites. The issue of greed primarily deals with the rich and the poor. During his time on earth, Jesus dealt mostly with the poor, but the rich were proportionately welcomed to associate with Him.

"For it is easier for a camel to go through a needle's eye, than for a rich man to enter into the kingdom of God,"- Luke 18 verse 25.

Holding a grudge because of racism and slavery

Rush uttered, "Racism, as an American original sin would not end. It would only get worse." Racism and slavery are tests of God's commandments in loving our neighbors as ourselves.

Israelites were slaves to Egypt and Pharaoh. It was God's design for the Israelites to be in bondage and under assault for years at the hands of the Egyptians. It was God's design for the Israelites to struggle and wander in the wilderness for 40 years amid battles with oppositions. So the slavery that the blacks went through was also God's design. By and large, African Americans hate and despise Caucasions because of slavery. With or without a just reason, it is profoundly wrong to hate a fellow human being that God created. Leave every evil deed to vengeance, but remember that vengeance is of the Lord.

God is the Word, and the Word is God. Every single word that God/ Christ had proclaimed would be accounted for. Christ abated the Ten Commandments to just two easy commandments.

Remember the two commandments:

"Thou shalt love the Lord thy God with all thy heart, and with all thy soul, and with all thy mind. This is the first and great commandment. And the second is like unto it, Thou shalt love thy neighbor as thyself. On these two commandments hang all the law and the prophets,"- Matthew 22 verses 37-40.

Thy neighbor is any person that we have come in contact with. That is one of the reasons God divided blacks and whites. With division came racism, bigotry and prejudice, which the devil begot. If you can overcome that, then you are a child of God and are readying yourself for his kingdom. If you don't take heed to those two commandments, there is no place for you in heaven. The word of God wouldn't go in vain, God won't go in vain.

Conclusion

Human beings shouldn't take their last breath holding grudges against a fellow human being. Instead, take your last breath knowing full well that you believed in God, and that you loved your neighbors and in return, beyond the shadow of a doubt, God will prepare you for death.[11]

Rush Limbaugh does what he does best, but does it against the best

Jesus Christ used words to convert sinners. Christ didn't, by any stretch of the imagination, use force to convert the multitudes.

Rush Limbaugh is an utmost example in that perspective of how Jesus used words instead of force. Christ came and he denied himself as the King of the world, even though the people knew he was. They just couldn't come to terms with the fact that Christ was the Messiah because Christ wasn't riding on a chariot with a brigade of horsemen. It's the word that makes Rush the most dangerous person in America. Rush has no executive authority like a President, a King or a Prime Minister. Rush has no judicial or legislative authority like a Senator, a Judge or a Parliament leader. Rush is no Military commander. Yet he commands more respect, and he has the support of masses. He has the most supporters and followers. And Rush is no Julius Caesar or no Adolf Hitler.

Rush's power comes from his knowledge, his understanding and his wisdom. Rush's authority comes from the word that he utters. What is the word? The word is God. God gave Rush wisdom and understanding. God specifically and uniquely created Rush. Rush Limbaugh denounced himself to be called a hero or a celebrity. Rush doesn't want his supporters bowing down to him because Rush knows full well that he's a sinner. He knows he took a bite of the forbidden fruit. Rush knows that the only hero in this world is Jesus Christ.

The worldwide hatred for Rush Limbaugh is way beyond evil. Most of that hatred is blind hatred and secondhand hatred.

But the genuine hatred for Rush is predicated on the fact that Rush says what they (the haters) don't want to hear. To those millions if not billions of people, they live a lie. The truth is bitter for them. The truth is hard to swallow.

"The Lord will cause your enemies who rise against you to be defeated before your face; they shall come out against you one way and flee before you seven ways," Deuteronomy 28 verse 7.

The enemies of Rush came initially to attack Rush one way, but they were scattered seven ways. They weren't able to reunite to attack him again because they had been unceremoniously discredited, thereby causing an indefinite and perhaps in some quarters irreparable damage to their repute countrywide. Take for instance, the impeached Bill Clinton's 90's feud with Rush Limbaugh. At the end of the day, Clinton fled away with a salacious scandal which led him to forswear his country.

Al Gore, Howard Dean, Al Sharpton, Tom Daschle, Jesse Jackson and Harry Reid: all these prominent Americans have all openly tried to condemn Rush Limbaugh. They approached him with all sorts of obnoxious and despicable issues. However, embarrassment, disgrace, abashment, shame, odium, demotion and humiliation all boomeranged against them.

Rush Limbaugh's dialogue with the Bush dynasty

In late 2008, President George Bush (Bush 43) hailed Rush Limbaugh's 20 years of broadcasting: "President George W. Bush calling to congratulate you on 20 years of important and excellent broadcasting."
Rush Limbaugh was surprised to get an unexpected call from the President: "Well, thank you, sir. You've stunned me! I'm shocked. But thank you so much."

George Bush went on: "I'm here with a room full of admirers. There are two others that would like to speak to you and congratulate you, people who consider you friends and really appreciate the contribution you've made."

Rush Limbaugh responded: "Thank you, sir, very much. Put 'em on."

George Bush continued: "Well, I'm just calling along with President 41 and the former governor of Florida. We're fixing to have lunch here, and I said, "Listen, we ought to call our pal and let him know that we care" for you. So this is as much as anything, a nice verbal letter to a guy we really care for."

Rush Limbaugh thanked the outgoing President: "Well, thank you, sir, very much. I'm overwhelmed. I can't tell you how much I appreciate this and how much you've surprised me."

Rush then talked to President Walker Bush (Bush 41) after his conversation with George Bush. Walker Bush sent his greetings: "Hey, Rush? How are you doing?

Rush Limbaugh responded: "Mr. President, sir. I am never better. I'm so glad that you three called me. I'm stunned here. It's great to hear from you."

Walker Bush had advice for Rush: "I've got some advice for you."

Rush Limbaugh replied: "Tell me."

Walker Bush uttered: "Slow down your backswing. That's what I'm doing is giving advice. I remember playing with you and enjoying it. How are you?"

Rush Limbaugh, while laughing, said: "I'm great."

Walker Bush spoke on: "Proud of you, always."

Rush appreciated the warm words from Bush senior: "Well, thank you. I'm doing great. And you? You're looking well, too."

Walker Bush responded: "Well, yeah. I'm kind of on the sidelines, but I can't do golf and all that stuff anymore. But life is good. It's wonderful, and it's great having the family up here in Maine, and all is well."

Rush ended his conversation by talking briefly to Governor Jeb Bush, the junior brother to President George Bush.

Jesus Christ was a true leader. Rush is the embodiment of Him. He epitomizes the leader. Rush is a natural leader of men. Hitler didn't epitomize the leader. Hitler led effectively predominantly because he commanded a powerful army.

We all know the saying, "Actions speak louder than words." But the Word of God, the Word that Jesus spoke, speaks louder than actions.

Rush is original, a thoroughbred. Nothing that Rush is made up of is manufactured. Rush has been at the forefront of America's positive causes for years.

Many politicians and political figures have tried earnestly and eagerly to be like Rush. They want to walk in his shoes.

They envied Rush's achievements. Because of Rush's unprecedented success, they have a niche for it. They want to be recognized as a chief leader of a renowned movement. They have tried to take on Rush, they have tried to take on the leader of the GOP. They want to pit their wits against Rush. They want to punch above their weight against Rush. These stuffed shirt politicians will need to take a course to learn to be like Rush.

They have been trying to be what they weren't meant to be. Every human created has their purposes and duties here on earth. Leading the GOP was destiny for Rush, and no one can do it better. That is why Rush is a cut above all the carbon copies.

The dues that Rush paid contributed heavily to his accomplishments.

God put him at the pedestal. God consolidated Rush's leadership ability.

Rush's critics have no clue whatsoever as to what Rush goes through on a daily basis. Volleys of abuse, spewing vile contempt and sweeping accusations of racism are pitched daily against Rush. Yet Rush maintains his composure. "The things that a dog sees and remain calm are more severe and atrocious than when a hen sees a hawk and start crowing angrily," said Celestine Mohammed. They have no clue what it feels like to be on the receiving end of unadulterated hatred. For security purposes, being reclusive and being in undisclosed locations as if one is a leper is paramount for Rush.

From the conception, from Adam, no human being ever born has been subjected to the trials and the tribulations that Jesus Christ was subjected to during his time on earth.

Jesus Christ eluded arrests. Christ went through struggles and temptations. The suffering that Jesus endured at Calvary was the culmination of His struggles. Christ cried in Matthew 27 v 46: "My God, my God, why hast thou forsaken me?"

Remember what Christ said: "Verily, verily, I say unto you, He that believeth on me, the works that I do shall he do also; and greater works than these shall he do; because I go unto my Father," John 14 verse 12.

Rush Limbaugh claimed to be "a talent on loan from God." He couldn't be more right. Rush also claimed to be a prophet. He's one of the greatest prophets in this generation. The most listened to radio host in the whole wide world and the leader of the Republican Party, with multi-million copies sold of his two bestselling books, Rush has since reached the pinnacle of his achievements. With more achievements certainly on the horizon, Rush acknowledged that he pays his ten percent tithes to God. Rush daily appreciates the talent from God. Utilizing that talent made Rush who he is.[12]

God bless those that believe in God.
God bless Rush Limbaugh.
God bless God in heaven.

End.

Notes

CHAPTER ONE

1

Huffington Post, Rachel Sklar, The Next First Family Of The United States, November 5, 2008;

abcnews.go.com, Sam Donaldson, Commentary: Conservative Attacks on Obama Could Backfire, June 24, 2008;

The Venezuelan Missile Crisis?, The Rush Limbaugh Show® Premiere Radio Networks, October 21, 2008;

Bill Ayers Audio Unearthed, The Rush Limbaugh Show® Premiere Radio Networks, October 22, 2008;

Obama's Real Problem with Ayers, The Rush Limbaugh Show® Premiere Radio Networks, October 8, 2008;

Radical Marxists Weeks Away from Electing One of Their Own, The Rush Limbaugh Show® Premiere Radio Networks, October 14, 2008;

Compare: O.J. Simpson vs. Bill Ayers, The Rush Limbaugh Show® Premiere Radio Networks, October 7, 2008;

foxnews.com, 'H&C' Panel Reacts to Bill Ayers' Interview With 'Good Morning America,' November 17, 2008;

usatoday.com, Liz Sidoti, Gerald Herbert, McCain TV ad raises Obama's links to ex-radical, October 9, 2008;

Obama's Double Life Exposed: His Racist, Hatemonger Pastor, The Rush Limbaugh Show® Premiere Radio Networks, March 13, 2008;

Barack Obama and Pastor Wright: Far More Than Guilt by Association, The Rush Limbaugh Show® Premiere Radio Networks, March 14, 2008;

Why Obama Can't Be President, The Rush Limbaugh Show® Premiere Radio Networks, October 2, 2008;

Damning Archival Audio Barack Obama Doesn't Want You to Hear, The Rush Limbaugh Show® Premiere Radio Networks, October 29, 2008;

Washington Post, Howard Kurtz, Collateral Damage, April 30, 2008;

cnn.com, Transcript of Obama's speech, March 18, 2008;

cnn.com, Obama 'outraged' by Wright's remark, April 29, 2008;

The Boston Globe, Scott Helman, Obama tagged with comments of another cleric, May 31, 2008;

Farrakhan Calls Obama "Messiah", The Rush Limbaugh Show® Premiere Radio Networks, October 10, 2008;

chicagobreakingnews.com, Farrakhan calls Obama a 'new beginning', November 9, 2008;

newsmax.com, Ken Timmerman, Obama-Farrakhan Ties Are Close, Ex-Aide Says, November, 3, 2008

2

This Election is All About Race, The Rush Limbaugh Show® Premiere Radio Networks, October 22, 2008;

newsbusters.org, Noel Sheppard, Hannity to Obama: Do You Have The Guts To Come On My Show? July 19, 2008;

telegraph.co.uk, Alex Spillius, Michelle Obama attacked over patriotism gaffe, February, 19 2008;

Rush Blamed for "Whitey" Rumor, The Rush Limbaugh Show® Premiere Radio Networks, June 12, 2008;

Messiah to Child: America Sucks, The Rush Limbaugh Show® Premiere Radio Networks, August 7, 2008;

Obama Flip-Flops on DC Vouchers, The Rush Limbaugh Show® Premiere Radio Networks, May 6, 2009;

time.com, Barack Obama, Barack Obama: My Spiritual Journey, October 16, 2006;

drudge.com, 12 stories About Palin on Front Page Here, September 02, 2008;

Obama Practices the Low Art of Political Seduction at Notre Dame, The Rush Limbaugh Show® Premiere Radio Networks, May 18, 2009;

Senator Obama's Inhuman Voting Record on Infanticide, The Rush Limbaugh Show® Premiere Radio Networks, August 18, 2008;

Conservatism Can Win Hispanics, The Rush Limbaugh Show® Premiere Radio Networks, November 19, 2008;

Why Obama Can't Be President, The Rush Limbaugh Show® Premiere Radio Networks, October 2, 2008;

Critique Obamaism, Not Obama, The Rush Limbaugh Show® Premiere Radio Networks, November 18, 2008;

foxnews.com, Greta Van Susteren, Exclusive: Rush Unleashed, Parts 1 and 2, July 25, 2009;

Mo: What's Wrong with America, The Rush Limbaugh Show® Premiere Radio Networks, June 11, 2009;

Steve Wants His Schadenfreude, The Rush Limbaugh Show® Premiere Radio Networks, November 4, 2008;

Obama "Rushes" to Grandmother's Bedside (After Just a Few Days), The Rush Limbaugh Show® Premiere Radio Networks, October 23, 2008;

Obama's Aunt Found in Slum, The Rush Limbaugh Show® Premiere Radio Networks, October 30, 2008;

The Times, Found in a rundown Boston estate: Barack Obama's aunt Zeituni Onyango, October 30, 2008;

Obama's Aunt Found in Slum, The Rush Limbaugh Show® Premiere Radio Networks, October 30, 2008;

Bureaucrat: Obama's Aunt Zeituni is an "Exemplary" Slum Resident, The Rush Limbaugh Show® Premiere Radio Networks, October 31, 2008;

findarticles.com, Ann Coulter, Obama: Lucifer Is My Homeboy, September 22, 2008

3

drudge.com, PEW "The Gold Standard" - Obama 52% McCain 38%, October 21, 2008;

Let's Tweak the Media: Obama to Campaign in 57 Islamic States, The Rush Limbaugh Show® Premiere Radio Networks, May 12, 2008;

Fox News, Rush's Interview with Greta Van Susteren on Fox, September 19, 2008;

Abcnews.com, Obama's Former Minister Breaks Silence, Rips Fox News during Funeral Service, April 13, 2008;

foxnews.com, Embattled Reverend Takes Shot at Hannity, August 12, 2008;

foxnews.com, Obama's Pastor's Controversial Remarks, March 13, 2008;

Joe Biden to Man in Wheechair: "Stand Up, Chuck. Let 'Em See Ya!", The Rush Limbaugh Show® Premiere Radio Networks, September 10, 2008;

The Boston Globe, Biden on Obama, August 24, 2008;

Abcnews.com Rick Klein, Obama's Evolving Take on Meeting With Iran, May 20, 2008;

washingtonpost.com, Biden Not Worried About Southern Dems, August 27, 2006;

time.com, Diversity in Delaware? - The Screwups of Campaign '08, June 17, 2006;

Biden's Three-Letter Word: J-O-B-S, The Rush Limbaugh Show® Premiere Radio Networks, October 16, 2008;

NPR: Open Thread: Obama's 'Bitter' Remarks, The Rush Limbaugh Show® Premiere Radio Networks, April 13, 2008;

The Lesson of Joe the Plumber, The Rush Limbaugh Show® Premiere Radio Networks, October 17, 2008;

Who Paid for Hillary's Pantsuits, Pelosi's Pearls, or Biden's Plugs?, The Rush Limbaugh Show® Premiere Radio Networks, October 23, 2008;

What is Barack Obama's Endgame?, The Rush Limbaugh Show® Premiere Radio, Networks, May 5, 2009

4

Why'd Catholics Vote for Obama?, The Rush Limbaugh Show® Premiere Radio Networks, November 21, 2008;

quotes.liberty-tree, Theodore Roosevelt Quote with Comments

telegraph.co.uk, Toby Harnden, Barack Obama meets John McCain, November 2008;

Yes We Can: The Reestablishment of Principled Conservatism Begins, The Rush Limbaugh Show® Premiere Radio Networks, November 5, 2008;

Exit Poll Data: Twenty Percent of "Conservatives" Voted for Obama, The Rush Limbaugh Show® Premiere Radio Networks, November 5, 2008;

Emanuel Has "Sharp Elbows," But We Have "Right-Wing Rage", The Rush Limbaugh Show® Premiere Radio Networks, November 7, 2008;

Why Doesn't Liberalism Have to Change When Democrats Lose?, The Rush Limbaugh Show® Premiere Radio Networks, November 19, 2008;

Open Line Friday on Wednesday, The Rush Limbaugh Show® Premiere Radio Networks, November 12, 2008;

Will the Pendulum Swing Back?, The Rush Limbaugh Show® Premiere Radio Networks, May 12, 2009;

Fear: American Industry Preps for Obama Win by Laying Off Workers, The Rush Limbaugh Show® Premiere Radio Networks, October 22, 2008

5

Your President-Elect Isn't Corrupt; He Just Has Corrupt Associations, The Rush Limbaugh Show® Premiere Radio Networks, December 10, 2008;

The Obama Pardon List Starts Early, The Rush Limbaugh Show® Premiere Radio Networks, December 9, 2008;

Fitzgerald on Obama's Chicago: "In the Middle of a Crime Spree", The Rush Limbaugh Show® Premiere Radio Networks, December 9, 2008;

Shocker: Senate Seats for Sale, The Rush Limbaugh Show® Premiere Radio Networks, December 10, 2008;

Obama's America: Corruption, Nationalization, and Propaganda, The Rush Limbaugh Show® Premiere Radio Networks, December 10, 2008;

cbs2chicago.com, Jury Finds Tony Rezko Guilty on 16 of 24 Charges, June 4, 2008;

What Tony Rezko Did Obama Know?, The Rush Limbaugh Show® Premiere Radio Networks, June 5, 2008;

Obama Throws ACORN Under Bus, The Rush Limbaugh Show® Premiere Radio Networks, October 15, 2008;

Obama-Blago Scandal Timeline, The Rush Limbaugh Show® Premiere Radio Networks, December 10, 2008

6

Why Obama Can't Be President, The Rush Limbaugh Show® Premiere Radio Networks, October 2, 2008;

Messiah Loses at Warren Forum; Dems Accuse McCain of Cheating, The Rush Limbaugh Show® Premiere Radio Networks, August 18, 2008;

Sean Hannity, Fox News, Rush on Fox News Channel with Sean Hannity Interview Taped on, January 19, 2009;

cnn.com, GOP chastises Obama's speech over Israeli-Palestinian issue; June 4, 2009;

Can You Negotiate with a Religion?, The Rush Limbaugh Show® Premiere Radio Networks, June 5, 2009;

Obama Claims Credit for Iraq Win, The Rush Limbaugh Show® Premiere Radio Networks, July 1, 2009;

Cheney Puts Obama on Defensive, The Rush Limbaugh Show® Premiere Radio Networks, May 21, 2009;

abcnews, Kirit Radia, Jason Ryan, and Karen Travers, Cheney Slams Obama Decision to Investigate CIA Interrogators, August 25, 2009;

Obama Manipulates the Emotional Attachment of His Cult Followers, The Rush Limbaugh Show® Premiere Radio Networks, April 20, 2009;

Anti-Americanism Isn't Cool? It's the Central Tenet of Obamaism!, The Rush Limbaugh Show® Premiere Radio Networks, April 21, 2009;

Rush Rocks Milken Institute Forum, The Rush Limbaugh Show® Premiere Radio Networks, April 29, 2009;

President Obama's Cairo Speech: Outrageous, Absurd, Embarrassing, The Rush Limbaugh Show® Premiere Radio Networks, June 4, 2009;

Biden Guarantees World Crisis Under Obama within Six Months, The Rush Limbaugh Show® Premiere Radio Networks, October 20, 2008;

Why Did a Muslim in Touch with Al-Qaeda Do It? We Know Why!, The Rush Limbaugh Show® Premiere Radio Networks, November 9, 2009;

www.nationalreview.com, Jonah Goldberg, Durbin and Hitler, June 22, 2005;

boston.com, Libby Quaid and Mike Glover, McCain criticizes Obama over Iran comments, May 19, 2008;

huffingtonpost.com, Chavez: Obama "A Poor Ignoramus," April, 22, 2009

Obama Shatters Our Self-Esteem; Denies American Exceptionalism, The Rush Limbaugh Show® Premiere Radio Networks, September 23, 2009;

huffingtonpost.com, Marines' Evidence Proves Murtha Is Right That US Troops, May 18, 2006;

Boston Globe, Obama's stance on troops attacked, October 7, 2008;

Cbsnews .com, Joel Roberts, Senator Reid On Iraq: "This War Is Lost", April, 20, 2007;

freerepublic.com, Condoleezza Rice Blast Obama, September 22, 2009;

cnn.com, Gadhafi talks of U.N. 'inequality,' conspiracies at U.N ..., September 23, 2009

7

Shocking 1995 Obama Audio Found, The Rush Limbaugh Show® Premiere Radio Networks, October 24, 2008;

Obama to MTV: My Tax Hike Will Be "Chump Change" for Rich, The Rush Limbaugh Show® Premiere Radio Networks, November 4, 2008;

AP 2006: Wall Street Bonuses "Trickle Through" NYC Economy, The Rush Limbaugh Show® Premiere Radio Networks, November 26, 2008;

On the Record, Greta Van Susteren; Fox news, interview with Rush Limbaugh, July 23, 2009;

Stop-Start Analysis of Obama Ad: It's an Address from the Dictator, The Rush Limbaugh Show® Premiere Radio Networks, September 17, 2008;

What is Barack Obama's Endgame?, The Rush Limbaugh Show® Premiere Radio Networks, May 5, 2009;

foxnews.com, Obama Slams Financial Sector While Government Salaries ..., December 15, 2009;

Barney Frank Can't Find a Villain!, The Rush Limbaugh Show® Premiere Radio Networks, July 21, 2009;

Obama Claims He Won't Run GM, Then Explains How He Will Run GM, The Rush Limbaugh Show® Premiere Radio Networks, June 1, 2009;

The War on Prosperity Rolls On, The Rush Limbaugh Show® Premiere Radio Networks, July 1, 2009;

America's Piñata Strikes Back: We Won't Shut Up on Sotomayor, The Rush Limbaugh Show® Premiere Radio Networks, May 29, 2009;

Obama Attacks America Again Ahead of Muslim Apology Tour, The Rush Limbaugh Show® Premiere Radio Networks, June 2, 2009;

Obama Rips CEO Bonuses. Soon, He Will Decide What You Can Earn, The Rush Limbaugh Show® Premiere Radio Networks, November 26, 2008;

Durbin: Bring Terrorists to Illinois, The Rush Limbaugh Show® Premiere Radio Networks, November 17, 2009;

Story #3: Bam Puts Safety Net Under His Economic Casualties Stack of Stuff Quick Hits Page, The Rush Limbaugh Show® Premiere Radio Networks, October 6, 2009;

Obama Will Bumble into Solutions?, The Rush Limbaugh Show® Premiere Radio Networks, November 26, 2008;

Insane Obama Plan: The Biggest Economic Blunder in Our History, The Rush Limbaugh Show® Premiere Radio Networks, January 8, 2009;

Obama to Stock Market: Drop Dead, The Rush Limbaugh Show® Premiere Radio Networks, March 3, 2009;

Dem Strategy: Ram Obamacare Through, Implement It After 2012, The Rush Limbaugh Show® Premiere Radio Networks; September 28, 2009

Dark Days: Democrats in Midst of a Giant Health Care Con Game, The Rush Limbaugh Show® Premiere Radio Networks, October 8, 2009

8

Barack Obama: Naïve or Devious?, The Rush Limbaugh Show® Premiere Radio Networks, January 9, 2009;

An Opportunity for Conservatism, The Rush Limbaugh Show® Premiere Radio Networks, September 30, 2008;

RINOs Want to Wave the White Flag on Sotomayor and Embrace Obama, The Rush Limbaugh Show® Premiere Radio Networks, May 27, 2009;

Stack of Stuff Quick Hits Page, Story #3: Does Anyone Believe Holiday Spending is Really Up?, The Rush Limbaugh Show® Premiere Radio Networks, December 21, 2009;

Reestablishing Conservatism 101: Be Who You Are and Be Confident, The Rush Limbaugh Show® Premiere Radio Networks, January 8, 2009;

Drive-By Media in the Tank for '09: It's a Whole New Obama Ballgame, The Rush Limbaugh Show® Premiere Radio Networks, January 5, 2009;

Stack of Stuff Quick Hits Page Story #5: Teachers' Unions Uneasy with President Obama?, The Rush Limbaugh Show® Premiere Radio Networks, October 19, 2009

9

Sotomayor Nomination is a Chance to Highlight Obama's Radical Views, The Rush Limbaugh Show® Premiere Radio Networks, May 27, 2009;

Rush Interviewed by Sean Hannity, Part One Recorded:, The Rush Limbaugh Show® Premiere Radio Networks, June 3, 2009;

Flashback: How Vicious Liberals Lied About Conservative Judges, The Rush Limbaugh Show® Premiere Radio Networks, May 29, 2009;

State-Run Media Reports Limbaugh Effect at Sonia Sotomayor Hearings, The Rush Limbaugh Show® Premiere Radio Networks, July 15, 2009;

Michelle Obama Tells Us She Identifies with Sotomayor's Rage, The Rush Limbaugh Show® Premiere Radio Networks, June 4, 2009

10

Barack Obama Seeks to Turn America into a Third World Country, The Rush Limbaugh Show® Premiere Radio Networks, June 26, 2009;

Our Miraculous Declaration of Independence (and Rush's Clubs), The Rush Limbaugh Show® Premiere Radio Networks, July 3, 2009;

Obama Administration Moves to Cap Pay All Across Private Sector, The Rush Limbaugh Show® Premiere Radio Networks, June 11, 2009;

A Prebuttal to Obama's Infomercial, The Rush Limbaugh Show® Premiere Radio Networks, October 29, 2008;

Happy Dependence Day, America, The Rush Limbaugh Show® Premiere Radio Networks, July 2, 2009;

Obama Attacks America Again Ahead of Muslim Apology Tour, The Rush Limbaugh Show® Premiere Radio Networks, June 2, 2009;

Rush's Speech at Hillsdale College Churchill Dinner in Washington, DC, The Rush Limbaugh Show® Premiere Radio Networks, December 5, 2008;

Obama's America: Corruption, Nationalization, and Propaganda, The Rush Limbaugh Show® Premiere Radio Networks, December 10, 2008;

Let's Not Ignore Sotomayor's Negative View of the Constitution, The Rush Limbaugh Show® Premiere Radio Networks, May 29, 2009;

Sotomayor Nomination is a Chance to Highlight Obama's Radical Views, The Rush Limbaugh Show® Premiere Radio Networks, May 27, 2009;

Stack of Stuff Quick Hits Page, The Rush Limbaugh Show® Premiere Radio Networks, Story #2: Most Americans Don't Know What "Rights" Really Are, July 22, 2009;

2001 Audio: Obama Shows His Disdain for the US Constitution, The Rush Limbaugh Show® Premiere Radio Networks, October 27, 2008;

Left Creates a Crisis Mentality, Uses It to Abrogate Constitution, The Rush Limbaugh Show® Premiere Radio Networks, September 29, 2008;

"The Simplistic Notion That People with Wealth are Entitled to Keep It", The Rush Limbaugh Show® Premiere Radio Networks, November 4, 2008

11

Obama Calls Joint Session of Congress to Save Political Face, The Rush Limbaugh Show® Premiere Radio Networks, September 8, 2009;

Dung Heap Builds a Starter Home, The Rush Limbaugh Show® Premiere Radio Networks, December 22, 2009;

Dingy Harry's Universe of Lies, The Rush Limbaugh Show® Premiere Radio Networks, December 7, 2009;

The Democrat Health Care Bill is an Unmitigated Disaster, The Rush Limbaugh Show®
Premiere Radio Networks, December 14, 2009;

Where's the Outrage? Obama's Ego Sucks Up the Whole World's Wealth, The Rush Limbaugh
Show® Premiere Radio Networks, December 21, 2009

12

John Harris Sees Obama Landslide, The Rush Limbaugh Show® Premiere Radio Networks,
October 14, 2008;

Redistribution is not a Distraction, It's the Core Issue of This Election, The Rush Limbaugh
Show® Premiere Radio Networks, October 27, 2008;

Barack Obama is an Illusionist, The Rush Limbaugh Show® Premiere Radio Networks, July
20, 2009;

Obama Change: 81-Year-Old Carter Appointee Volcker is a Fresh Face?, The Rush Limbaugh
Show® Premiere Radio Networks, November 26, 2008;

A Prebuttal to Obama's Infomercial, The Rush Limbaugh Show® Premiere Radio Networks,
October 29, 2008;

Shocking 1995 Obama Audio Found, The Rush Limbaugh Show® Premiere Radio Networks,
October 24, 2008;

Angry Obama Aims to Get Even, The Rush Limbaugh Show® Premiere Radio Networks,
June 29, 2009;

On the Record, Greta Van Susteren; Fox news, Rush Unleashed, Part 1and Part 2 interview
with Rush Limbaugh, July 25, 2009;

Shhh! Don't Tell Robert Gibbs: We're Talking About Sotomayor, The Rush Limbaugh Show®
Premiere Radio Networks, May 28, 2009;

Biden: We'll Give You a Toaster September 16, 2008Cheney Puts Obama on Defensive, The
Rush Limbaugh Show® Premiere Radio Networks, May 21, 2009;

Obama's School Speech Explained, The Rush Limbaugh Show® Premiere Radio Networks,
September 8, 2009;

Anti-Americanism Isn't Cool? It's the Central Tenet of Obamaism!, The Rush Limbaugh Show® Premiere Radio Networks, April 21, 2009;

Can GOP Win Back the House in 2010? The Rush Limbaugh Show® Premiere Radio Networks, April 20, 2009;

Barack Obama Seeks to Turn America into a Third World Country, The Rush Limbaugh Show® Premiere Radio Networks, June 26, 2009;

Hanniy, Sean Hannity, Part 2 of Limbaugh on 'Hannity', Fox News, June 03, 2009;

Stand Up and Take Sides, GOP!, The Rush Limbaugh Show® Premiere Radio Networks, July 15, 2009;

Your President Wants You to Suffer, The Rush Limbaugh Show® Premiere Radio Networks, June 1, 2009;

Democrats Face Informed Citizens; Obama Doesn't Know What's in Bill, The Rush Limbaugh Show® Premiere Radio Networks, July 21, 2009;

Our President is a Laughingstock: Obama Awarded Nobel Peace Prize, The Rush Limbaugh Show® Premiere Radio Networks, October 9, 2009;

Open Line Friday on Wednesday, The Rush Limbaugh Show® Premiere Radio Networks, November 12, 2008;

Obama Will Bumble into Solutions?, The Rush Limbaugh Show® Premiere Radio Networks, November 26, 2008;

Community Organizer Obama Attacks Community Organizers!, The Rush Limbaugh Show® Premiere Radio Networks, August 5, 2009;

CHAPTER TWO

1

Al-Qaeda Finally Offends Drive-Bys, The Rush Limbaugh Show® Premiere Radio Networks, November 20, 2008;

Bone Brothers; Koch Records, "Dick Riders", February 22, 2005;

President Obama's Cairo Speech: Outrageous, Absurd, Embarrassing, The Rush Limbaugh Show® Premiere Radio Networks, June 4, 2009;

foxnews.com, Obama: Quit Listening to Rush Limbaugh if You Want to Get Things Done, January 23, 2009;

Rush Discusses His Bipartisan Stimulus Plan on Fox & Friends, The Rush Limbaugh Show® Premiere Radio Networks, January 29, 2009;

Drive-Bys Declare: Rush Leads GOP, The Rush Limbaugh Show® Premiere Radio Networks, January 28, 2009

2

Cbsnews.com, Michelle Levi, Emanuel: Rush Prays For Obama's Failure, March 1, 2009;

FOXNews.com, Sean Hannity, Rush Limbaugh on 'Hannity' – Hannity, June 04, 2009;

The Left is Afraid of Us, Folks, The Rush Limbaugh Show® Premiere Radio Networks, May 5, 2009;

Q: Why Do the Big 3 Need Money?, The Rush Limbaugh Show® Premiere Radio Networks, November 25, 2008;

CNN: Cheney/Limbaugh 2012?, The Rush Limbaugh Show® Premiere Radio Networks, May 28, 2009;

Rush on Your World with Neil Cavuto, The Rush Limbaugh Show® Premiere Radio Networks, April 8, 2009;

Stack of Stuff Quick Hits Page, The Rush Limbaugh Show® Premiere Radio Networks, Story #4: New York Post: Betsy McCaughey Nukes Obamacare July 20, 2009;

Cities Line Up to Woo El Rushbo, The Rush Limbaugh Show® Premiere Radio Networks, March 31, 2009;

Gallup Polls Rush Approval Rating, The Rush Limbaugh Show® Premiere Radio Networks, February 9, 2009;

Rush's Message to the Media, The Rush Limbaugh Show® Premiere Radio Networks, October 20, 2008;

Rush Donates $300,000 to Lead 2009; Leukemia & Lymphoma Society Cure-A-Thon, The Rush Limbaugh Show® Premiere Radio Networks, April 17, 2009;

Matthew 27: 60, King James Bible

The Role of Government is to Secure Our Liberty, Not to Seize It, The Rush Limbaugh Show® Premiere Radio Networks, June 26, 2009;

Libs Attack Blacks on Gay Marriage, The Rush Limbaugh Show® Premiere Radio Networks, November 12, 2008

3

Why Doesn't Liberalism Have to Change When Democrats Lose?, The Rush Limbaugh Show® Premiere Radio Networks, November 19, 2008;

Arlen Specter's Defection Says Nothing About the State of the GOP, The Rush Limbaugh Show® Premiere Radio Networks, April 29, 2009;

Will Republican Wizards of Smart Learn the Joe Lieberman Lesson?, The Rush Limbaugh Show® Premiere Radio Networks, November 18, 2008;

Critique Obamaism, Not Obama, The Rush Limbaugh Show® Premiere Radio Networks, November 18, 2008;

Rush's Speech at Hillsdale College Churchill Dinner in Washington, DC, The Rush Limbaugh Show® Premiere Radio Networks, December 5, 2008;

Unconscionable: McCain Staffers Attempting to Destroy Sarah Palin, The Rush Limbaugh Show® Premiere Radio Networks, November 6, 2008;

Hearings Aren't Helping Sotomayor, The Rush Limbaugh Show® Premiere Radio Networks, July 16, 2009;

God Bless the House Republicans, The Rush Limbaugh Show® Premiere Radio Networks, September 30, 2008;

An Opportunity for Conservatism, The Rush Limbaugh Show® Premiere Radio Networks, September 30, 2008;

Rush Responds to General Powell, The Rush Limbaugh Show® Premiere Radio Networks, December 15, 2008;

FOXNews.com, Sean hannity, Rush Limbaugh on 'Hannity' – Hannity, June 04, 2009;

America's Piñata Strikes Back: We Won't Shut Up on Sotomayor, The Rush Limbaugh Show® Premiere Radio Networks, May 29, 2009;

Too Many Washington Republicans Seem Perfectly Content as Losers, The Rush Limbaugh Show® Premiere Radio Networks, May 29, 2009;

GOP Acts Like Oppressed Minority, The Rush Limbaugh Show® Premiere Radio Networks, May 27, 2009;

Listening, GOP? 40% of Americans Call Themselves Conservatives, The Rush Limbaugh Show® Premiere Radio Networks, June 15, 2009;

weeklystandard.com, William Kristol, Good News for Conservatives, February 18, 2008;

Attacks on Palin are Attacks on You, The Rush Limbaugh Show® Premiere Radio Networks, October 2, 2008;

Wake Up, GOP! Liberals Fear Sarah Palin Because the Voters Love Her, The Rush Limbaugh Show® Premiere Radio Networks, July 16, 2009;

The Left is Afraid of Us, Folks, The Rush Limbaugh Show® Premiere Radio Networks, May 5, 2009;

Sarah Six-Pack vs. Joe Doofus, The Rush Limbaugh Show® Premiere Radio Networks, October 1, 2008;

Hate-Filled Liberals Distort Our Sarah Palin Interview Instantly!, The Rush Limbaugh Show® Premiere Radio Networks, November 17, 2009;

Matthew 9:37, King James Bible
Mark 10: 27, King James Bible

4

Are Americans Smart Enough to Realize Barack Obama is a Fraud?, The Rush Limbaugh Show® Premiere Radio Networks, August 5, 2009;

Bone Brothers; Koch Records, "Real Life", February 22, 2005;

Cnsnews.com, Martin Kady II, Kerry Attacks Palin As "Cheney-esque," August 31, 2008;

John Kerry Gets It Right on Rush!, The Rush Limbaugh Show® Premiere Radio Networks, September 2, 2008;

weeklystandard.com, Stephen F. Hayes, Reformers versus Traditionalists? November 11, 2008;

David Brooks Finds His Rock, The Rush Limbaugh Show® Premiere Radio Networks, October 16, 2008;

edition.cnn.com, Steele talks to Limbaugh: 'We are all good' March 3, 2009;

Arlen Specter's Defection Says Nothing About the State of the GOP, The Rush Limbaugh Show® Premiere Radio Networks, April 29, 2009;

FOXNews.com, Cheney: Powell Left the Republican Party, May 10, 2009;

Luke 22: 33, King James Bible

Luke 17: 31, King James Bible

5

Yes We Can: The Reestablishment of Principled Conservatism Begins, The Rush Limbaugh Show® Premiere Radio Networks, November 5, 2008;

Good Riddance, GOP Moderates, The Rush Limbaugh Show® Premiere Radio Networks, October 24, 2008;

Why Doesn't Liberalism Have to Change When Democrats Lose?, The Rush Limbaugh Show® Premiere Radio Networks, November 19, 2008;

Try Doing Talk Radio, Senator Hagel, The Rush Limbaugh Show® Premiere Radio Networks, November 19, 2008;

Angry Obama Aims to Get Even, The Rush Limbaugh Show® Premiere Radio Networks, June 29, 2009;

Liberty Doesn't Go Out of Style, The Rush Limbaugh Show® Premiere Radio Networks, June 5, 2008;

Republicans in Rebuilding Phase: Stop Whining and Start Teaching!, The Rush Limbaugh Show® Premiere Radio Networks, May 5, 2009;

Our Nostalgia Isn't for Reagan, Jeb. It's for Conservatives with Courage, The Rush Limbaugh Show® Premiere Radio Networks, May 4, 2009;

The Left is Afraid of Us, Folks, The Rush Limbaugh Show® Premiere Radio Networks, May 5, 2009;

The California Ballot Initiatives, Federalism and Colin Powell's GOP, The Rush Limbaugh Show® Premiere Radio Networks, May 20, 2009;

Let's Replace the Listening Tour with a Conservative Teaching Tour, The Rush Limbaugh Show® Premiere Radio Networks, May 4, 2009;

Health Care, the UAW and the GOP, The Rush Limbaugh Show® Premiere Radio Networks, May 6, 2009;

;Oklahoma Man Pines for Palin, The Rush Limbaugh Show® Premiere Radio Networks, November 26, 2008

6

Stack of Stuff Quick Hits Page, The Rush Limbaugh Show® Premiere Radio Networks, Story #6: All's Not Well Between Obama and Hillary, November 20, 2008;

On the Record, Greta Van Susteren; Fox news, interview with Rush Limbaugh, July 23, 2009;

Palin Blasts State-Run Media, Big Government -- and Scares Liberals, The Rush Limbaugh Show® Premiere Radio Networks, July 27, 2009;

John Kerry Gets It Right on Rush!, The Rush Limbaugh Show® Premiere Radio Networks, September 2, 2008;

Salon.com, Vincent Rossmeier, Palin doesn't rule out Senate run, November 14, 2008;

Npr.org, Franks James, Sarah Palin Quits As Alaska's Governor, July 3, 2009;

Jeb and Huckabee: Conservatives?, The Rush Limbaugh Show® Premiere Radio Networks, May 5, 2000;

Huffingtonpost.com, Sam Stein, Barbour: I Can't "Just Say Flatly No" To Presidential Run, June 28 2008;

After Relentless Media Pounding, Sarah Palin Close to Obama in Poll, The Rush Limbaugh Show® Premiere Radio Networks, July 20, 2009;

usatoday.com, Jeb Bush won't run for Senate in 2010, January 6, 2009;

CNN.com - Transcripts, Situation Room, May 27, 2009;

Rush and The Obama Recession, The Rush Limbaugh Show® Premiere Radio Networks, November 17, 2008

7

Too Many Washington Republicans Seem Perfectly Content as Losers, The Rush Limbaugh Show® Premiere Radio Networks, May 29, 2009;

Hate-Promoting Left Seizes Chance to Falsely Blame Right for Violence, The Rush Limbaugh Show® Premiere Radio Networks, June 11, 2009;

Rush's Speech at Hillsdale College Churchill Dinner in Washington, DC, The Rush Limbaugh Show® Premiere Radio Networks, December 5, 2008;

GOP Acts Like Oppressed Minority, The Rush Limbaugh Show® Premiere Radio Networks, May 27, 2009;

The Left is Afraid of Us, Folks, The Rush Limbaugh Show® Premiere Radio Networks, May 5, 2009;

Listening, GOP? 40% of Americans Call Themselves Conservatives, The Rush Limbaugh Show® Premiere Radio Networks, June 15, 2009;

The Future of Conservatism, The Rush Limbaugh Show® Premiere Radio Networks, October 22, 2008

CHAPTER THREE

1

Sympathy for the Bamster?, The Rush Limbaugh Show® Premiere Radio Networks, January 6, 2009;

Whose Swastikas, Speaker Pelosi? The Rush Limbaugh Show® Premiere Radio Networks, August 6, 2009;

"Sue 'Em!" Liberal NFL Politics and Media Slander Sparks Outrage, The Rush Limbaugh Show® Premiere Radio Networks, October 15, 2009;

Democrat Party Marginalizes Itself, The Rush Limbaugh Show® Premiere Radio Networks, August 5, 2009;

Why Liberal Jews Support Obama, The Rush Limbaugh Show® Premiere Radio Networks, October 23, 2008;

usatoday.com, Sen. Clinton: Near zero chance of running for president again, October 14, 2008;

Why Mrs. Clinton as Secretary of State Makes Sense for Everyone, The Rush Limbaugh Show® Premiere Radio Networks, November 17, 2008;

Rush's Interview with Barbara Walters Fascinates the Drive-By Media, The Rush Limbaugh Show® Premiere Radio Networks; December 4, 2008;

Stack of Stuff Quick Hits Page Story #4: Hillary's Assignment: Spread Gay Rights Around World, The Rush Limbaugh Show® Premiere Radio Networks, June 2, 2009;

Joe Biden, the King of Comedy, The Rush Limbaugh Show® Premiere Radio Networks, September 11, 2008

2

On the Record, Greta Van Susteren; Fox news, interview with Rush Limbaugh, July 23, 2009;

Nancy Pelosi in 2006: Disrupting Protesters are "Very American", The Rush Limbaugh Show® Premiere Radio Networks, August 14, 2009;

huffingtonpost.com, Sam Stein, Bob Dole: Health Care Will Pass, GOP Should Be Open To Reform, October 07, 2009;

Dark Days: Democrats in Midst of a Giant Health Care Con Game, The Rush Limbaugh Show® Premiere Radio Networks, October 8, 2009;

Senate Democrat Hacks Discuss Rush During Health Care Debate, The Rush Limbaugh Show® Premiere Radio Networks, December 11, 2009;

Democrats Pit Obama's Personal Likability Against Mean Old Rush, The Rush Limbaugh Show® Premiere Radio Networks, December 11, 2009;

Childish Bam Whines and Moans, The Rush Limbaugh Show® Premiere Radio Networks, July 29, 2009;

An Update on Barry's Hut Brother, The Rush Limbaugh Show® Premiere Radio Networks, September 15, 2009;

Greenspan Condemns Capitalism to Survive Among Washington Elite, The Rush Limbaugh Show® Premiere Radio Networks, October 24, 2008

Stack of Stuff Quick Hits Page, The Rush Limbaugh Show® Premiere Radio Networks, Story #3: McClatchy in the Tank, Excuses Fannie and Freddie, October 13, 2008;

An Opportunity for Conservatism, The Rush Limbaugh Show® Premiere Radio Networks, September 30, 2008;

Stack of Stuff Quick Hits Page, The Rush Limbaugh Show® Premiere Radio Networks, Story #10: Home Rescue Plan Delaying, Not Solving Crisis, October 13, 2009;

America 2008: Socialism Saves Us, The Rush Limbaugh Show® Premiere Radio Networks, October 3, 2008;

Ben Bernanke is Toast at the Fed, The Rush Limbaugh Show® Premiere Radio Networks, November 25, 2008;

A Full-Scale Assault on Capitalism, The Rush Limbaugh Show® Premiere Radio Networks, February 11, 2009

Lefty Elites Think They're Immune from the Havoc of Their Policies, The Rush Limbaugh Show® Premiere Radio Networks, July 3, 2009;

Hannity, Fox News, Rush on Fox News Channel with Sean Hannity Interview Taped on, January 19, 2009;

Stack of Stuff Quick Hits Page, The Rush Limbaugh Show® Premiere Radio Networks, Story #6: Misery Spread Equally: Recession Delays Divorces, November 24, 2008;

Q: Why Do the Big 3 Need Money, The Rush Limbaugh Show® Premiere Radio Networks, November 25, 2008;

Khalid Sheikh Mohammed to Plead Not Guilty, Attack US Foreign Policy, The Rush Limbaugh Show® Premiere Radio Networks, November 23, 2009;

From the Climate Hoax to Health Care to "Hope," Liberalism is Lies, The Rush Limbaugh Show® Premiere Radio Networks, November 23, 2009;

Obama Flip-Flops on DC Vouchers, The Rush Limbaugh Show® Premiere Radio Networks, May 6, 2009;

The California Ballot Initiatives, Federalism and Colin Powell's GOP, The Rush Limbaugh Show® Premiere Radio Networks, May 20, 2009;

Hate-Promoting Left Seizes Chance to Falsely Blame Right for Violence, The Rush Limbaugh Show® Premiere Radio Networks, June 11, 2009;

Rush Rocks Milken Institute Forum, The Rush Limbaugh Show® Premiere Radio Networks, April 29, 2009;

Barney Frank Can't Find a Villain!, The Rush Limbaugh Show® Premiere Radio Networks, July 21, 2009;

Obama Lied and the Economy Died, The Rush Limbaugh Show® Premiere Radio Networks, July 14, 2009;

A Look Inside the Liberal Mind, The Rush Limbaugh Show® Premiere Radio Networks, June 30, 2009;

Emanuel Has "Sharp Elbows," But We Have "Right-Wing Rage", The Rush Limbaugh Show® Premiere Radio Networks, November 7, 2008;

Drive-Bys Can't Wait for Obama to Take Over, But He's in No Hurry, The Rush Limbaugh Show® Premiere Radio Networks, December 8, 2008;

Obama: I'll Bankrupt Coal Industry; Your Energy Prices Will Skyrocket, The Rush Limbaugh Show® Premiere Radio Networks, November 3, 2008;

Angry Obama Aims to Get Even, The Rush Limbaugh Show® Premiere Radio Networks, June 29, 2009;

Exit Poll Data: Twenty Percent of "Conservatives" Voted for Obama, The Rush Limbaugh Show® Premiere Radio Networks, November 5, 2008;

Fox news, Who's Blaming Limbaugh, Hannity and Ingraham for Failings of, November 24, 2008...www.foxnews.com/story/0,2933,457005,00.html

Kondracke: GOP Should Fire Rush, The Rush Limbaugh Show® Premiere Radio Networks, November 24, 2008;

Hanniy, Sean Hannity, Part 2 of Limbaugh on 'Hannity', Fox News, June 05, 2009;

Get Off the Ledge, Conservatives! We Have Two Battles on Our Hands, The Rush Limbaugh Show® Premiere Radio Networks, November 6, 2008;

After Relentless Media Pounding, Sarah Palin Close to Obama in Poll, The Rush Limbaugh Show® Premiere Radio Networks, July 20, 2009;

If Any Republican Wins, Then They've Attracted Independents!, The Rush Limbaugh Show® Premiere Radio Networks, November 3, 2009;

Chris Shays Tells Us How to Win, The Rush Limbaugh Show® Premiere Radio Networks, November 7, 2008;

Too Many Washington Republicans Seem Perfectly Content as Losers, The Rush Limbaugh Show® Premiere Radio Networks, May 29, 2009;

What Does El Rusbo's Gut Say?, The Rush Limbaugh Show® Premiere Radio Networks, October 29, 2008;

McCain Won't Fight, So We Have to Drag Him Over the Finish Line, The Rush Limbaugh Show® Premiere Radio Networks, October 8, 2008;

Top Ten GOP Moderate Moments, The Rush Limbaugh Show® Premiere Radio Networks, November 3, 2009;

Snowe Votes Yes on Baucus Bill Tax Increases and Medicare Cuts, The Rush Limbaugh Show® Premiere Radio Networks, October 13, 2009;

Time to Name Names, Senator McCain, The Rush Limbaugh Show® Premiere Radio Networks, October 7, 2008;

Liberal Rejoinder: Bush Did It Too!, The Rush Limbaugh Show® Premiere Radio Networks, November 30, 2009;

What Motivates Dick Cheney? The Rush Limbaugh Show® Premiere Radio Networks, May 11, 2009;

Dr. Dean Plugs Communitarianism, The Rush Limbaugh Show® Premiere Radio Networks, December 1, 2009

4

newsbusters.org, Kyle Drennen, CBS: Alec Baldwin 'Easy Target' for 'Conservative Junkyard Dog' Sean Hannity, May, 12, 2008;

newsbusters.org, Justin McCarthy, joy Behar: 'Rush Limbaugh is a Terrorist', October 22, 2008;

"Rush Limbaugh is a Terrorist", The Rush Limbaugh Show® Premiere Radio Networks, October 22, 2008;

newsbusters.org, Justin McCarthy, Joy Behar: Sean Hannity a 'Dangerous Force in America', October 13, 2008;

Home - The Sean Hannity Show, Sean Hannity's Top 10 Items for Victory

thinkexist.com/quotes/with/keyword/freedom_of_the_will, Freedom of the will quotes & quotations

FOXNews.com, Obama: Supporter Should Debate Hannity – Hannity, August 06, 2008

www.foxnews.com Ann Coulter weighs in on Conservative Commentator War, January 29, 2009;

The Herald-dispatch.com, Dave Lavender, Obama chats with local radio, October 09, 2008

5

Obama Rips CEO Bonuses. Soon, He Will Decide What You Can Earn, The Rush Limbaugh Show® Premiere Radio Networks, November 26, 2008;

The Plumber vs. The Messiah, The Rush Limbaugh Show® Premiere Radio Networks, October 15, 2008;

Obama Administration Moves to Cap Pay All Across Private Sector, The Rush Limbaugh Show® Premiere Radio Networks, June 11, 2009;

Socialist Obama Cannot Uphold the Constitution He Has Dismissed, The Rush Limbaugh Show® Premiere Radio Networks, October 28, 2008;

The Role of Government is to Secure Our Liberty, Not to Seize It, The Rush Limbaugh Show® Premiere Radio Networks, June 26, 2009;

It Took a Plumber to Flush Out Obama's Plan to Target Achievers, The Rush Limbaugh Show® Premiere Radio Networks, October 20, 2008;

The Simplistic Notion That People with Wealth are Entitled to Keep It", The Rush Limbaugh Show® Premiere Radio Networks, November 4, 2008;

Cnn.com, Interview with Barack Obama; Schwarzenegger Campaigns with McCain transcripts.cnn.com/TRANSCRIPTS/0810/31/sitroom.03.html

Rush Rocks Milken Institute Forum, The Rush Limbaugh Show® Premiere Radio Networks, April 29, 2009;

Socialist Obama Cannot Uphold the Constitution He Has Dismissed, The Rush Limbaugh Show® Premiere Radio Networks, October 28, 2008;

Suddenly, "Yes, We Can" is "No, We Can't. Lower Expectations.", The Rush Limbaugh Show® Premiere Radio Networks, November 21, 2008;

"The Simplistic Notion That People with Wealth are Entitled to Keep It", The Rush Limbaugh Show® Premiere Radio Networks, November 4, 2008;

www.brainyquote.com/quotes/authors/k/karl_marx.html -Karl Marx Quotes

----

6

A Prebuttal to Obama's Infomercial, The Rush Limbaugh Show® Premiere Radio Networks, October 29, 2008;

Happy Dependence Day, America, The Rush Limbaugh Show® Premiere Radio Networks, July 2, 2009;

Why Obama Can't Be President, The Rush Limbaugh Show® Premiere Radio Networks, October 2, 2008;

Socialism Doesn't Scare the Millions Who Don't Pay Taxes, The Rush Limbaugh Show® Premiere Radio Networks, November 5, 2008;

Matthew 10: 14/15, King James Bible

Fox News, Newt Gingrich, newt.org/tabid/102/articleType/ArticleView/articleId/... Newt discusses Health Care with Hannity, July 24, 2009

7

Matthew 15: 14, King James Bible

Heaven'z Movie, Bizzy Bone Ruthless/Relativity/Mo Thugs/Epic, "Waitin' for Warfare," October 6, 1998;

What's Headed Your Way in the "Centrist" Government of Obama, The Rush Limbaugh Show® Premiere Radio Networks, November 10, 2008;

Dems Lower Obama Expectations, The Rush Limbaugh Show® Premiere Radio Networks, December 22, 2008;

CNN.com, U.N. 'doesn't smell of sulfur anymore,' says Chavez, September 25, 2009

Suddenly, "Yes, We Can" is "No, We Can't. Lower Expectations", The Rush Limbaugh Show® Premiere Radio Networks, November 21, 2008;

Callers Attack Your Humble Host, The Rush Limbaugh Show® Premiere Radio Networks, June 10, 2009;

Opening Monologue Delivered Flawlessly Despite Little Sleep
The Rush Limbaugh Show® Premiere Radio Networks, October 27, 2009;

Axelrod and Biden Attack Rush,
The Rush Limbaugh Show® Premiere Radio Networks, November 2, 2009

8

online.wsj.com, James Taranto, Leave Barack Alone!, August 6, 2009;

Saturday Afternoon in Washington: Conservatism on the Ascendancy, The Rush Limbaugh Show® Premiere Radio Networks, September 14, 2009;

Community Organizer Obama Attacks Community Organizers!, The Rush Limbaugh Show® Premiere Radio Networks, August 5, 2009;

Callers Report from Tea Parties, The Rush Limbaugh Show® Premiere Radio Networks, April 15, 2009;

Tea Parties Were a Great Success, But Resist Third-Party Temptations, The Rush Limbaugh Show® Premiere Radio Networks, April 16, 2009

9

www.foxnews.com, Obama: America Not What It Once Was; Friday, August 08, 2008;

washingtonmonthly.com, Steve Benen, Washington monthly, February 28, 2009;

greenpagan.newsvine.com, Vitter: Limbaugh Is Saying 'What I Am Saying' — 'I Hope' Obama 'Fails in Advancing Leftist Policy, March 4, 2009;

blogs.salon.com, The Liberal Perspective/Joe Sheridan's Radio Weblog, March 4, 2009;

Congressman Phil Gingrey to Rush: "I Regret Those Stupid Comments", The Rush Limbaugh Show® Premiere Radio Networks, January 28, 2009;

Huffington Post Nicholas Graham, Sanford Implies Rush Limbaugh Is An "Idiot", February 25, 2009;

Connie Schultz, Ignorant Ditz, The Rush Limbaugh Show® Premiere Radio Networks, May 4, 2009;

Obama Manipulates the Emotional Attachment of His Cult Followers, The Rush Limbaugh Show® Premiere Radio Networks, April 20, 2009;

What the Drive-Bys Don't Know About Barack Obama? Everything, The Rush Limbaugh Show® Premiere Radio Networks, January 22, 2009;

Unpresidential Obama Loses Cool, Flees DC to Push the Porkulus Bill, The Rush Limbaugh Show® Premiere Radio Networks, February 9, 2009;

If You Want Obama to Succeed, Then This is What You Endorse..., The Rush Limbaugh Show® Premiere Radio Networks, June 2, 2009;

Obama Manipulates the Emotional Attachment of His Cult Followers, The Rush Limbaugh Show® Premiere Radio Networks, April 20, 2009;

This Country is Failing Because President Obama is Succeeding, The Rush Limbaugh Show® Premiere Radio Networks, May 28, 2009;

Obama Press Conference: Listless, Lifeless, Lying -- and Very Valuable, July 23, 2009; Liberalism Thrives on Deception, The Rush Limbaugh Show® Premiere Radio Networks, July 23, 2009;

Sean Hannity, Rush on Fox News Channel with Sean Hannity, Fox News, January 19, 2009;

Last Man Standing Assaulted by Kool-Aid Drinking Drive-By Media, The Rush Limbaugh Show® Premiere Radio Networks, January 23, 2009;

www.nbcchicago.com, Rahm Emanuel: Limbaugh Is "Force" Behind GOP, March 2, 2009;

Limbaugh: I Hope Obama Fails, The Rush Limbaugh Show® Premiere Radio Networks, January 16, 2009;

Callers Grade Obama's 100 Days, The Rush Limbaugh Show® Premiere Radio Networks, April 29, 2009

10

Attacks on Palin are Attacks on You, The Rush Limbaugh Show® Premiere Radio Networks, October 2, 2008;

Biden: We'll Give You a Toaster, The Rush Limbaugh Show® Premiere Radio Networks, September 16, 2008;

Acts 17: 29-30, King James Bible

www.worldofquotes.com/author/William-Shakespeare/1 William Shakespeare Quotes

news.bbc.co.uk, BBC NEWS | Business | Bush talks tough on business, July 10, 2002;

Luke 20: 18, King James Bible

Will Obama Soon Self-Destruct?, The Rush Limbaugh Show® Premiere Radio Networks, June 12, 2009;

Lefty Elites Think They're Immune from the Havoc of Their Policies, The Rush Limbaugh Show® Premiere Radio Networks, July 3, 2009;

GOP Acts Like Oppressed Minority, The Rush Limbaugh Show® Premiere Radio Networks, May 27, 2009;

Good Riddance, GOP Moderates, The Rush Limbaugh Show® Premiere Radio Networks, October 24, 2008;

Hypocrisy, Charity and Perception, The Rush Limbaugh Show® Premiere Radio Networks, December 22, 2008;

Rush's Speech at Hillsdale College Churchill Dinner in Washington, DC, The Rush Limbaugh Show® Premiere Radio Networks, December 5, 2008;

Liberty Doesn't Go Out of Style, The Rush Limbaugh Show® Premiere Radio Networks, June 5, 2008

11

REID: GOP Run by Talk Show Host, The Rush Limbaugh Show® Premiere Radio Networks, August 6, 2009;

Sean Hannity, Home - The Sean Hannity Show;

State-Run Media Misinterprets Sarah Palin, The Rush Limbaugh Show® Premiere Radio Networks, July 13, 2009;

Obama "Enchanted" by El Rushbo, The Rush Limbaugh Show® Premiere Radio Networks, April 30, 2009;

Record Number of Affluent Voters Made by Bush Years, Voted Obama, The Rush Limbaugh Show® Premiere Radio Networks, November 11, 2008;

Huffington Post, Susan Crile, Schwarzenegger Pokes Fun At Limbaugh's Weight, May 28, 2009;

Fighting Against Dependence Day, The Rush Limbaugh Show® Premiere Radio Networks, July 3, 2009;

On the Record, Greta Van Susteren; Fox news, Rush Unleashed, Part 1and Part 2 interview with Rush Limbaugh, July 25, 2009;

Yes We Can: The Reestablishment of Principled Conservatism Begins, The Rush Limbaugh Show® Premiere Radio Networks, November 5, 2008;

The Future of Conservatism, The Rush Limbaugh Show® Premiere Radio Networks, October 22, 2008;

Rush's Speech at Hillsdale College Churchill Dinner in Washington, DC, The Rush Limbaugh Show® Premiere Radio Networks, December 5, 2008;

Saxby Chambliss Shows the Way, The Rush Limbaugh Show® Premiere Radio Networks, December 4, 2008;

Luke 9: 62, King James Bible

Genesis 19: 26, King James Bible

McCain Won't Fight, So We Have to Drag Him Over the Finish Line, The Rush Limbaugh Show® Premiere Radio Networks, October 8, 2008;

Los Angeles Times, Peter Wallsten Tug of war in the GOP, October 28, 2008;

House Democrat Plan Outlaws Individual Private Health Insurance, The Rush Limbaugh Show® Premiere Radio Networks, July 16, 2009;

Let's Replace the Listening Tour with a Conservative Teaching Tour, The Rush Limbaugh Show® Premiere Radio Networks, May 4, 2009;

Republicans in Rebuilding Phase: Stop Whining and Start Teaching!, The Rush Limbaugh Show® Premiere Radio Networks, May 5, 2009;

Arlen Specter's Defection Says Nothing About the State of the GOP, The Rush Limbaugh Show® Premiere Radio Networks, April 29, 2009

12

The Drive-Bys Go Berserk Over Cheney, Powell and El Rushbo, The Rush Limbaugh Show® Premiere Radio Networks, May 12, 2009;

Day Two: Rush and General Powell, The Rush Limbaugh Show® Premiere Radio Networks, October 21, 2008;

Powell Endorsement of Obama Has Everything to do with Race, Elitism, The Rush Limbaugh Show® Premiere Radio Networks, October 20, 2008;

Rush's Message to the Media, The Rush Limbaugh Show® Premiere Radio Networks, October 20, 2008;

Powell Has "Mr. Limbow" on Brain, The Rush Limbaugh Show® Premiere Radio Networks, July 13, 2009;

Why Colin Powell is Mad at Me, The Rush Limbaugh Show® Premiere Radio Networks, May 6, 2009;

www.pbs.org/newshour, Online NewsHour: Convention Speeches -- General Colin Powell, August 12, 1996;

Colin Powell Does 180 from 1996, The Rush Limbaugh Show® Premiere Radio Networks, June 11, 2009;

Rush Responds to General Powell, The Rush Limbaugh Show® Premiere Radio Networks, December 15, 2008;

CNN.com - Transcripts, December 15, 2008;

newsbusters.org/blogs/noel-sheppard/2008/12/12Noel Sheppard, Colin Powell Bashes Rush Limbaugh and Sarah Palin, December 12, 2008;

Foxnews.com, Powell Bashes Limbaugh in GOP Diatribe Thursday, May 07, 2009;

Where's the Outrage? Obama's Ego Sucks Up the Whole World's Wealth, The Rush Limbaugh Show® Premiere Radio Networks, December 21, 2009;

The California Ballot Initiatives, Federalism and Colin Powell's GOP, The Rush Limbaugh Show® Premiere Radio Networks, May 20, 2009;

Foxnews.com, Exclusive: Rush Unleashed, Parts 1 and 2 - Greta Van Susteren ...July 25, 2009;

Day Two: Rush and General Powell, The Rush Limbaugh Show® Premiere Radio Networks, October 21, 2008;

We're Conservatives, Not Purists, The Rush Limbaugh Show® Premiere Radio Networks June 8, 2009;

America's Piñata Strikes Back: We Won't Shut Up on Sotomayor, The Rush Limbaugh Show® Premiere Radio Networks, May 29, 2009;

washingtonpost.com, E.J. Dionne Jr. - Rush and Newt Are Winning, June 4, 2009;

Moderate GOP Got the Campaign They Wanted and They Don't Like It, The Rush Limbaugh Show® Premiere Radio Networks, October 13, 2008;

Why Does GOP Want to Get Along?, The Rush Limbaugh Show® Premiere Radio Networks, June 18, 2009;

Why Doesn't Liberalism Have to Change When Democrats Lose?, The Rush Limbaugh Show® Premiere Radio Networks, November 19, 2008;

Try Doing Talk Radio, Senator Hagel, The Rush Limbaugh Show® Premiere Radio Networks, November 19, 2008

13

Chuck Norris Does the Job the State-Controlled Media Used to Do, The Rush Limbaugh Show® Premiere Radio Networks, August 11, 2009;

Obamacare: It's All About Control, The Rush Limbaugh Show® Premiere Radio Networks, July 31, 2009;

The "Best" Health Care Isn't a Right, The Rush Limbaugh Show® Premiere Radio Networks, December 7, 2009;

Chavez Rips Capitalism, Draws Cheers from Copenhagen Confab, The Rush Limbaugh Show® Premiere Radio Networks, December 17, 2009;

It's Not a Consensus, It's a Cabal, The Rush Limbaugh Show® Premiere Radio Networks, November 30, 2009;

On the Record, Greta Van Susteren; Fox news, interview with Rush Limbaugh, July 23, 2009;

How Did America Become Great?, The Rush Limbaugh Show® Premiere Radio Networks, October 28, 2008;

Heed Ronald Reagan's Warning, The Rush Limbaugh Show® Premiere Radio Networks, August 14, 2009;

Obama's Mission: Government Command and Control of Economy, The Rush Limbaugh Show® Premiere Radio Networks, December 9, 2009;

Dingy Harry's Universe of Lies, The Rush Limbaugh Show® Premiere Radio Networks, December 7, 2009;

The Obamas are the King and Queen in the Universe of Lies, The Rush Limbaugh Show® Premiere Radio Networks, December 10, 2009;

The Obama-Biden Depression: Welcome to the "New Normal", The Rush Limbaugh Show® Premiere Radio Networks, October 20, 2009

CHAPTER FOUR

1

BTNHResurrection, Bone Thugs n Harmony, Ruthless Records, "Change the world," February 29, 2000;

Obama Disowns His Whiteness, The Rush Limbaugh Show® Premiere Radio Networks, March 21, 2008;

huffingtonpost.com, Taylor Marsh, Obama: Grandmother "Typical White Person," March 20, 2008;

www.slate.com, Richard Thompson Ford, "George Bush doesn't care about black people, January 23, 2008;

Matthew 22: 29b, King James Bible

Obama Exacerbates Racial Divide, The Rush Limbaugh Show® Premiere Radio Networks, July 24, 2009;

Rush Baby Asks Advice on Battling the Stereotyping of Conservatives, The Rush Limbaugh Show® Premiere Radio Networks, June 4, 2009;

Why Liberal Jews Support Obama, The Rush Limbaugh Show® Premiere Radio Networks, October 23, 2008;

FOXNews.com Talk-Radio Host Don Imus Apologizes for On-Air, April 6, 2007

www.poligazette.com, Michael van der Galien, MSNBC Fires Imus, April 12th, 2007;

abcnews.go.com, Jake Tapper, Obama: Fire Imus, April 11, 2007;

www.cnsnews.com, Melanie Hunter, Congressman Calls for Suspension of Talk Show, September 29, 2005;

Matthew 7: 12, King James Bible

2

boes.org/docs2/mking01.html Martin Luther King Jr: "I have a dream"

FOXNews.com Joseph Abrams, Billboard Claiming Martin Luther King Was, July 14 2009;

www.reuters.com, Bob Tourtellotte Update 1-Family members turn out for BET Jackson tribute ...June 29, 2009;

Michelle Obama Tells Us She Identifies with Sotomayor's Rage, The Rush Limbaugh Show® Premiere Radio Networks, June 4, 2009;

President Obama Comes Alive When the Topic Turns to Racism, The Rush Limbaugh Show® Premiere Radio Networks, July 23, 2009;

boston.com, Matt Viser and Andrew Ryan, Gov. Patrick: Arrest 'every black man's nightmare', July 23, 2009;

Luke 20:17, King James Bible

3

cnsnews.com,Obama's Former Pastor Says 'Jews' Are Keeping Him from Obama, June 11, 2009;

Paterson Takes Rush's Advice, Blames Obama for His Own Failure, The Rush Limbaugh Show® Premiere Radio Networks, September 23, 2009;

3news.co.nz, Diddy 'scared' of Sarah Palin - Story – Entertainment, October 6, 2008;

essenceofpolitics, The Essence of Politics: Remarks by Michael Steele: RNC, May 19, 2009;

www.telegram.com, A product of the Worcester Telegram & Gazette, December 31, 2008;

abcnews.go.com, Louise Schiavone, Reid to Meet With Burris as Showdown Looms, January 3, 2008;

cbs2chicago.com, Roland Burris Goes To Washington, Denied Entry To U.S. Senate January 7, 2009

4

Stack of Stuff Quick Hits Page, Story #6: African-Americans See Hope, Doubt in Obama Victory, The Rush Limbaugh Show® Premiere Radio Networks, November 3, 2008;

transcripts.cnn.com, State of the Union with John King Interview with Colin Powell, July 5, 2009

5

Michelle Obama Tells Us She Identifies with Sotomayor's Rage, The Rush Limbaugh Show® Premiere Radio Networks, June 4, 2009;

BTNHResurrection, Bone Thugs n Harmony, Ruthless Records, "Don't worry," February 29, 2000;

Obama Stokes Racism at NAALCP, The Rush Limbaugh Show® Premiere Radio Networks, July 20, 2009;

Farrakhan Calls Obama "Messiah", The Rush Limbaugh Show® Premiere Radio Networks, October 10, 2008;

abcnews.go.com, Jake Tapper, Obama Parses Wright & Wrong in Race Speech, March 18, 2008;

blogs.abcnews.com Jake Tapper,Philly Blunt: PA Gov. Says Some Keystone Staters Won't Vote for a Black Man, February 12, 2008;

Murtha: Western PA is "Redneck", The Rush Limbaugh Show® Premiere Radio Networks, October 21, 2008;

Messiah Loses at Warren Forum; Dems Accuse McCain of Cheating, The Rush Limbaugh Show® Premiere Radio Networks, August 18, 2008;

The Perfect Peace Prize Choice, The Rush Limbaugh Show® Premiere Radio Networks, December 10, 2009;

Matthew 7: 3-5, King James Bible

See, I Told You So: Obama's Election Didn't End Race Business, The Rush Limbaugh Show® Premiere Radio Networks, June 18, 2009;

Shhh! Don't Tell Robert Gibbs: We're Talking About Sotomayor, The Rush Limbaugh Show® Premiere Radio Networks, May 28, 2009

6

nytimes.com, Richard l. Berke the 1998 Campaign: The Overview; Clinton and Gingrich Press Cases, November 2, 1998;

Radical Marxists Weeks Away from Electing One of Their Own, The Rush Limbaugh Show® Premiere Radio Networks, October 14, 2008;

New York City Union Layoffs Prove Liberal Welfare States Do Not Work, The Rush Limbaugh Show® Premiere Radio Networks, April 10, 2009;

Liberals and the Dependent Class, The Rush Limbaugh Show® Premiere Radio Networks, October 23, 2008;

Washingtonpost.com, Michael A. Fletcher, Gore: Wide Disparity in Prosperity, July 17, 1998;

Stack of Stuff Quick Hits Page Story #6: African-Americans See Hope, Doubt in Obama Victory, The Rush Limbaugh Show® Premiere Radio Networks, November 3, 2008;

Juan Williams on Judging Obama, The Rush Limbaugh Show® Premiere Radio Networks, January 21, 2009;

Trouble Brews on Sharpton Show, The Rush Limbaugh Show® Premiere Radio Networks, July 22, 2009

7

Liberals and the Dependent Class, The Rush Limbaugh Show® Premiere Radio Networks, October 23, 2008;

Rep. Steve King (R-IA) Exposes Commissioner Goodell as a Weasel, The Rush Limbaugh Show® Premiere Radio Networks, October 29, 2009;

Smear Campaign Against Rush is Attempt to Discredit Conservatism, The Rush Limbaugh Show® Premiere Radio Networks, October 14, 2009;

Rush Tells All About the Rams Deal, The Rush Limbaugh Show® Premiere Radio Networks, October 15, 2009;

State-Run Media Scum Smear Rush Using Fabricated Quotes, The Rush Limbaugh Show® Premiere Radio Networks, October 13, 2009;

State-Run Media Scum Smear Rush Using Fabricated Quotes, The Rush Limbaugh Show® Premiere Radio Networks, October 13, 2009;

Don't Wallow in Depression, Just Stop Obama's Radical Agenda, The Rush Limbaugh Show® Premiere Radio Networks, October 30, 2009;

The NFL Controversy Revisited, The Rush Limbaugh Show® Premiere Radio Networks, October 23, 2009

8

Obama Manipulates the Emotional Attachment of His Cult Followers, The Rush Limbaugh Show® Premiere Radio Networks, April 20, 2009;

This Country is Failing Because President Obama is Succeeding, The Rush Limbaugh Show® Premiere Radio Networks, May 28, 2009;

Obama Plans to Implement FDR's Socialist "Second Bill of Rights", The Rush Limbaugh Show® Premiere Radio Networks, October 29, 2008;

Liberals and the Dependent Class, The Rush Limbaugh Show® Premiere Radio Networks, October 23, 2008;

Drive-Bys Can't Wait for Obama to Take Over, But He's in No Hurry, The Rush Limbaugh Show® Premiere Radio Networks, December 8, 2008;

Democrats Copy Russia's Putin, Move in to Claim Private Industries, The Rush Limbaugh Show® Premiere Radio Networks, December 8, 2008;

Liars and Prostitutes Pass Fraud Health Care Bill Tribute to Obama, The Rush Limbaugh Show® Premiere Radio Networks, December 21, 2009;

The Washington Political Class Does Not Care What You Think, The Rush Limbaugh Show® Premiere Radio Networks, December 21, 2009

9

Steve Wants His Schadenfreude, The Rush Limbaugh Show® Premiere Radio Networks, November 4, 2008;

Bureaucrat: Obama's Aunt Zeituni is an "Exemplary" Slum Resident, The Rush Limbaugh Show® Premiere Radio Networks, October 31, 2008;

Snowe Votes Yes on Baucus Bill Tax Increases and Medicare Cuts, The Rush Limbaugh Show® Premiere Radio Networks, October 13, 2009;

Obama Tears Down US Economy, Mikhail Gorbachev Endorses Plan, The Rush Limbaugh Show® Premiere Radio Networks, June 8, 2009;

Libs Tweaked by MJ and Reagan, The Rush Limbaugh Show® Premiere Radio Networks, July 2, 2009;

Michael Jackson's Individuality Flourished During the Reagan Era, The Rush Limbaugh Show® Premiere Radio Networks, July 1, 2009

10

www.foxnews.com, Sean Hannity, Sharpton on Jackson's Obama Remarks, July 10, 2008

cbsnews.com, Jesse Jackson Used N-Word In Obama Remarks July 17, 2008;

boston.com, Sophia Tareen, Jackson apologizes for comment about Obama, July 9, 2008;

huffingtonpost.com, Obama's Father's Day Speech Urges Black Fathers To Be More, June 15, 2008;

cbs5.com, Jesse Jackson Caught Bad-Mouthing Obama; Remarks Caught On, July 9, 2008;

Messiah Loses at Warren Forum; Dems Accuse McCain of Cheating, The Rush Limbaugh Show® Premiere Radio Networks, August 18, 2008;

huffingtonpost.com, Sam Stein, Obama: I Would Not Have Nominated Clarence Thomas, August 16, 2008

313

11

Proverbs 5: 23, King James Bible

www.slate.com, Mickey Kaus "White Man's Greed" Obama's very first service at Wright's, March 30, 2008;

Liberals and the Dependent Class, The Rush Limbaugh Show® Premiere Radio Networks, October 23, 2008;

Luke 18: 25, King James Bible

Matthew 22:37-40, King James Bible

Luke 18: 25, King James Bible

12

The Bush Family Calls Rush, The Rush Limbaugh Show® Premiere Radio Networks, August 1, 2008;

John 14:12, King James Bible

Deuteronomy 28: 7, King James Bible

Matthew 27: 46, King James Bible

Author Bio

Rush Limbaugh, "I hope he Fails," Bailed out America: is the author's second book in as many years.

The author is a political junkie who majored in Politics and Economic at a certain State University in New York.

The author, Ndyfreke Nenty is also a God fearing English Limbaugh conservative who believes that conservatism is rooted to Christianity. Conservatism is all about the truth and the truth is all about God.

The book is a continuation of Nenty's first book "American Politics 001." It uses the tenets of God's word to define the politics of today. A Church built on the Rock of Jesus Christ will last forever. America was built on the rock of conservatism and capitalism. Therefore, any other philosophies, for example liberalism and socialism, are foreign to America and thus detrimental and threatening to this great country.